A PIECE OF

Cake

A Piece of

Cake

CAKE

Recipes
for Female
Sexual
Pleasure

MELINDA GALLAGHER, M.A.,
and EMILY SCARLET KRAMER

FOUNDERS OF CAKE

ATRIA BOOKS
New York London Toronto Sydney

ATRIA BOOKS
1230 Avenue of the Americas
New York, NY 10020

Copyright © 2005 by Melinda Gallagher and Emily Kramer

Chapter opener graphics by Emily Scarlet Kramer and Aron Wahl
Medical illustrations copyright © 2005 by JN Graphics

Library of Congress Cataloging-in-Publication Data

Gallagher, Melinda
  A piece of cake : recipes for female sexual pleasure / Melinda Gallagher
and Emily Kramer.
       p. cm.
    1. Sex instruction for women. 2. Women—Sexual behavior. I. Kramer,
Emily. II. Title.

 HQ46.G33 2005
 613.9'6'082—dc22

                                                            2005053013

 ISBN-13: 978-0-7434-9625-4
 ISBN-10: 0-7434-9625-6

First Atria Books hardcover edition November 2005

10 9 8 7 6 5 4 3 2 1

ATRIA BOOKS is a trademark of Simon & Schuster, Inc.

Manufactured in the United States of America

For information regarding special discounts for bulk purchases,
please contact Simon & Schuster Special Sales: 1-800-456-6798 or
business@simonandschuster.com.

To all the CAKE Girls who entrusted us
with their experiences, thoughts, and desires, presenting
a new, empowered vision of female sexuality to the world.

Main Entry: CAKE

n.

1: a sweet baked food made from a dough or thick batter, usually containing flour and sugar and often shortening, eggs, and a raising agent

2: a euphemism for a woman's sexual anatomy; silky smooth on the outside, tender and moist on the inside

---

I want to be the girl with the most cake.

—COURTNEY LOVE

Contents

A PIECE OF

The World According to Cake

Women today are leading vibrant and diverse sexual lives. We are evolving in our relationships and our careers, entertaining a never-ending variety of fantasies and realizing pleasure-filled adventures. A distinct and powerful female sexual culture is emerging, wherein women are more satisfied and in control than ever before.

Despite this progress, many age-old myths and misconceptions about women and sex still abound. Female pleasure is discussed in antiquated terms, when it's discussed at all. We are supposedly less sexual than men, labeled either "bad girls" or "good girls," sexy babes or sexless mothers, sluts or virgins. Moreover, we're expected to just "look good" rather than "feel good," encouraged to fake it if we can't "make it," and generally discouraged from getting off.

There is a huge disconnect between how women are portrayed and how women really live, fantasize, think, and act. In 2000, we created CAKE to set the record straight. We began producing events in New York City and later expanded to London. We launched the CAKE website—

1

www.cakenyc.com—and asked women from around the world to share their sexual experiences with us. Our goal was to create a forum, to begin a dialogue, and to allow women to integrate sexuality into all aspects of their lives. From our first CAKE event, where naughty excerpts from 100 of the best erotic films were projected on 40-foot screens, we knew we were on to something! We watched as the floodgates opened and women started talking . . . dirty!

Over the past five years we have talked to, worked with, and entertained thousands of women, in person and online. We created the CAKE Report, an online sex survey that included demographics, personal sexual histories, body image, masturbation habits, orgasm techniques, fantasy lives, partner explorations, contraception preferences, and sexual health practices. Slowly but surely, a fresh vision of female sexuality emerged.

Many of the women we interviewed live in New York City. Others are scattered throughout the United States, and the rest hail from the UK and abroad. Some are married, and some are single. They come from a wide variety of religious backgrounds. A majority have college or graduate degrees, some have children, and most identify as "straight," though they are not always fond of labels.

What follows is a profile of a new generation of women, and the birth of the CAKE philosophy of female sexuality.

RECIPES FOR FEMALE
SEXUAL PLEASURE

We have chosen to highlight positive ways that women seek and find sexual pleasure. We do not claim that all women have experienced or must explore sexuality in every way we suggest. Our agenda is to provide more options for women and to show the many ways that women get turned on and get off.

Let's get started. Here are recipes for you to expand your repertoire. Female sexuality is about to come out of the closet.

2

THE CAKE PHILOSOPHY

- Women like to initiate sex.
- We get turned on every day of the week.
- We are visual.
- We fantasize.

- We know how to get ourselves off.
- We like sex (better than shopping!).
- We know how our bodies work.
- Sex isn't over with until we orgasm.

From so simple a beginning endless forms
so beautiful and most wonderful have been,
and are being evolved.

—CHARLES DARWIN, *ON THE ORIGIN OF SPECIES*

On Your Own

Sweet and Sticky Hot Buns

Difficulty: Beginner

Yield: One Confident Woman

Ingredients:

5 memories about your childhood

8 kick-ass body image exercises

7 masturbation techniques

4 small to large vibrators

8 different ways to experience orgasm

Directions: Combine these ingredients and mix well. Let cool overnight and eat daily. Pass along to your friends.

CHAPTER 1

From Birth to Babe

It was the summer between 6th and 7th grade when I read *Are You There God? It's Me, Margaret* by Judy Blume. Margaret always talked about finding her "special spot," and I read the book, like, twice, trying to figure out where the hell that was. Finally I just started exploring my own body and found my clitoris right away. We've been best friends ever since!

—ELIZABETH, 22

We start our journey with the origins of women's sexual lives—our childhood years. This time is all about self-discovery; as kids, we dream, feel, touch, and explore. Long before your "first time," you had a first fantasy. Indeed, your first kiss may have come *after* your first orgasm. There were movies that made you hot (remember *Grease?*) before you even knew about real turn-on material. These were the moments when we first encountered sexual *pleasure*. And then there was light. . . .

But it wasn't all good. Just as our curiosity compelled us to explore, we learned that our role was to be sexually passive, ultimately monogamous, and more emotional than sexual. Now, that's no fun! Despite these messages, we forged on in secret, when no one was watching. We searched, scrounged, and sometimes begged for more information about what was going on with our bodies. With determination and luck, we found our own paths to pleasure, and our sexual evolution began.

Looking back on these primitive times, we find it's quite clear that our capacity to be sexual doesn't just pop into the picture when we are adults. We've been sexual all along. Let's go back behind the scenes and take a brief look at how our first experiences with sexuality affect who we are today. Join us for a trip down memory lane—from birth to babe.

GIRLS WILL BE GIRLS

You're no more than eleven years old, in bed with your silky "My Pretty Pony" comforter snuggled around you. The pillow is between your legs and you curiously start rubbing rhythmically up against it. The sensation is like an itch that feels better the more you scratch it; you rock against the soft fluffiness, faster and harder, until you explode. You are shocked and amazed, but you don't tell anyone about your new favorite bedtime routine. Not long after, you decide to touch yourself with your fingers to see how that feels, and you find your sensitive clitoris. Your nightly ritual evolves, and you learn that you love your smell, that your nipples like to be squeezed, and that the air from the ceiling fan feels good blowing across your body—the same things you love to this very day.

Oh, the places we'll go! Renee (27) wishes she had been taught that her first sexual feelings (and she had a lot of them) were natural. Little did she know, at age 7, that she wasn't the only girl who loved to climb the rope in gym class! No one, not even her friends, had ever talked to her about sex, let alone masturbation, so she tried to stop her hands from heading south of the border. In junior high, she heard about a "nasty" thing called jerking off that only boys did, but since what she did felt so good, she figured that must be something else entirely.

The female body is obviously not so difficult if a six-year-old can work it out sans instructions. Roberta (23) found her clitoris when she was wiping herself after she peed. Going about her business, she felt something that was different than usual. She repeated the motion and discovered her clitoris, and moments later she had her first orgasm. All of this occurred before she even knew what was happening to her; all she cared about was that it felt great! Once we experience arousal, the natural next steps are masturbation and hopefully orgasm—and that's exactly the path many girls take, like ducks to water.

Sure, it's not always so easy. Maggie (35) tried touching herself early on. It felt really nice, but the magic never happened. When she was 14, her boyfriend convinced her to try it out again. So one day she kept rubbing, determined to figure out what he was so excited about. During an after-school nap, she alternated between her left index finger and her middle finger and her left index finger, because each one kept getting tired, until after over an hour her right middle finger did the job. She remembers thinking, "My head is exploding, I am going to die here, and this is how they are going to find me, with my hand down my pants!"

It's cause for celebration when women learn to masturbate early, and masturbate often. After our first orgasm, there's just no turning back. In one moment, we truly begin to understand the relationship between sexual thoughts, that feeling "down there," our body's capability to experience pleasure, and the positive power of it all. We may not know what it all means, but we're sure we want to do it again . . . and again . . .

Pleasure Tip: Remember one technique you discovered on your own that felt good when you were a kid (maybe that time in your basement, springing up and down on the bouncy ball . . .) and try it again now.

FAMILY TIME

You're taking your time in the tub when your mom barges in and yells, "Stop touching yourself! Get out of that tub and stop thinking naughty thoughts!" You knew it! You're going straight to hell for your evil ways. But instead of atoning for your sins, you simply learn to be more secretive.

When masturbation is forced to hide out at home, it's easy to feel ashamed of our sexual development. Even when we're not explicitly discouraged, we still know that our habit is considered "bad." If we have little outside encouragement, we go off on our own lonesome journeys toward figuring out how to actively experience pleasure. But with just a shove in the right direction, we're off to the races. Yeehaw!

When Melissa was thirteen, her mother had the unusual foresight to give her daughter her first vibrator! Her mom instructed her to "go to it, and figure out what makes you feel good before you share yourself with another person." This motherly deed made Melissa (now 31) feel that her body and her pleasure were hers to own and that it was up to her to decide how and when she would share them with someone else. Many years, and thousands of orgasms later, Melissa's mom's advice has worked extremely well.

Melissa, consider yourself a lucky, lucky girl! Many of us don't get such positive direction from our families and are, instead, sent directly on a road devoid of sexual fulfillment, or left to discover a path on our own. We heard all about the birds and the bees, but we weren't looking for an explanation on how the animal kingdom procreates! We wanted someone to clue us in on the *human* orgasm and why we just couldn't keep our hands out of our Underoos.

Lula (35) recalls that her mother made one valiant attempt to teach her about sex, but promptly got embarrassed. Her mother brought home a book one day to read to her and her sister, but when she got to the first page, they all started laughing, and that was that. Lula's mom slammed the book shut and said, "All right, damn it, figure it out for yourselves!" And that is exactly what Lula did.

Both girls and boys experience arousal at a very young age; it is purely a physical reaction. There does not have to be shame attached to early exploration, or fear that these feelings may immediately lead to relationships and intercourse. When we are young, sexual pleasure is not compartmentalized or taboo—it just is.

Pleasure Tip: Tell your partner or a girlfriend one fun thing about your sexual development that you think he or she would never guess about you—like, yes, you masturbated every afternoon after getting home from high school.

10

SEX NOT SO ED

Remember those fun sex-ed classes we all were required to attend—the girls in one class, the boys in the other? While we are not exactly sure what happened in the boys' room, for us girls the entire world of female sexuality was contained in menstrual kits. So you mean to tell us that we are going to bleed soon, have to stick some weird cotton thing up there, and pray we don't die from toxic shock? Puberty sucks!

Two-dimensional pictures of the uterus look more like a cow's head with fallopian tubes for ears and horns than a part of our bodies. Boring at best, scary at worst. Pretty pink pads in Ziploc bags, and off we go to recess. Later, we learn that getting it on with the boys is something to fear.

Our gym teacher instructs the high school sex-ed class, which is kind of strange. Wearing her purple terry-cloth warm-up suit, she tells us all about the horrors of teen pregnancy and shows us positively frightening pictures of every STD under the sun. This is what happens to girls who give it up too early. You bad, bad girl, you. Of course, there is no mention of masturbation, of how sex can be fun, or of orgasm. In fact, there's no reference to pleasure at all.

INPUT → OUTPUT

Back in your bedroom, you plaster your walls with boy band pinups and press your lips against the cool, glossy paper. *Mmm . . . hmm.* Then you close your eyes, roll your head back and forth, and wrap your arms around your body as if Simon LeBon were right there in the room with you. What . . . exactly . . . are you doing? As creative as we may be, we don't just come up with these moves on our own. When we're young, we're little information suckers, taking in everything around us and running it through our bodies to see how it feels. We can respond to overtly sexual images or ideas before we have any idea what we are looking at or reading.

A remarkable number of women first experience sexual thoughts upon finding our father's *Playboy* and *Penthouse* magazines, hidden in the depths of underwear drawers, the backs of closets, or down in the basement. Just as common is inadvertently catching a peek of racy late-night cable television or our brother's stash of porn videos. When we stumble upon this "adult" entertainment, we are hit by a sense of wonder, awe, titillation, and unparalleled curiosity. We learn immediately that sex is, among other things, a visually exciting experience.

Rose (34) was dislodging a tennis ball from the rafters of her parents' garage when her dad's entire collection of *Penthouse* came crashing down upon her, leaving her in a virtual pile of porn. She went through at least six issues that afternoon, sitting on the cold cement floor, mesmerized by the photos of nude women. They seemed powerful and confident to her, like superheroes or goddesses, looking happy and satisfied and even dominant. She learned from the juicy pages that you could have sex in costume, and as a 12-year-old, dressing up was appealing! The possibilities seemed endless; you could apparently get it on in a dentist's chair with the hygienist watching, over the hood of the car when you take it in for a tune-up, or on a haystack during horseback riding lessons . . . all of which looked great to her.

As girls, we're too young to make judgments on the politics of porn. These images are simply an open window revealing a part of sex-

12

uality that would otherwise remain hidden. They were sexual, powerful, forbidden, and—butt naked! One might assume that we'd be negatively impressed by mock poses and airbrushed "beauties." But our first reaction to these images was to be more intrigued than intimidated.

Bright and dramatic, with barely clad women front and center, a whole new world unfolds within these inviting pages. The experience of opening up a magazine and seeing women or couples in a sexual situation for the first time sparks an instantaneous physical reaction. Judi (39) first felt that tingle between her legs at her sister and brother-in-law's house. She went down to the game room, which was built like a bar complete with "Gentlemen's" and "Ladies'" bathrooms. She opened the door to the men's room and found walls filled with dirty posters, and magazines that made her feel light-headed. Her hand naturally traveled down her pants, and she orgasmed quickly. You can bet that she returned to that bathroom many times throughout those young years.

After discovering the idealized curves of breasts and hips in *Penthouse,* Violet (26) was caught creating her own pictures of enormous rainbow-colored penises and breasts outlined in red Crayola. "I don't remember why I'd done it as much as the embarrassment I felt when my friend's sister snatched the ingenuous renderings off the table. 'I'm telling Mom!' she chanted as she skipped down the hall. I knew I was in trouble, that what I'd done was wrong. Her mother immediately drove me home and made me agree that I would tell my mom what I had done. I never did tell her, though, and I remember thinking how thankful I was that my 'mischief' would go unpunished; I would never, my adolescent mind decided, draw another picture of a naked person again! The lesson was so warped for me. I feared I'd be punished by my parents for imitating the very images that my father so relished in secret."

In the 1980s, "video killed the radio star," and our sexual learning curve changed forever. We all want our MTV. The cable guy comes to the house and installs the magic box. Suddenly we no longer need the bunny rabbit ears or the bent wire hanger looming large in the living room. The possibilities are endless. Good Lord, there are almost sixty channels!

13

Wait, what's this one? You can't see anything but wavy lines, and colors, and blips of . . . entangled naked bodies. There's something that sounds like elevator music, but cooler, and there are vague intimations of moaning, squealing—"Oh, God. Oh, yeah, baby. Give it to me." What is going on? Wait, is that real? What are they doing? And why is it making my crotch tingle?

Bianca (21) always loved to watch sex scenes on late-night TV when her parents were asleep, and she had her first orgasm when she was fifteen while watching a girl masturbate on the Playboy Channel. She watched in awe as the female star moaned and groaned solo style, and she reached down between her own legs to imitate the motions.

As exciting as your new discovery is, you know that you have to keep it hidden. You develop techniques for quickly changing the channel, or you keep the volume low in case your parents come home sooner than expected. This only adds to the fun! Suzie (32) was always sort of excited by the idea of getting caught masturbating to forbidden images—a fantasy that gets her hot even still.

The search for more material has begun. You get your hands on trashy romance paperbacks whose heroines are taken by force by mad and dangerous men, and you imagine being literally swept off your feet by your hero on a horse. Inspired by *Indiana Jones*, Rebecca's (20) first sexual thoughts were about being tied up and helpless on a wheel-like contraption. Vivianna (32) imagined all sorts of action-movie scenarios, like being tied up on a ship, or having to hide and sleep in fields in attempts to rescue her hero from the forest. Alexandra (28) read a lot of Anne Rice and dreamed about being seduced by a vampire in her sleep.

When Jennifer (32) was eight or nine, she was obsessed with *Chip 'n' Dale, Rescue Rangers,* and she used to fantasize about Chip—who, we might add, is a cartoon chipmunk. She imagined that he was hurt and that she'd have to take care of him, taking off his little bomber jacket and tucking him into her bed. Rachel (24) and a friend found a fan dancers segment of a documentary about Japanese culture so erotic, they rushed out to their tree house to reenact what they had seen. So even if you were allowed to watch only PBS, you were still in for some fun!

The images Betsy (28) found by sneaking peeks at her parents' video collection led to thoughts with a naughty edge: Spankings, pink bottoms, and glorious submission took her to the point of climax at an early age. As an adult, she's explored those turn-ons and has sought out partners who enjoy these same fantasies.

Pleasure Tip: Go find that movie, book, or magazine that made you tingle for the first time, and experience that lovin' feelin' all over again. For inspiration, check out *Child's Play* for our all-time faves.

KIDS R US

"I don't want to grow up, I'm a Toys R Us Kid. . . . More bikes, more trains, more video games!" And why would anyone, really? Childhood is the time when the whole world seems like one big adventure to explore. There is a joyous, almost sticky, pleasurable sense of just about everything. While the range of experience is virtually endless, it would be hard to find a woman who didn't undress Barbie and Ken and tuck them in under the covers. Most of us had intentional exploration during basement Truth or Dare, Spin the Bottle, Five Minutes in the Closet, and slumber parties. Playing doctor and patient comes as natural as cutting the crusts off PB and J—why would you want to play with clothes on?

Some of the "facts of life" are introduced through juvenile jokes that can be very revealing. In seventh grade math class, Terri (34) learned about what boys had "down there" from a dirty joke—you know, the one about Daddy putting his "car" into Mommy's "garage." She suddenly realized that all the boys sitting in class possessed a penis . . . making each and every one of them a potential sex partner. She just couldn't get over all those penises hiding behind all those zippers!

Of course, this type of experience makes the imagination run wild at that age. Terri started wondering how she could make out with the boys,

15

CHILD'S PLAY

- Afternoon delight with the soaps
- Peeping Toms from *Porky's*
- Sharon Stone's crotch shot in *Basic Instinct*
- The voodoo rituals of *Eleven Days, Eleven Nights*
- Breathless conversations on the radio on *Love Phones* with Dr. Judy
- The forbidden lust of *West Side Story*
- A young Richard Gere in *American Gigolo*
- Jane Fonda having a blast in the orgasm machine in *Barbarella*
- The modern-day fairy tale of *Pretty Woman*
- The dirty moves in *Dirty Dancing*
- Ralph Macchio's karate kicks
- Golden boy Shaun Cassidy
- John Taylor playing bass in Duran Duran
- Jabba the Hutt dominating Princess Leia
- Ronald McDonald's perma-grin
- Davy Jones crooning Monkees tunes
- Donny Osmond singing it up with his sister
- 1970s cops Starsky and Hutch, chasing criminals in their hot rod
- Batman's tight, dark outfit
- James Bond with Pussy Galore
- Prince's sex fiend, "masturbating with a magazine"
- Kermit the Frog . . . naked underneath his trench coat
- Steven Tyler's big lips
- "Me Jane, you Tarzan"
- The guy masturbating on the lawn in Judy Blume's *Wifey*
- Looking up "sex" in the *Encyclopaedia Britannica*
- Anne Rice's bloodthirsty, homoerotic vampires
- The taboo brotherly-sisterly love of *Flowers in the Attic* and *The Blue Lagoon*
- The candid descriptions of masturbation in *Our Bodies, Ourselves*
- The hokey 1970s illustrations in *The Joy of Sex*
- Neanderthal courtship in *The Clan of the Cave Bear*
- Ping the duck getting spanked in *The Story About Ping*
- The Happy Hooker's sex column explaining blow jobs in *Penthouse*
- The how-to book *A Doctor Talks to 5-to-8-Year-Olds*
- Madonna hitchhiking naked in her *Sex* book
- The prolonged embrace of *Pride and Prejudice*
- *Emmanuelle*'s sexual romps in the Thai countryside
- Lady Chatterley being dominated by her lover
- The bra section of the JCPenney catalog

16

masturbating to these thoughts with a round toothbrush travel case. In high school, she fell for Andre, whose moves on the half-pike, sinewy skater looks, and beautiful penis turned her on. He was her first blow job, and later on she lost it to him on a couch at his father's house. Years later, his is still her favorite penis! What started as a joke became late-night exploration, and the male member was a hot commodity from then on.

Innocent games go along with innocent jokes, and even just the utterance of an adult word sends us into fits of laughter. Who needs Candyland when you've got Sexland, a game invented by Jesse (22) and her kindergarten friends involving the act of sneaking into bathroom stalls, kissing and giggling? They were vaguely aware of the idea of sex, but they didn't connect it to their physical feelings.

The playground is fertile ground for hating boys and loving them at the same time. Your crush dashes around as you run away, excited by the thought of him catching up to you. The first sexual thoughts Julie (33) had were during games of Cowboys and Indians or Cops and Robbers with the other kids in her neighborhood. As an adult, she looks back and sees that she was always the one who loved getting caught and tied to a tree, or handcuffed and dragged away to jail! And, yes, she still loves to be tied up—just not to a tree.

Even if you grow up being interested only in men, you might begin your exploration with girls. Although Pam (21) has been with men for most of her life, her first sexual thoughts were about her girlfriends, at around the fifth grade. Boys were mean, gross, and ugly, so it seemed natural to be physical with the nice, loving girls she spent all her time with.

You trade newfound sexual knowledge with friends the way you trade baseball cards or bubble gum. You put what you've got out on the table to see who's got something new to share with you. At 9 years old, Margaret (28) discussed sex with her girlfriends, and sometimes they imitated sex or foreplay with one another. They'd take turns playing the part of the man and the woman and hold and caress each other, soaking up all the stimulation. Margaret's first sexual thoughts were inspired by a group tutorial of the uninformed.

Buried deep in your sexual past may be memories of really going for it before you knew exactly what you were going for. Karena (19) had a friend named Jodi, who was a tomboy with two older brothers. She smelled like Hot Pockets and she seemed to know a lot about sex. One night when they were playing, Jodi gently laid Karena down on the floor behind her bed and got on top of her, touching her in ways she had never imagined. They are still friends now, though they have never talked about how they used to play when they were young.

For girls who like boys, the opposite sex doesn't stay out of the picture for long. Sports may be segregated, but nothing stops you from checking out the boys on the opposite field, sweating it up in uniform. Every Saturday, Missi (24) would watch from her bedroom window as her neighbor mowed the lawn, and she would feel warm and cold all over. He would get all sweaty in the sun as he made his way from his house to under her window. She'd never tried masturbating before, but the day she watched him pour the remainder of his glass of water over his face and chest, she just had to touch herself.

Your adolescent attractions have a clear link to the tingling between your legs. Dating and more intense sexual relationships begin and deepen; you move from thinking about and discussing romance to dating, kissing, and sexual petting. What started as purely a tingling feeling is now imbued with social meaning and expectation. It's all very daunting and confusing: a time filled with good, wholesome teenage angst. No one understands you. Much to the dismay of your parents, the phone is your new best friend. Hours are spent twirling the cord around your fingers, telling your girlfriends about your latest crush. A boy signs the sixteenth page of your yearbook, you start wearing lipstick, and a rebel is born.

With no one around to teach us the goods, we reach out to the one reliable source we know must have the answer—1-900-HOT-SEXX. Julie (25) and her girlfriend decided to secretly call the hotline to try dirty talk for the first time when they were 14 years old. Little did Julie know that her father was standing by her bedroom door, listening to his adorable young daughter deliver a litany of sexual innuendo to the stranger on the other end of the line. He marched over, took the receiver out of her hands, hung up the phone, and said, "Julie, I need to speak with you, *now*."

As soon as you start getting physical, the questions of who with, when, where, and how you are going to lose your virginity begin. There are some major conflicting social messages: sexual innocence, inexperience, and ignorance are culturally valuable qualities for girls. We are instructed to hold our virginity close to our hearts, as if we were saving up money in a piggy bank, and we realize that our "innocence" is the ultimate value. When the right man (that's our husband) comes along with the promise of financial stability, love, and happiness, and literally sweeps us off our feet, then we can open our legs.

At the same time, you're faced with peer pressure, both good and bad. Everyone around you is either doing it or not doing it, and suffering the social consequences either way. You want to keep it because it's yours, because you're supposed to wait, because it's scary, but you want to lose it to be cool, to enjoy it, and to just get it over with already!

When guys lose their virginity, they get the big high five and the "Way to go!" For women, losing our virginity is introduced with a grin-and-bear-it attitude. Listen, girl, it's going to hurt, so just buck up and take it. For guys, the theory is, the earlier the better; but the first girl to lose it is labeled a slut. On average, sexual relationships and intercourse begin for both men and women around "the edge of seventeen," to quote Stevie Nicks. But almost no women have an orgasm during their first time.

"Okay . . . owww . . . Stop . . . All right, a little more. *Ow!* Okay, go ahead . . . *Slowly!*"

Sound familiar? Susan (26) describes her first time as ending with "Sorry, I came. You're too damn tight!" Now, that's hardly the fantasy we were prepared for! Three minutes to some guys is hitting big numbers the first time, and we all know how much pleasure that leaves the girls. What an underwhelming, pointless operation!

To be fair, the first time can just be hard and awkward. Nerves take hold, technique eludes you, he slips out as easily as he slips in . . . how is that thing supposed to work, anyway? Of course there are some physical challenges. It can hurt. You can bleed. The hymen's a reality, and if you didn't ride enough horses or bikes, yours may well have been intact. But enjoyable, pleasurable, positive first times are totally possible and, with the right attitude and armed with knowledge, are becoming all the rage.

Monique's (23) fairy-tale first time was when she was 17, with her long-term boyfriend while his parents were out of town. She was comfortable with her body and had been having orgasms since she started masturbating at 11. Monique's mother talked to her about sex when she was 8 years old by reading her a book on the subject. Instead of leaving Monique to figure out everything on her own, she answered questions like "Mom, what is a penis?," while advising Monique to wait to have sex with someone until she knew she cared about him and knew that it would be right for her. Interestingly, despite hearing that every girl's first time was awful, Monique had an orgasm the first time she had sex, and even felt ready to try positions other than the good ol' missionary. Monique's comfort level and knowledge of her own body made her first sexual experience a positive and enjoyable one—all because of Mom! That's more than beginner's luck.

Pleasure Tip: Get a group together at your home for a fun night of Spin the Bottle to relive those wild younger years.

CHAPTER 2

Rock Your Body and Reap the Rewards

> I have breasts and an ass, and I'm keeping 'em! I like to walk
> around naked in my room and look at myself. This ritual makes
> me continually aware of the changes my body is going through
> and is essential to keeping a positive sense of my sexuality. I
> have watched the perils of body image, and the "feminine
> ideal." I have witnessed my mother, my sister, and my friends
> battle unnatural ideals, and have once beaten an eating disorder
> myself. I am now determined never to fall prey to that again.
>
> —JULIE, 21

So you've got your good-body-image days and your bad-body-image
days. On a good day, the shower feels nice and hot when you hop in,
and you enjoy the way it looks when the water runs over your body.
Stepping out onto the mat, you wrap a cozy towel around you and
relax on the couch with a bottle of your favorite body moisturizer, just
loving your curves and the way your skin feels. You look in the mirror
and your tits look perky, your tummy is smooth, your bottom looks

rounded, and you think, "Ohhh, yeah, take *that!*" Turning on some funky music, you slip into heels and dance with yourself, without anyone around to watch or judge.

Then you've got your bad-body-image days. You avoid the mirror on your way out of the shower, and any glimpse of your figure reminds you of the things you hate. Why, oh why, is one breast bigger than the other? Are those *more* stretch marks appearing across your thighs? The thought of revealing these flaws to someone else makes you want to jump back into bed and hide under the covers.

The psychology behind these days can take total hold of our sex life. Insecurity eats up our appetite for sex, whereas confidence makes us hungry for all the pleasure we know our hot bod deserves. It's quite a simple matter: When we love our tits, asses, vulvas, and everything in between, we are going to come more often. On the other hand, if we are overwhelmed by a sense of inadequacy and shame about the way our body looks and feels, then we can't possibly express our sexual needs and desires. Sucking in your stomach while having an orgasm just does not work!

THE GOOD, THE BAD, AND THE UGLY
Take back your body image

Some of us are incredibly enthusiastic about our bodies. But for many of us it's a long and hard internal battle that we fight every day.

The promise of a "new sexy you" is the basis of the entire beauty and fashion industry. We are continually encouraged to "find our perfect palette," complete the "6-week body makeover," and change our hair color to "transform our life." The traditional makeover inevitably injects us with a serious dose of insecurity and inadequacy. Why must we feel prospectively bad about ourselves so that we can retrospectively feel better? Hmm. Something about the whole damn concept seems rather backward. We are plucked, buffed, preened, and altered. But at

22

the end of this elaborate, time-consuming, and often painful makeover experience, are we experiencing more sexual pleasure? We think not.

Our culture is obsessed with the female body. Today the bar for normality is set in the pages of *InStyle*, *Vogue*, and *Elle*. We should look just like celebrities and models. We need to be perfect. Free of cellulite. Free of wrinkles. Free of blemishes. Free of anything unsightly. Simply divine.

Let's get real!

This model of the female body is pure fantasy. Our bodies go through changes every day and every year as we grow as women. Some of these changes are related to our cycles, and others are unpredictable. We get PMS, we ovulate, we get pregnant, get fit, get sick, get tattoos, have surgery—and our libidos are rolled up in all of these transformations. In fact, our reproductive capacity necessitates that our weight and bodily proportions naturally change from puberty to menopause, and for good reason. Ironically, most women spend their entire adult lives struggling against nature.

Pleasure Tip: Redefining what a sexy woman looks like is up to us. Let those women's magazines know how tired you are of the unrealistic images in their glossy pages. Sign an open letter to the editors of your favorite women's magazine, and cut the last strings of your bad-body-image dependencies.

OPEN LETTER

TO: All Editors of Women's Magazines

FROM: CAKE Girls

RE: Get Real!

When we look at the pages in your magazines, we feel the pressure to be "perfect," please our man in "10 Easy Steps," and buy the new best skin cream to erase those unsightly wrinkles. Suddenly, we find ourselves looking in the mirror and thinking, "something just doesn't add up here." We can understand a little color contrast and some reddening of the lips—but distorting body parts to make the perfect image? Now, that's sort of twisted. By presenting manipulated, unrealistic standards, your industry has completely warped the female image and adversely affected our images of ourselves.

You have gone beyond being arbiters of good taste and have become master artistes, airbrushing us to death, "saving" the public from having to endure photos that would show the imperfections of the female body. Thanks to you, the manipulation of the female form is held in high esteem. You ignore the negative effects that this imagery has on women's perception of our own bodies, our confidence, and ultimately our sexuality. The hyper-surreal way the female body is portrayed has gone so far overboard that our eyes are trained to *reject* natural, real bodies on the rare chance we see them.

Responding to this phenomenon, Kate Winslet (star of *Titanic* and other Hollywood blockbusters) commented on how she found herself taken aback by the images published after one photo shoot. Outspoken on the issue, she was shocked by the degree to which her body had been manipulated—slimmed, sculpted, and resized according to the current fashion.

Instead of praising the masters of airbrushing, why don't you put an end to this charade?

Almost all of the editors and writers at your magazines are *women*, who have the power to change how our culture defines what is considered "beautiful," "sexy," and "feminine." As Betty Friedan wrote a generation ago, "The feminine mystique says that the highest value and the only commitment for women is the fulfillment of their own femininity." You are promoting a new unhealthy version of the feminine mystique. You can change the standards and create an entire revolution in how pop culture defines female beauty by simply printing images of real women.

But until that happens, kindly cancel my subscription.

Sincerely,

[YOUR NAME]

OBJECTIFY YOURSELF
Find pleasure in your own image

For just a moment, let's ignore our arms, stomach, thighs, and calves and focus on the most directly pleasurable part of our own bodies: pussy, beaver, vagina, cunt, yoni, coochie, vulva, labia, clit, lips, flower, fruit, bud, rose, cherry muff, muffin, kitten, wee-wee, mee-mee, love canal, hole, snatch, twat, cooter box, poonany, bush, poontang, powderbox, honey pot. Did we miss your favorite euphemism? You might want to try "cake" on for size. No more excuses for calling it "down there"—what are you, lost in Australia without a map?

> Dear CAKE,
> I look at my vagina every single day. It really intrigues me. It pulls me in and begs me to examine it. I have grown to absolutely love it. I used to get freaked out, thinking it was a strange color, or get upset about a sudden shaving irritation. But my vagina has been so good to me in the past. It's like a wonder of the world to me. I think because I am so in touch with it (literally), it really treats me well. Is this normal?
> —KATHERINE, 19

Indeed, Katherine, this is very normal, and you are not alone. There's always time to sit down and take another look at your love muffin—to get to know your vulva like you know your fingers and toes—and treat it with all the lovin' it deserves.

Why are we supposed to constantly observe ourselves in the mirror to get great abs or a great butt, but never supposed to observe our vaginas so as to have great orgasms? Our vaginas not only give us great pleasure but also are the passageway through which all new life comes. The vagina truly deserves our respect, and yes, if you treat it well, it will reward you a thousand times over.

The good old hand mirror between the legs is a simple way to check in and feel around for visual and physical stimulation. You slide your back down the bathroom wall and sit on the bath mat with your toes touching and your knees open and lean the mirror at the perfect angle so all is easy to see. This is when it's time for some "Vagina Dialogues," when you and your cake have a serious heart-to-heart. You say: "Sorry, baby, I know I've been ignoring you, but I've been busy with work, and I've barely had time to take out the trash. But I know our relationship needs to be more of a priority, and I'm really going to make some time to hang out with you, starting right now." She blushes and glows in response.

Since we rarely see the insides of vaginas outside of porn or a medical room, these face-to-face sessions are mixed with admiration and awe. Not knowing whether what she had looked "right," Roberta (23) used to compare what she saw with porn pictures. Luckily, each vagina has its own personality, and it'd be quite a scavenger hunt to find two alike.

When Nancy (24) was growing up, she loved to just lie in bed and look at her vagina with a hand mirror, and she has continued this practice as an adult. She admires her colors, smell, and curves and likes to check out her clitoris up close. She even got a clitoral-hood piercing to accentuate the positive—of her pleasure, that is.

Pleasure Tip: Quick—grab a digital or Polaroid camera for immediate gratification. Make your cake this year's starlet, though she won't be gracing any covers save the one on your bed. Think less about what anyone else would see in the photos and more about what would turn you on to look at. When you're done, keep your clothes off and fall asleep naked, holding on to the crotch that's yours, all yours.

27

NIP/TUCK?

Let's start with the B's. Breasts, boobs, bosoms. The "Barbie doll" body, which does not exist in nature, has become the baseline ideal, and women are splurging big-time on breast implants. According to the American Society of Plastic Surgeons, in 2004 alone, more than 260,000 women got breast implants, a 20 percent increase from the previous year. We are bombarded by ceaseless displays of "before" and "after" shots. With the advent of plastic surgery television—*Extreme Makeover, I Want a Famous Face,* and *Nip/Tuck* are the mainstays—it would seem that the entire nation is going under the knife.

The sell goes something like this: "Feeling bad about your breast size and shape? Maybe you are inadequate. So why not indulge in a little 'fixer-upper'? Everybody's doing it."

Mainstream actresses, adult starlets, models, and hundreds of thousands of everyday women have learned that there is a boob-based equation—the bigger your boobs, the bigger your tips, the better your chances of landing a magazine cover, the more money you are likely to bring in, and it goes on ad infinitum. More titty equals more attention and more moolah.

In a disturbing turn of events, body perfection has moved southward, and there's a brand-new booming market for labia surgery. Now you can match your perky boobs with nipped and tucked labia. Any sign of inner lips "drooping" down below the outer ones can be quickly snipped away, leaving you with the new "ideal" pussy. In direct contrast to penis enlargement, there's a new, distorted, and distinctly pleasure-draining standard for women whereby our genitals are visually more appealing when they are smaller. Huh?

In an ideal world, we would be more richly rewarded for our bodies as they are. The choice is yours—but before you go under the knife, ask yourself: Why is there just one standard image of what the body should look like, when in reality every woman's body is naturally different? Whatever your decision, we like you just the way you are.

THE BRAZILIAN

There's just one word to describe the "strip"—not the Las Vegas strip, but the little runway strip of hair left over from a Brazilian wax . . . *ouch!* If the Brazilian leaves us begging for our mommies, why are so many of us standing in line to take it off?

The answer comes approximately twenty-four hours after the procedure, when we discover the unexpected suppleness of our newly waxed skin—we are talking baby's-bottom soft. Removing the pubic hair on our labia can increase the sensitivity of tongue-to-skin, hand-to-skin, vibrator-to-skin contact so much that we forget the painful pulling, tugging, and tweezing (yes, tweezing) of the 30-minute procedure. The final result is a bare underside, and we mean all the way under, with nary a hair to stand in your way.

Bottom line? It's sort of like your first acid trip: While it's going on, you keep asking yourself, "Why am I doing this, *why* am I doing this?," but afterward you feel like a champ for getting through it, and you discover a part of yourself that you never knew existed. But, also like an acid trip, it's not a daily necessity, and we can stand proud and true to our roots by staying au naturel.

NATURAL HIGHS
Understand sexual functioning

Some days you just wake up intensely horny. You're ravenous with lust, ready to jump on anything, given the chance. The doorknob starts to look good, and it's difficult to concentrate on life outside of sex. You are predatory, howling at the moon, and you get cranky when you can't get laid. Don't fight it, work with it. When you are aroused, go with it. When you are not, *c'est la vie.*

Some women are labeled sexually dysfunctional when we have problems with desire and arousal. Hold up—before we accept that we're damaged goods, let's first define what female sexual function is all about. You know how people say that men think about sex every 6 seconds? Well, even though we never hear about the quantity or quality of women's daily sexual thoughts, your active mind is a part of a healthy sex life.

With a little encouragement, exploration, and confidence, we can fine-tune our libidos and have sex on the brain every day. Become attuned to your body's arousal signals; figure out what makes you hot and what dulls your senses. Our libidos are there and ready for the picking!

While Prince Charming can make our panties wet, and a loving relationship is a big turn-on, female arousal is not always dependent on romance or a relationship. In fact, it may not even be dependent on a man—or a woman. When we are open to what turns us on, sometimes arousal can take us by surprise even while we're sitting in the office, working out, or hanging at home. Jessica (32) gets turned on by the darnedest things. Some are outright sexy, like reading erotica before bedtime and self-love sessions in front of her bathroom mirror in the morning before work, while others are quite tame, like her post-work bathing ritual. Arousal to her is as natural as sipping her "organic blend of Pete's coffee each morning."

When we are aroused, blood rushes to our breasts and genitals. Muscle tension builds up throughout the body and continues to build until we have an orgasm and the tension releases. There's wetness, tingling, warmth, itching, acceleration of heartbeat, and lightness of body, all of which can come over us with hardly any heads-up. In the process, the clit and our other erectile tissue wake up and stand at attention! Yes, women get wood, just like the boys.

In several studies, women who watched erotic videos showed physical signs of arousal but didn't consciously realize they were raring to go. How absurd is that? Psychologists think it happens because the women's minds weren't in tune with their bodies. Enough—let's get tuned in.

Pleasure Tip: Pay close attention to the things that make you wet and warm. Respect your erection—there is no denying its presence, and heck, why should you? It is there for a reason: It wants to get off. Sure, we don't have a large long handle that points straight out and says, "Hey, I'm here, pay attention to me," but if you think there are no arousal signs in women, it's only because you're not lookin'. The physical signs are actually hard to ignore.

TRACK IT
Get to know your cycle

Certain things are just not under your control. When desire hits you so hard you have to lock yourself in the house and fight the urge to seduce the pizza boy, your body is in charge. While we may not all have cycles that are constant from month to month, our arousal cycle can follow right along with our ovulation and menstrual cycle.

About a week before the first day of her period, Paris (35) gets like a cat in heat. Her body gets more voluptuous, she can survive on four hours of sleep, and she can have sex repeatedly. At other times of the month, she doesn't think about sex as much and is less driven to go after it. After reading that ovaries alternate in dropping eggs every other month, Heather (22) joked that her right ovary makes her horny, and her left ovary makes her bitchy, because she alternates between these intense feelings from month to month. Now that she's on the contraceptive patch, her arousal cycle tends to have more to do with levels of stress in her life.

About ten days before ovulation, Mirta (48) found her sense of touch as well as her appetite heightened. By the time she started ovulating, she "could eat a horse, probably after fucking it first." Then, after three or four days, "She-Hulk" would subside and "Working Suburban Mom" would reappear. Now that she's premenopausal, Mirta's cycle has totally changed, and she's still trying to figure out what her new body signals mean.

On average (but certainly all women differ) women are most often hornballs in the days leading up to and around ovulation, and many, many women report that they get really, really wet during their periods. Regardless of the peaks, a rule of thumb with the female libido is that, when given the opportunity to be sexual creatures 24/7, we give in to the pursuit of pleasure whenever and wherever humanly possible.

31

EGG DROP SOUP

"But wait," you say, "I don't really know when I ovulate, let alone what happens when I do. I only know when I get my period, duh."

What is ovulation? Ovulation is the release of a single, mature egg that develops in your ovary each menstrual cycle. The process of ovulation is triggered by the release of luteinizing hormone (LH). The levels of this hormone increase significantly about a day or two before ovulation, causing the egg to be released from your ovary. The egg travels down the fallopian tube toward the uterus. If fertilization does not occur within 24 to 48 hours after ovulation, the egg disintegrates and is expelled with the uterine lining at the start of your next period, usually 12 to 16 days later. If fertilization occurs, the egg implants itself in the lining of the uterus and begins its growth, resulting in a pregnancy.

When does ovulation occur? The time of ovulation within the menstrual cycle is determined by the luteal phase, which is usually 12 to 16 days long, the average being 14 days. So, on average, you will get your period 14 days after you ovulate. To find out when you ovulated in your last cycle, subtract 14 days from the first day of your period. This will be the day that your egg dropped. If the last day of your period began on October 14, you probably ovulated on October 1. To account for the range of your luteal phase, add 2 days on either side. So you can be pretty sure that you ovulated somewhere between September 29 and October 3.

Now you will want to figure out when you will ovulate next. First count the length of your typical cycle—28, 30, 35 days; whatever. Considering an October 14 period and a 30-day cycle, you should get your next period on November 12. That means you will likely ovulate next between October 28 and November 1.

What happens to your body during ovulation? A week or so prior to ovulation, your cervical discharge, which you can check out with your fingers, is cloudy and thick. Right before ovulation it becomes clear, slippery, and stretchy, like raw egg whites. Immediately following ovulation, your body temperature can increase by 0.4 to 1.0 degrees. Some women feel discomfort or pain in their lower abdomen as the egg leaves the ovary. This condition is known as "mittelschmerz," or "middle pain," and it usually lasts from a few minutes to several hours.

*The exact time of ovulation may vary within your cycle, because ovulation can be delayed by a number of factors such as stress, illness, diet, or increased physical activity, but it should not vary more than a day or two.

32

How long does the egg live after ovulation? Once released, the egg is capable of being fertilized for 12 to 48 hours before it begins to disintegrate. This is the most fertile period of your cycle. Knowing your fertile days can help you increase your chances of getting pregnant, or of avoiding an unwanted pregnancy.

How long do sperm live in the body? Estimates vary, but it's generally agreed that sperm can live for 4 days in the female body after internal ejaculation.

How long are you fertile during your menstrual cycle? Your fertile period starts about 4 or 5 days before ovulation—due to the potential life of sperm—and ends about 24 to 48 hours after it, due to the life of the egg. Doing the math: There are roughly 7 fertile days over a woman's cycle.

*If you are on the pill or other hormonal contraception, surprise, surprise, you do *not* ovulate, because the hormones prevent your body from releasing an egg altogether!

YOUR GYNO, YOUR FRIEND
Take care of your sexual health

You go for your regularly scheduled, not so desirable, but necessary annual gynecological exam expecting the same old, same old—a few pats here and a few strokes to the breasts, a quick finger up the ass (who knew?), an unexciting pelvic exam, that strange feeling when the cold metal speculum is inserted and your doc Q-tips your cervix for the Pap smear, *et voilà, c'est fini, n'est pas?* But wait . . . a week or so later, your gyno calls with some unnerving news: Your Pap smear came back positive for abnormal cell growth, or that discharge turned out to be more than just a yeast infection. For many women, this means one thing—you have been exposed to an STD! What is a sexually active girl to do?

If you have an abnormal Pap smear, chances are you have been exposed to HPV, and you fear the worst: developing warts that . . . take over your body . . . and never go away . . . and you'll *never be able to have sex again,* and on top of it all, you'll probably get cervical cancer.

Whoa, there! Don't get ahead of yourself . . . it won't go down like that. Take the reality step by step.

33

Pleasure Tip: If you have an STD, don't freak out: You are not alone. The worst part about STDs is the total lack of public dialogue. Many of us keep our negative sexual experiences very private and feel stigmatized and alone. Women who feel isolated by their STDs may ignore the problem, fail to get information and help, and stop feeling sexual. To be totally confident about your body, be on top of your sexual health. Go see your gyno every year to get your annual Pap smear and check for human papillomavirus (HPV) and other STDs. Be sure to ask questions about anything that's unclear and bring up any concerns you might have. This is an integral part of being a sexual woman, so do it. For more information on STDs, check out *Our Bodies, Ourselves: A New Edition for a New Era* by the Boston Women's Health Book Collective.

CHAPTER 3

Play Solitaire

I masturbated last night for the first time. I'm a virgin, for
numerous reasons, and I have no intention of changing my
virginal status until I get married. Even so, a girl still needs
some pleasuring, so I took things into my own hands
(literally!). I started out by rubbing my hands down my body,
over my breasts, around my belly button, and down my hip
bones until I reached my inner thighs. I explored my clitoris,
stroking it, pinching it, pushing on it. I moved my hands down
to my vaginal opening, spreading the lips and putting my
fingers inside myself. My nerves were so alive, so on fire. I felt
more aching and desiring between my legs than ever before—
it felt so good! I put two fingers inside myself and used the
heel of the same hand to rub the head of my clitoris. I rubbed,
harder, harder, faster, faster, breathing heavier, heavier, sweat
breaking out all over my body. I felt so empowered, so in
control, so fucking sexy as I shuddered with my first orgasm!

—ERIN, 21

Oh, oh, oh, oh, ooohhhhh—the female orgasm. While it may be a myth
that there's no such thing as a bad blow job, we can say for certain that
there is no bad orgasm. Stress-relieving, body-cleansing, emotionally
bonding, mind-clearing, and pleasure-filling—orgasms have a place in
each and every day of our lives. They have health benefits, like relieving
headaches and curing the menstrual blues. They help you sleep. They

relieve tension and stress. As Mae West said decades ago, "An orgasm a day keeps the doctor away."

We've come a long way, baby. From a time when our mothers' generation had to fight for the right to orgasm, to our current generation, who demand them on a daily basis. Unfortunately, while we have experienced a positive paradigm shift, we still have a way to go to make the orgasm a staple of women's sexual diets.

Even among the pleasure-seeking bunch of women who responded to the CAKE Report, over 80 percent do not always experience orgasms during sexual intercourse, and 70 percent have faked an orgasm with a partner. We also heard from women who have never had an orgasm. Whoa. Now, you *know* that if a significant fraction of all men had never had an orgasm, the world would come to a stop and there would be a international campaign to overcome the tragic condition!

Sure, guys have reproduction on their side, but the female orgasm also facilitates the process. Increased lubrication and blood flow prepare the vagina to safely accept the penis, and orgasmic contractions aid in propelling semen up through the cervix. First and foremost, though, the female orgasm is about pleasure—and we like it like that.

The female orgasm is commonly thought of as both more difficult and more complex to achieve than the male orgasm. While women may in fact be coming less frequently than men, there's no anatomical reason for this to be so. Those of us who masturbate regularly can often orgasm in under a minute if we so desire, and several times a day. There's nothing technically or psychologically difficult about that.

FLY SOLO
Be the pilot and the passenger

Dear CAKE,
I'm 24 and I have never had an orgasm. I consider myself
a sexual person and have had plenty of sexual experiences.
This just doesn't seem fair. Please let me know what I am
doing wrong.

—ERICA, 24

Damn straight, that is not fair! Too often the female orgasm
is treated as just icing on the cake, that is, when and if it
happens. And no, Erica, you are not doing anything wrong.
Don't fret; you do not have to accept an orgasmless fate. Take
immediate action to learn your own body through daily
exploration—learn to fly solo!

Now women are embracing masturbation more and more because
it allows us to know our bodies, discover what we want, and express
that want to our partners—a collective pleasure principle if ever there
was one. Masturbation is a first step in our personal sexual evolution,
and it enhances our sexual self-esteem. The styles, the props, the times,
the places, and the fantasies differ from one woman to the next, but all
masturbation is the common pursuit of self-love.

I was home from college for the summer, hanging out with
old high school friends, playing drinking games and Truth
or Dare. I got asked if I had ever had an orgasm. The room
was noticeably quiet as I hung my head and uttered a quiet
no. A friend asked, "Didn't anybody ever tell you about the
removable showerhead?" So the next day, when I got home
from the beach, I sat down in the bathtub with the removable
showerhead in my hand and played with the different settings.
I began washing the sand off my legs, with the water temperature

just right. After stroking my inner thighs with the water, I aimed the spray at the top of my vagina, nervously knowing that something amazing was about to happen. The feeling started small and then grew, and I was almost too scared to continue, terrified that my parents, who were watching TV in the next room, would knock on the door and discover what I was doing. When it was over, I was suddenly aware of how warm and salty my skin felt. I was shocked at how easy it was and how quickly it happened, since I had heard and believed that it was harder and took longer for women to come than men. A voice in my head told me it was wrong, but I got hooked on the feeling.

—JULIA, 25

Unfortunately, "taking a walk through the valley of love" is still considered a moral no-no by some. Somewhere along the way, some of us got the idea that touching ourselves is bad, whether that came from our parents, our peers, or those pearlized tampon applicators that keep our fingers "safe" from our bodies. While what is publicly shunned may be privately embraced, masturbation still remains hidden behind closed doors even by adults.

According to Thomas Laqueur's book *Solitary Sex: A Cultural History of Masturbation*, masturbation has a long history of social shame. Interpretations of the story of Onan, who was struck down after spilling his seed on the ground rather than into the wife of his dead brother, posited masturbation as a sin. One author sold this story in a pamphlet that circulated throughout the 1700s alongside ads for products like "strengthening tincture" and "prolific powder" as cure-alls. This approach to self-love grew even stronger, and we developed all sorts of anti-masturbation devices; men could buy armor, cages, bandages, and rings to block their wandering hands.

Though men have usually been the focus of the negative sentiment, this same sentiment, in a way, also legitimized men's need to jerk off. Male self-satisfaction was an irresistible urge that needed to be controlled, but it was something common to every man—a physical inevitability. Female masturbation drew a lot less public attention. Unluckily, Sigmund Freud included us girls in the deal and defined masturbation as an immature act that one has to get through to become an independent, worthy adult. He called it "resolutely antithetical to the process of civilization, especially for women."

Thankfully, sexuality researchers Alfred Kinsey (in the '40s) and Masters and Johnson (in the '50s and '60s) sent the private reality of masturbation as positive and healthy into the public forum. According to our research, women are now rubbing one out on a regular basis, some daily, and with an undeniable fervor. Ninety-seven percent of women who responded to the CAKE survey masturbate regularly, averaging 3 to 5 times a week (and sometimes 10 times a day!). Tellingly, 95 percent of those women experience orgasm when with a partner. Knowing what turns *you* on, and what gets *you* off, increases the likelihood that you'll engage successfully with a partner. Heck, if you don't know how to give yourself an orgasm, how can you expect your partner to take on the task?

Carrie (32) had her first masturbation moment in her 20s, when she started to open up conversations with other women and checked out explicit porn, naughty websites, and educational books. The sparks really started to fly a few years later when she ordered the Rabbit Pearl vibrator at a toy party hosted by a friend. "Icing your cake" for the first time is surely more pleasurable, and often more significant, than "popping your cherry." After that, you wonder how you ever went without dessert.

At first masturbation was a mechanical ritual for Susan (24). She started very young and would stimulate her clitoris the same way night after night. As she got older, she found that she could get off without the formerly required dab of lotion, by rubbing up against bike seats. Today she has a full repertoire of techniques to match her changing needs.

Pleasure Tip: Not experiencing as much pleasure as you'd like? Don't get mad, get even. Take matters into your own hands and slip down under those undies, for the first . . . second . . . or third time today. . . .

TURN YOURSELF ON

You're sitting at your desk and you glance over at your mildly attractive neighbor. You just can't help yourself. Your eyes glaze over, your mind begins to wander, and before you know it, you are in the bathroom stall clutching the door and coming in your casual Friday attire. Calling up arousal at will involves tricky mind maneuvers—otherwise known as sexual fantasies.

Whether they involve far-fetched adventures or steamy real-life-like encounters, our fantasies are, at bottom, thoughts, words, and images that we find hot and exciting. These sexual thoughts are diverse, kinky, and creative, stemming from unfulfilled or fulfilled experiences,

---

Cake Bite

TOP 10 LIST OF CLASSIC READS TO STIMULATE YOUR MIND AND CROTCH

1. *My Secret Garden,* by Nancy Friday

2. *The Story of O,* by Pauline Réage

3. *Tropic of Capricorn,* by Henry Miller

4. *Aqua Erotica: 18 Stories for a Steamy Bath,* edited by Mary Anne Mohanraj

5. *Delta of Venus,* by Anaïs Nin

6. *The Story of the Eye,* by Georges Bataille

7. *The Surrender: An Erotic Memoir,* by Toni Bentley

8. *100 Strokes of the Brush Before Bed,* by Melissa P.

9. *The Best American Erotica,* edited by Susie Bright

10. *Sex,* by Madonna

---

or taboo scenarios that we would never want to try out in reality but that turn us on in our minds. There are always new techniques to learn and new toys to be bought, but no masturbation method is complete without the element of mental stimulation.

"What subjects are normal and appropriate?" you ask. *All* of them! There's no need to censor ourselves when no one can hear. Anything and everything that may enter our thoughts is appropriate. No one can mess with, take away, or control these private thoughts. We may choose to share them or not, but in the end they give us the nourishment we need.

Pleasure Tip: We know you've got something on your mind that you're just dying to share with the world. Contribute your real-live fantasies, stories, and pleasures to CAKE, www.cakenyc.com. Need some inspiration? Look for all the juicy Surrender the Pink submissions throughout the book,

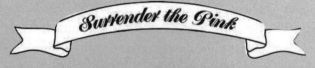

THE TOP FEMALE MASTURBATION FANTASIES

Three-way Street—Threesomes in all possible gender combinations

Girls, Girls, Girls—Straight girls exploring with other girls

Casual Encounters—Getting it on with a stranger, or having a one-night stand

Dominance and Submission—Taking control and being taken

Exhibition and Voyeurism—Watching and being watched

Trading Places—Gender-bending and/or role play

Fantasia—XXX fairy tales

41

GET GRAPHIC

Fantasies of every ilk bring us to a "ready for pleasure" state in no time. Lisa (31) finds that touching herself is much better when the mind and the body are stimulated together. After the first time she read erotica while masturbating, she realized that a good fantasy is vital to her masturbation practice. Picturing two men by her side, she imagines one of the men talking to her, telling her what to do and explaining what it's like to watch her with the other man, all in graphic detail. "I'm sucking his dick and he's talking to the other guy, asking how my pussy feels, how close he is. Eventually the talker takes control and I am left alone with him. He's telling me how much he wants to fuck me, and he only stops talking to go down on me." The idea of the words, hearing the graphic details as she imagines each feeling, is what gets her off.

Play up a plot

Leigh Ann (23) has two major fantasies that can be played out on their own or in combination to make a third. The first involves her boyfriend going down on her in that perfect, ever-so-soft way. He teases her with his tongue until he can sense she can't take it anymore, then he shifts his head to the side and puts his tongue inside her, making her come immediately. The second involves 69ing a lovely female stranger on the floor of a dance club. She imagines dancing with her and grinding against her. Then she slides down until she is on her knees, kissing the girl's thighs and crotch. Once the girl can't take it any longer, she falls down, and they kiss and rub their breasts up against each other until the girl pushes Leigh Ann down and eats her out on the dance floor while grinding her crotch on Leigh Ann's face. And the third fantasy? Why, that involves her boyfriend and the girl together, of course.

Rewind and replay

An eventful and fulfilling sex session fuels the thoughts Nina (31) enjoys while masturbating. She lies flat on her back, legs spread and eyes closed, while she rubs her clit and massages her breasts. Images of her sex life flash in her mind, and she gets turned on remembering it all. To get off, she fantasizes about the first time she was with two bisexual men. She recalls the arousal she felt while watching the two men kiss each other and stroke each other and the incredible orgasm she experienced when they both ate her pussy, after which they shared her juices in a wet three-way kiss. The image of the three of them fucking at the same time, her on all fours, while the man screwing her got fucked by the man behind him is what makes her come hard while she probes her pussy with her fingers. When sex is that good, it's good enough to repeat in our minds over and over again!

Edit and record

We can also take a situation and alter it to make it better than it was the first time around. One night, Kathryn (24) was out at a bar, and things started getting pretty hot while she was dancing with a stranger. Before she knew it, they were in the bathroom and she was going down on him. That experience didn't sit right with her, so she decided not to do anything like it again. But . . . the situation is just what fuels her current fantasy. She always imagines giving oral sex when she climaxes, even during sex with her boyfriend. She likes to have his fingers in her mouth when she comes. Picturing the bar scene after the fact, she heightens the circumstances, imagining that there are more men present and that she is taking it from behind while she has one man in her mouth. She likes to think of them being amazed by her bad-girl behavior, their sense of disbelief turning into animalistic lust.

Watch it in reverse

Growing up among feminist women, Jocelyn (29) never felt that masturbating was wrong. The confusion arose when she discovered that her own particular fantasies were generally about aggression or force. She likes hair-pulling, hands on throat, nails, biting, pinching, and restriction in bed, but she pushes herself to think about the even darker and rougher when she flies solo. In one scenario, she is in an empty classroom and her male professor and one of his students force her to go at it with them before the class shows up. She thinks that because she's a bold, aggressive person in her everyday life, the typical submissive fantasy does it for her. Like any true fantasy, it takes her out of her own world to a place she never could be in reality.

Lola (31) has a persistent fantasy about switching sides and getting to be a man having sex. Part of her attraction to men has to do with her fascination with their "otherness," and she's always wondered what it would feel like to have a cock, to feel it get stiff, and feel the weight of a pair of balls swinging below it. Imagining that she has the body of a man—a smooth chest and a hard cock—is usually enough to get her most of the way there. Add to that any basic scenario, like a foxy woman sucking her, another guy stroking her, or some straight-up penetration, and she's ready to come. Part of the appeal is playing a traditional, old-school male role by being the "fucker" rather than the "fuckee."

Pull the trigger

Your body's warm, your cake is wet, you're fully turned on. It's time to bring out the big guns and pull your trigger. Mental triggers are the images and thoughts you use to get over that last hurdle, from the moments before orgasm to orgasm itself. To identify one trigger, pick a fantasy and isolate the hottest moment. Call on this moment in the moment of bliss and replay it over and over in your mind, increasing its power, as you move toward climax.

To get over the orgasmic barrier, Daphne (30) always visualizes the way her man's tongue looks when it flicks across her clit. Sometimes she imagines that someone quietly sneaks into the room to spy on her. Her trigger is to picture what the spy would see and how turned on he would be by watching her. Lisa's (31) trigger begins with a man lying beneath her, sucking her clit. She imagines telling him she won't come in his mouth. And then she does it anyway. She slows the process

OUT ON THE TOWN

OUTLANDISH PLACES
FOR PETTING THE PUSS

While fantasies are confined to our minds, they are not confined to the bedroom. We often can't wait to return to the privacy of our own homes to get our rocks off. It might even be worth the risk of getting caught . . . oh, so hot. Here are a few places, scenarios, and altogether nutty situations in which we play solitaire.

- In the classroom, under the desk, during a physics lecture
- Under the blanket in the seat on an airplane
- In the back of a New York City cab
- In a conference room, under the desk, in the bathroom stall . . . at work
- Outdoors, in nature
- On the Amtrak train
- In front of the three-way mirror in a dressing room at Macy's
- In the waiting room at a doctor's office
- In the front row at the movie theater

down, savoring each stage—sucking, promising, and coming—playing it over and over again until she explodes.

Pleasure Tip: Fantasies come through your mind naturally and easily; you just have to recognize them for what they are. To fantasize purposefully for the first time, think of your last pleasurable sex experience and replay it in your mind. When reality isn't enough, direct the characters in your mind to do whatever you'd like, feeling free to think of things you might not want to experience for real. If you are an experienced fantasizer, jot down your fantasies when you have them, so you can refer back to them at other times for inspiration. No patience for plot? Just choose a simple moment, object, or person, and replay the image over and over again in your head.

PLEASURE HUNT
Find your body's booty

You've finally found some peace and quiet; no one else is home and you've got a few free moments to yourself. After a quick rinse-off in the tub or shower, you pop on a relaxing sound track and stretch out on your bed. To get more in the mood before you go for the big kahuna, you use your hands to caress your body, top to bottom. As you conjure up your favorite fantasy, warmth starts to spread around your body and you're ready to get down.

Moving your fingers southward, you explore to find what areas are most sensitive, how much pressure you want, and what motion suits your mood today. Having recently read about the G-spot, you change up your regular clit-based method and start by massaging from the inside out. With one finger inserted inside you and the other rubbing your labia, you come hard and fast. Now, how about that? You've found a new technique.

Self-exploration is where it's at, since a lot of the existing information on female anatomy is contradictory and confusing. Some publications show the clitoris as a small isolated nub at the front of the body, and ignore the presence of internal erectile tissue all together. Other publications lead women to believe there is reason to shoot for "vaginal" orgasms from internal stimulation alone. Much of this confusion is due to a century-old debate over whether the vagina or the clitoris is ultimately responsible for the female orgasm. How absurd!

Over the years, we've learned that women have an extensive, responsive, and interactive sexual system—a pleasure system, if you will. Now we have to get to know the ins and outs of that system and all the different varieties of stimulation that women enjoy. There is no one surefire way to get every girl off, but there is a whole bag of tricks to choose from, depending on the day and your mood (and on the phase of the moon), so reach in and grab one for your own game of solitaire.

THE ONGOING SAGA

VAGINA VS. CLITORIS

Early 1900s Sigmund Freud: The vaginal orgasm is mature; the clitoral orgasm is immature.

1950s and **1960s** Alfred Kinsey and Masters and Johnson: The clitoris is where it's at!

1966 Mary Jane Sherfey: The clitoral system is a large structure of female erectile tissue, and the male and female genitalia are homologous.

1970 Anne Koedt: The vaginal orgasm is a myth! The problem's not our inability to transfer our orgasm to the vagina, but rather that conventional sex positions and practices are focused on male pleasure and don't address the clitoris as they should.

1981 Federation of Feminist Women's Health Centers: We have an extensive network of erectile tissue that includes the *urethral sponge* and the *perineal body.*

1982 Alice Ladas, Beverly Whipple, and John Perry: There's a sensitive "spot" behind the pubic bone. Let's call it the G-spot, after a Dr. G who knew about it in the '50s!

1987 Josephine Lowndes Sevely: No one "spot" dominates female response, but the prostatic glands are responsible for female ejaculation.

1999 Dr. Milan Zaviacic: Women have a prostate that makes fluid!

2000 Rebecca Chalker: The clitoris has 18 parts!

2003 Fanny Fatale (aka Deb Sundahl): The G-spot is the female prostate!

Present day Betty Dodson: Don't divide between the clit girls and the G-spot girls. Let's all be combo girls. Pleasure rules! CAKE couldn't agree more.

The pleasure system

The female pleasure system is a network of erectile tissue, nerves, muscles, ducts, and glands that relate to our sexual response. When we are turned on, all this erectile tissue fills with blood, and we get engorged and hard. While you may orgasm by just touching one area of the system, all the other areas are also a part of your pleasure.

The male and female genitals are analogous structures. All people start out with the same embryonic tissue, which develops into either male or female genitalia after about 7 or 8 weeks in the womb. In women, a portion of this tissue rounds out and forms the outer labia to surround the genital area, whereas in men it drops and becomes the scrotum. The tissue that spreads out to create the inner labia for women fuses to form the shaft of the penis for men. We all have clitoral bodies, urethras, and prostates.

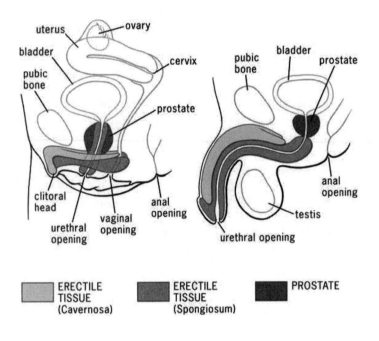

ERECTILE TISSUE (Cavernosa)

ERECTILE TISSUE (Spongiosum)

PROSTATE

The clitoris

There are more nerve endings concentrated in the area of the external clitoris than in any other part of the male or female body. The visible part of the clitoris is the head of a larger body of erectile tissue. Behind the head is a shaft, which extends back internally about half an inch to an inch and then splits into two legs, which travel down the sides of the pelvic bone in a wishbone shape. Underneath these legs are two bulbs of erectile tissue that curve down and surround the vaginal opening.

The G-spot (aka the female prostate)

All women have erectile tissue that surrounds the urethra, running parallel to the upper wall of the vagina. It can feel good to stroke this tissue through the upper wall of the vagina. This tissue has glands that can produce fluid, and ducts that lead this fluid out the body through the urethra. By definition we now call this network of ducts, glands, and tissue the female prostate, and we call the fluid female ejaculate.

The concentration of glands and ducts within the erectile tissue differs from woman to woman. Your G-spot is the area along the erectile tissue that you find most pleasurable when stimulated through the vaginal wall. It's common for women to have glands most concentrated near the opening of the urethra, but some have glands concentrated back near the cervix, and others have a more even distribution of glands from front to back. You may find that where your erectile tissue is more concentrated with prostatic ducts and glands, you are more sensitive.

The perineal sponge

The erectile tissue between the lower vaginal wall and the anus is known as the perineal sponge. The walls of the anal canal are also made up of erectile tissue and nerve endings that make anal stimulation pleasurable for many women.

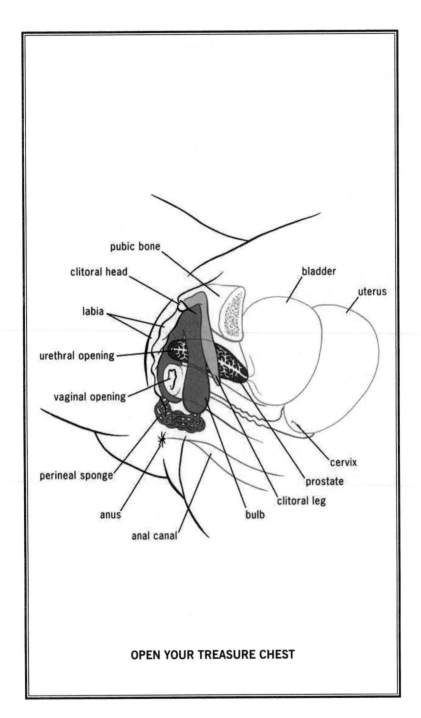

pubic bone

clitoral head

labia

urethral opening

vaginal opening

perineal sponge

anus

anal canal

bladder

uterus

cervix

prostate

clitoral leg

bulb

OPEN YOUR TREASURE CHEST

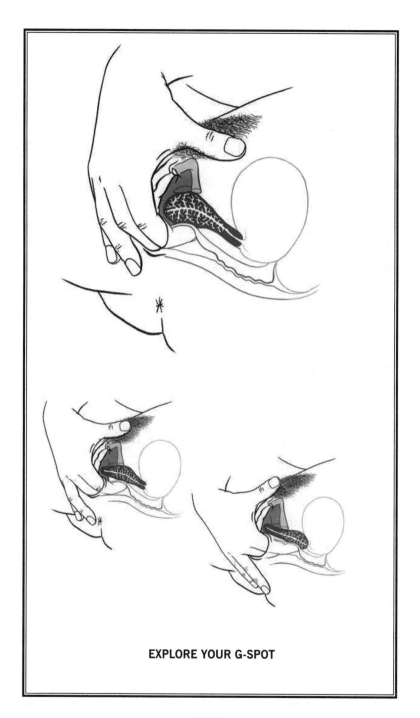

EXPLORE YOUR G-SPOT

TIPS, TRICKS, AND TECHNIQUES
Around the clock

Some women like to touch the external clit directly, while others choose to rub the hood because it is so sensitive. Hand motion and speed are two key components to getting off; experiment with what feels best for you.

Find one part of the external clitoris—left side, right side, bottom, or top—that is particularly sensitive. Try and make that the first point of your circular motion. Put pressure on this first point and then let up on the pressure as you make a light circle around your clitoris, until you get back to the first point and apply pressure there again. Keep your fingers moist with your natural juices or some lube. Change up the speed and see if you like a slower or quicker motion. Stay with it, pause, and try again. Repeat. Continue repeated motions on the clitoris till you orgasm. Don't give up, no matter how much your hand cramps!

Other common paths around the clitoris include figure 8s, flicking, up and down, side to side, and pulsating. Rachel (23) even finds that her orgasms vary depending on what side of her clit she stimulates. If she focuses on the right side, the orgasm is quick and pleasurable. The left side takes longer, but once she was brought to tears because of the intensity of the orgasm.

Kisha (30) uses a basic technique in which her fingers stroke her external clitoris and lips and occasionally travel inside. She uses a circular motion to distribute her juices and takes pauses when she's at the brink, to increase the intensity. She also pinches her nipples occasionally to increase pressure on her body. She alternates hands and tastes herself, which turns her on to no end. She tightens her body when she's at the point of orgasm, then slowly releases, squeezing occasionally, drifting asleep with spasms of pleasure.

The hand job

Pinch the skin above the hood of the exposed clitoris and roll the skin back and forth between your fingers to feel the hard cylindrical shaft. As you touch it, notice how it gets harder and bigger as it fills up with blood. As your entire clitoris begins to get engorged, your outer labia will puff forward and you can press down and feel the erectile tissue through the skin.

Try pinching all the skin of the vulva together, with your thumb on one side and your fingers on the other side. Give yourself a hand job by massaging all the internal tissue of the clitoris through your inner and outer lips, rubbing up and down as you would the shaft of a penis.

Lying on her stomach, Sharmila (28) likes to put a pillow between her legs and pull it forward. Reaching down, she rubs her external clitoris directly with her first finger, alternating between gently teasing the area and pushing hard on it. Then she moves her hand to the other side of the pillow and pushes through the material, putting lots of pressure and force on her clitoris. She gyrates against the pillow while pulling it up from behind to stimulate as much surface area as she can.

The infamous come-hither

To explore internal stimulation, take one finger and touch the top of the entrance of your vagina. Instead of inserting your finger straight back, push it up and follow the tissue on the upper wall back until you can't go any further. Curve your fingers toward your belly button, as if you were going to try to rub it from the inside. Move your finger back and forth along this wall in a "come-hither" motion. Pushing up against the top wall of the vagina stimulates the erectile tissue that surrounds the urethra—otherwise know as the G-spot or the prostate.

Just as you can find the penis through pants more easily when it is hard, the female prostate is easier to feel through the vaginal wall when we are turned on. If you're aroused, the erectile tissue increases in size and part of it presses down on the upper wall of the vaginal canal. If you are not at all turned on, you might not have much sensation at all in this area. This is most likely because your tissue isn't engorged enough to be as sensitive as it might be. Try heading back up and out to the clitoris for a little stimulation, and then return inside to the vaginal wall. Use any means necessary to get hard so you can notice the difference. You will clearly feel the tissue swelling.

When you are feeling turned on, make sure to check in with your urethral opening. This external area can be really sensitive, and just moving your fingers up and down over it can feel good, especially if you hit the external clitoris, move over the urethra, go down to the vaginal opening, and then head back up again.

Insert your finger into your vaginal canal again and rotate it around to feel how the top wall has a texture different from the otherwise smooth walls. What's most notably different is how the wall over the prostate is bumpy and ridged. You may feel the ridges close to the vaginal opening, all the way through toward the back, or more concentrated in the back of the vaginal canal, up toward the belly button. Also try hooking your finger inside, around the pubic bone. You might find ridges up and around this area as well.

The exact location of your glands and ducts will also have an impact on which techniques you use. Some women find that prostate stimulation works best with a fully inserted finger wrapped up and around the pubic bone. Others, who have glands concentrated near the opening of the urethra, happily stimulate their prostate with a large external vibrator, like the Hitachi Magic Wand, whereby vibration stimulates the external clitoris as well as the prostate.

You can control and move this body of erectile tissue using the muscles inside your vagina. Contract your vaginal muscles, as if you were trying to suck something into yourself, and see how the walls grab your finger when it's inside. Now remove your finger, sit up, grab a mirror, and spread your lips so you can see your vaginal opening. Use your muscles to push out, as if you were trying really hard to pee, and you may be able to see the erectile tissue of the prostate as it moves forward.

Palming it

When a few fingers are busy working the prostate from the inside, use the rest of your hand's surface area to massage the whole clitoris from the outside. Use the top of your palm to target the top of your clitoris for some serious double stimulation. While you move your fingers in and out, move your whole hand up and down in the same rhythm.

Barbara (21) begins by focusing on her vagina. Moving her fingers in and out, she focuses on the front wall, rubbing harder and harder with the heel of her palm on her clit. After that orgasm, she moves on to caress her clitoris because it's screaming with sensitivity. Flicking faster and faster with just her pointer finger, she then grabs a nipple with the other hand and has the most explosive orgasm.

The two-handed approach

Elizabeth (32) uses both hands: one to keep pressure on her sensitive prostate, and the other to massage her vulva. With her left middle finger inside, curved strongly against the front wall of her vagina, she uses her whole right hand to rub wide circles around her clitoris. Occasionally she massages her whole vulva while pushing her finger harder against her prostate. When she feels ready to come, she rubs the top of her clitoris with one hand, and the area of her prostate right near the opening of the vagina with the other.

Behind the scenes

If you insert one finger and press down toward your ass instead of up toward your belly button, you will feel another area of sensitive tissue. Using lubrication from your body or some lube, head back out and down between your cheeks. If you want, try this part in the tub. Gently massage around the outside of your anal opening and try inserting a finger. Combine anal stimulation with other techniques for additional pleasure potential.

Position yourself

One of the best masturbation positions is on your back, but you might also get off lying facedown on your stomach or on your side. Usually Jennifer (28) lies on her back with her legs open, stroking the G-spot and the clitoris with the same speed and motion, but recently she discovered a new trick. By lying on her side, she can move her body on her fingers, like she's fucking her hand. This also means her legs are closed, so the rest of her vulva gets stimulated at the same time. When she comes, she likes to leave her fingers inside to feel her vaginal contractions.

Also try kneeling or standing up and bending over, as if you're doing it doggie style. Clench your butt and push your pelvis forward, and move your hips back and forth against your hand.

Rub-a-dub-dub

There comes a time when every girl realizes the extra-special reward of sinking into a nice warm bath: the water-induced orgasm. When it comes to ease of use and a quick fix, one of the best places to fire up your engine is the tub! There are three basic options, depending on how your bath is configured: the tub faucet; the detachable shower head; the Jacuzzi/pool jet.

The faucet. The bathtub is a refuge for female masturbation—warm, moist, soft, and caressing. Start with a nice warm bath and wait until you feel good and relaxed. When you are feeling oh-so-nice, slide your body down, wrap your legs around the faucet, and let the water pour over your crotch. It may take a little maneuvering, but the procedure is well worth the results. Don't worry about looking a bit silly, because you will actually look pretty sexy. Experiment with the temperature and pressure of the water to see what feels best to you. Move your body around to see what part of your vulva you want the water pressure to fall on. When you find a spot that feels good, keep the water flowing on that area. Running water mimics the feeling of a warm, wet tongue as it consistently pours over the vulva. You may want to read some sexy stories while in the tub to get your juices flowing.

The detachable showerhead. The innocuous-looking but irresistible detachable showerhead is a Bed, Bath & Beyond mega masturbation tool just waiting to be put to good use. It's easier to bring the water to you than to bring yourself to the water. This snazzy prop also has different settings for varying pressures (pulsating, gyrating, and spraying) and speeds that give you access to an endless variety of water-powered experimentation.

The Jacuzzi. A description of water-induced orgasms would be incomplete without a mention of the ever-popular and well-utilized Jacuzzi! Jump in and press yourself up against the wall—right on the jet—and let the water do the work. Experiment with how close you like to be to where the water streams out. Hands down, the Jacuzzi wins for the most likely place women find their masturbation potential. We guarantee an orgasm in thirty seconds, or your money back!

We all have the same basic equipment, but in the end we all come to an understanding of our own individual bodies. You are the expert. The secrets of your body may be just what another woman needs to hear to unlock the secrets of her own. At the end of the day, whatever you find works for you, babycakes, is gold.

Pleasure Tip: Masturbation techniques can include all areas of your body. Nipple pinching, lip biting, thigh caressing, or ass rubbing—that unabashed, unashamed, I'm-gonna-get-'em-tiger kind of pure sexual desire—makes nothing off limits. When flying solo, we can be as loud or as soft, as wild or as calm, as contorted or as relaxed, as we want. Get noisy and shock your neighbors into thinking you've got a wild man hiding in your closet, ready to please you at your will.

THE BIG O
Enjoy the payoff

Let us be perfectly clear: There is absolutely, positively no mistaking an orgasm. There is an explosive release that surprises even the tried-and-true orgasm veterans every time because of how damn good it feels. From a technical perspective, the big O in orgasm is actually the physical release of sexual tension that has built up, and, boy, does that release feel so good! Overall, an orgasm is one of the most pleasurable, indulgent, and important experiences a woman can have.

When you've increased the speed and intensity of your own masturbation technique, and you're ready to pull your mental trigger, there are a few physical triggers to tack on to the process. Different combinations of muscle tension and breathing bring varied results and affect the way an orgasm feels. Lots of women say that clenching, squeezing, and tensing help them to go from turned on to getting off. By paying attention to what you feel like when you orgasm, and how you get there, you can add variety to your orgasms.

Remember, achieving orgasm is not a passive body function. You have a lot of control over when and how you come. You can tense up your whole body until you come, or try coming with your body completely relaxed, breathing through any muscle tension. See what happens when you hold your breath as you begin to come, or continue taking deep breaths all the way through your orgasm.

Many non-Western philosophies about the body address ways to use your breath to move and control your sexual energy flow before and during orgasm. A Tantric breathing exercise is what helped Anne (26) to experience her first orgasm. When she focused just on what she was doing with her hands, she frustratingly couldn't get off. Her body reacts best when she focuses on breathing the pleasure throughout her body—that gives her lots of space, and permission to get in tune with what her body needs.

Usually Jennifer (23) screams and moans when she is coming, but recently she discovered something new. If she takes a deep breath just when her orgasm hits, she gets what feels like an electrical shock through her body. The orgasm goes from her groin, like a lightning bolt, straight up to her head.

There's a building of tension between wanting it now and not wanting it to happen because then it will be over. Your push your tits in the air and spread your legs as wide as possible, and get the deepest penetration you can. Right before you come, you know nothing can stop you from stepping over the edge; if your roommate walks in on you now, c'est la vie. An explosion jolts through you. Your toes curl, your tongue goes numb, and your mind's eye flashes a million unnamed colors.

There's a sharp contraction of pleasure and then rhythmic throbbing, mostly concentrated within your clitoris, vagina, and uterus. You feel anywhere from 5 to 12 synchronized contractions of the uterine, vaginal, anal, and lower abdominal muscles for about 10 seconds. Your nipples will become erect and you will have a hard time keeping your eyes open. And, oh yeah, it feels really, really outstanding, exquisite, remarkable—waves of pleasure rolling through your body!

A light wash of warmth spreads from your clit out to your body's extremities. When it reaches your cheeks, your whole body feels like it's floating off the bed into little pink clouds. As your orgasm subsides, you are gently lowered back onto your bed and you slowly come out of your trance.

Pleasure Tip: Have you seen *your* orgasm face? Check yourself out in the mirror while you come. Are you a clencher, a smiler, a brow-frowner, or a shock-and-awe-er? Think you know what you look like smack dab in the middle of an orgasm? Think again. Challenge yourself by keeping your eyes open for the entire time you are coming. We guarantee you will be surprised by how fucking cool you look.

CHAPTER 4

It's a Vibe Thing

After many hours of extensive and pleasurable product testing, I have concluded that the Hitachi Magic Wand wins the "best vibrator" award. Adored for both its speed and intensity, the Magic Wand also says "I'm unashamed of my sexuality so I bought a big ol' vibrator that plugs in the wall and refuses to be hidden!" I like my vibrator to be bold, with loads of extra vibration. I'm getting shivers just thinking about it.

—SARAH, 23

Hands aside, vibrators work wonders and make us come. We use vibrators to orgasm for the first time, to orgasm at the end of a long day, and to orgasm with someone else in bed. Using a vibrator is a healthy and integral part of many women's everyday schedules, as simple and necessary as using a toothbrush.

The latest and greatest endorsement of a vibrator was the infamous Rabbit cameo on *Sex and the City.* On the first season, back in 1998, Miranda introduced Charlotte to her secret weapon, the Rabbit, a two-pronged, multispeed vibrating dildo with bunny ears for external stimulation, and rotating pearls for internal stimulation. Thanks to the ease and privacy of the Internet, women went straight from their TVs to their computers, and soon the Rabbit found its way onto many women's bedside tables.

More and more women-owned stores are following in the footsteps of trailblazers like Dell Williams, the founder of Eve's Garden, and Joani Blank, the founder of Good Vibrations, who in the 1970s offered women a new vibrator-shopping experience. Babeland in New York City and Seattle, and female-owned online retailers (like CAKE!), now give women an opportunity to buy the best-quality vibrators without shame.

Although our society is moving toward accepting the vibrator, we still have a ways to go before Martha Stewart admits that she owns one! Even though healthy and happy women and couples use vibrators all the time, they are publicly shunned as a kinky toy.

Despite an increase in female-focused sex stores, vibrators are still sold primarily by the porn industry as a novelty item marketed to men. The sexy women on the covers of most vibrator boxes are there to convince men that including a vibrator in their sex life will be good for them. (And in fact it will be!) The sale of vibrators is still outlawed in some states (even where Viagra is widely available), and women have been arrested for selling sex toys door-to-door.

As it stands, the vibrator plays two overlapping but contradictory roles in today's culture—one as a tool for sexual pleasure and empowerment, the other as a widget powering the billion-dollar "adult novelty" business. This little buzzer has become symbolic both of women's control of our own sexuality, and of how female pleasure has been manipulated and controlled.

FROM CURE-ALL TO ACCESSORY

A SHORT BUT SWEET HISTORY OF THE VIBRATOR

1860s As Rachel Maines explains in her book *The Technology of Orgasm,* the purpose of the vibrator has always been to get women off, but its roots are in the medical industry. George Taylor patented steam-powered vibrating devices for Western doctors treating women for "hysteria." Anxiety, irritability, sexual fantasies, and excessive vaginal lubrication were typical symptoms. What was the cure for "hysteria"? Why, female genital massage, of course! The result of this genital massage was called not orgasm but hysterical paroxysm, because the term "orgasm" was linked only with penetrative sex. Other possible remedies for this female malady included an innocuous bike or horseback ride, or an appointment at a spa offering water-stimulated release as a part of their service. Hysterical! Where have all the good times gone?

1880s Joseph Mortimer Granville, a British physician, improved on Taylor's invention and patented the electromechanical vibrator. This efficient and practical model enabled doctors to see more patients in an hour, and enlarge their profits in the process. Since vibrators stimulated the clitoris and not the vagina, the encounter was understood as purely medical. The introduction of the speculum as a gynecological instrument was more controversial than the practice of genital massage.

Early 1900s Soon enough, entrepreneurs began to offer the vibrator as a mainstream product that any woman could buy as a home appliance. No longer restricted to the doctor's office, popular women's magazines featured ads for mail-order vibrators with slogans like: "The pleasure of youth will throb within you!" and "Will be found to be very useful in many ways around the home!"

1920s Not so fast! As more pornographic films depicted women using vibrators for sexual self-stimulation, it became impossible for manufacturers to defend the polite fiction that they were simply innocent "massagers." Ads vanished from the journals and catalogs, and doctors found themselves unable to maintain the facade of medical propriety.

1970s Feminists reclaimed the vibrator as a tool for female sexual empowerment. Betty Dodson taught workshops for women on how to masturbate using a vibrator and distributed her independent booket *Liberating Masturbation*. She revitalized the mail-order business along with Dell Willams, who sold vibrators paired with Betty's booklet before she opened Eve's Garden, the first sex store for women, in 1975. In 1977 Joani Blank published *Good Vibrations: The Complete Guide to Vibrators* and opened Good Vibrations, the first sex store devoted entirely to the growing market of sex toys for women, and it's still successful today.

Present day Over the past 30 years, women like Betty, Dell, and Joani have put the vibe back in the hands of women by rejecting the notion that vibrators should be relegated to the back shelves of inaccessible and intimidating sex shops or euphemized as massagers or weight-loss devices. After a long and complicated history, the vibrator is only now getting the recognition it deserves.

START BUZZING
Get comfortable using a vibrator

Dear CAKE:

Aghh! I don't own a vibrator, though I know I should, and always fully verbally support every girl's right to own one. Why don't I own one? I think the answer is they are just too hard to come by. While I want one, I haven't taken the energy to get a few girls together for moral support, go down to a sex shop, and shop around. It always seems like it's so much trouble, and a little intimidating at that. There's still a stigma surrounding women's pleasure that I guess I've internalized. I have a growing frustration with the way it is just circumnavigated entirely by mainstream society, leaving women to come into their own, well, high and dry. For the longest time I didn't even terribly enjoy sexual experiences. I didn't hate them, but sometimes it just felt like a chore. When I was with my partners, I found myself wishing that sex would end as quickly as possible—I'd be

64

thinking, "Sigh . . . I just gotta keep at it until they get off." It's only recently that I've realized there is so much more to it. Maybe one of these days I will get up the courage to go out and buy myself a vibrator and take things into my own hands for once.

—RACHEL, 21

Will somebody send this girl a vibrator, for heaven's sake? Sweet Rachel, if you are reading this, give us your address and *we* will send you one! Your vibrator will pay attention to *you* every time, and it won't stop until you've come. The vibration, buzzing, and shaking take the pressure of orgasm off your mind and put it on your clit, where it should be.

Some vibes are made for external use and designed to focus on the clit; others are made for internal use and are designed to rub the G-spot, and there are vibrators ambitiously designed for simultaneous internal and external massage. You can even throw anal stimulation into the mix!

When my first real boyfriend (I was 21) asked me how to make me come, I said, "I don't know." He asked, "Well, don't you masturbate?" Almost with embarrassment and disgust, I answered, "No!" Somewhat offended, he decided there and then that we should go shopping for a vibrator. He bought me a Silver Bullet. It took me no time to warm up to the idea of it, once I realized how great it made me feel.

—JENNIFER, 32

Using a vibrator does not mean you need something extra. The act of sex, in its most basic reproductive form, doesn't even need a bed, let alone a vibrator, but that doesn't mean we have to have sex in the forest, now, does it? Vibrators are not natural, but neither are electric massage chairs, treadmills, or swimming pools. When it comes to all other aspects of our lives, we do not limit our pleasure to what nature provides us with, so why should sex be any different? While raw, animalistic, prop-free doin' it can feel great, so can a cozy solo session with your vibrator between the sheets.

When CAKE visited Princeton University to speak with members of the Organization of Women Leaders, a female student asked: "Like an alcoholic addicted to alcohol—can you get addicted to using a vibrator?"

Have no fear. The vibrator is a tool, not a drug. Of course, you can get *accustomed* to using it, but that is a good thing! A vibrator might get your body used to a certain type of stimulation, but it will not damage your tissue or nerves. Using a vibrator will not "numb" you, either—the idea that a vibrator desensitizes your clitoris is an overpublicized myth. There is no such thing as becoming physically addicted to it. Saying that vibrators are bad for you is like saying that using an electric razor is bad for your skin!

If you can get off fast and easy with a vibrator, you may get out of practice at getting off with your fingers. But masturbating with your fingers is like riding a bike: It will come back to you right away when you try it again. The trick is simply to retrain your body and your mind. If you want to rediscover your fingers-only orgasm, just give your vibrator a little vacation and put your hands back to work for a while, until they remember how to do their job.

Pleasure Tip: In the cab on your way to the airport, you reach into your Murakami Louis Vuitton handbag (you know, the one with the Japanese graffiti all over it that you bought for, like, $9 million), looking frantically for . . . it. Keys, yes. Cell phone, yes. Wallet, yes. Compact, yes. BlackBerry, yes. Lip gloss, yes . . . yes, yes, yes yes . . . the questions run through your mind: "Did I leave it at home? Did someone borrow it? Ugh! Where the fuck is my vibrator?" Now you're going to have to stop off at the drugstore for an electric toothbrush to tide you over on your trip. The vibrator: accessory and necessity. Don't leave home without it!

PUT YOUR VIBE TO WORK

Now that you've got your hands on the vibe of your choice, it's time to put that puppy to use. Keep your toy by your bed so you can break it out whenever you need it. What you want from your bad boy can differ all the time. Inner thigh massage with clitoral stimulation in the morning, or internal vibration in the evening . . . mix up your techniques just for kicks.

Alexandra (30) loves to warm up with her hands before diving in with a vibrator. She uses her middle finger to gently rub the clit, but when she is nice and wet, she inserts a small finger-sized vibrator into her vagina, pushing it in and out at varying speeds while maintaining the circular motion with her finger. (This technique can be a quick route to orgasm, but try enjoying the buildup by breathing slowly and relaxing your vaginal muscles.)

Once you have your tool in hand, there are many ways to use it. Expand your horizons. Use your vibrator for full-body stimulation—on all your personal erogenous zones! Try moving your vibrator up to your nipples, or around to stimulate the outside of your anus. For further exploration, you can always venture into strap-ons, butt plugs, and anal beads. We don't limit our wardrobe to just one pair of trusty sneakers, do we?

The 4 Ps for pleasure

Pressure. Try the full range between light and teasing, and hard and direct.

Placement. Go for the external clitoral area or the internal G-spot area, or rub all over your sexy self.

Grab a vibrator like the Rabbit, which has both an internal dildo to stimulate your vagina and an external vibrating attachment to stimulate your clit at the same time. Squeeze your vaginal muscles around it so that it is secured internally and externally. In this way your hands can be almost completely free to explore other parts of your body, like your nipples. Bring yourself close and pull away from orgasm several times before actually letting go. You will be rewarded with a more intense release—a trophy for all that hard work.

Position. Try legs spread and legs together; try standing up or kneeling on the ground.

Plethora. Since the female anatomy is sensitive to stimulation over a large area, try using more than one vibrator at once. Use an external vibrator along with a dildo: Gyrate your hips up against the external vibe and clench your vaginal muscles around the dildo. You will find that the combination of external buzzing and internal pressure creates an intense heat in your clit and sometimes a burning sensation so good that your vaginal muscles will contract against the dildo while your clit contracts happily with orgasm.

Exciting my clitoris is my favorite way to achieve orgasm. I begin by reading some erotic stories about men and women masturbating together. After that starts to get me aroused, I take out my Hitachi Magic Wand and place the top part of it on my clit. The first buzz sends me over the edge and starts to get me really riled up. I read more stories—some of them are very short. Once I start reading, I turn off my vibrator, put it to the side of me, and then take my dildo and ram it into my pussy. I always love to stop the vibrating while I'm using the dildo. After I play with my pussy for a few minutes, I stop, leave it in there, and begin to buzz again. I stop reading at this point and let my mind wander, thinking all sorts of erotic thoughts, such as being with another woman sexually, having a bunch of men masturbate and then come on my breasts all at the same time, or just having some fun in a orgy. That's when I start to feel my pleasure rising and decide to finish myself off. I turn the vibrator on the high setting and then lean my body back into my leather chair.

—NICOLE, 28

The elliptical trainer at the gym is only part of our workout, and the vibrator is just one component of our total sexual fitness program. We're really in tiptop shape once we combine our vibrator with everything we know about our bodies and our fantasies.

Whoever says that a dog is man's best friend and diamonds are a girl's has it all wrong. Canine love and bling-bling, step aside—the vibrator is truly loyal and increasingly valuable to men and women alike. On behalf of vibrators everywhere, we ask you to talk about your Rabbit, to leave your Pocket Rocket out in plain view, to display your Magic Wand in your bedroom, and to introduce your peers and partners to your new accessory! With a little help from our friends, we might just all get by.

Pleasure Tip: Keep all of your vibes together in a nice little—or big—box that lives somewhere very close to your bed so that everything is easily accessible. We recommend taking some time at this point to get the party started: Put down this book, pick up your favorite joy toy, and get better acquainted.

VIBES

There is no one vibrator that's perfect for everybody. But help is here in sorting through the array. There are indeed a number of top-quality vibes out there; you just need to know what to look for. We have listed the best of the best so that you will never again be without "a girl's best friend."

THE BULLET

Your first basic choice is the bullet: a little vibrating egg about the size of your thumb. The small mechanism inside the egg is connected to an AA battery pack with a long wire. You turn the vibration on by clicking the battery pack—and voilà, the egg begins to buzz. The metallic Silver Bullet is one of the cheapest and simplest vibes on the market. You can usually find it for around $10, so while it may break after a few months of use, you can always just go pick up a replacement. This vibe is best for external clitoral use.

Nicole (22) has been using the Silver Bullet for the past five years because she likes the nice, hard vibration of its small and sleek design directly on her clit. Its cold metal and distended ovular shape also allows her to occasionally insert it using an in-and-out motion. She loves it so much that she is currently on her tenth one!

THE STRAWBERRY KISS

The Strawberry Kiss is like the Bullet, but better. Its main vibrating component is a little larger than a strawberry—more like a plum—and is also connected to a battery pack. But instead of just one unit inside the strawberry, it's filled with small round balls that move around with the vibration, supplying additional stimulation on top of the overall big buzz. It's made out of soft plastic with little berrylike bumps. The tip of the berry is good for shallow vaginal play, which works especially well for women who have prostate sensitivity toward the opening of the vagina. It goes great with a bottle of champagne!

The high-quality Strawberry Kiss is made in Japan and comes in pink packaging, like a Hello Kitty toy, but cuter! Inside, the smell of new rubber reminds you of opening a new Barbie doll, bringing you back to your fifth birthday! The sound of the motor is a very faint, relaxing whir, like a ceiling fan. The speed control allows you to fine-tune the Strawberry to the perfect intensity.

THE POCKET ROCKET

You can ditch the unwieldy wire-and-battery pack that accompanies many vibes in exchange for the Pocket Rocket. It's a single compact unit with three rounded metal points at the tip that will deliver strong concentrated buzzing to wherever you place it, which for most woman is the clitoris. At just 4 inches, the Pocket Rocket comes up huge! While the vibrating tip is really made only for external clitoral stimulation, we haven't heard many complaints. Great especially when you need a quick fix.

Alice (28) likes the Pocket Rocket's discreet size, versatility, and subtlety. She can lie on her stomach and hold it tight to her clit while fantasizing about being grabbed from behind by Christian Bale and having Hugh Jackman (or the first guy she ever had sex with) in her mouth.

THE HITACHI MAGIC WAND

The mother of all vibrators is about a foot long, with a head the size of a tennis ball. The Hitachi has life-changing possibilities. It's big, like a power tool, and vibrates as strongly as one too. It can deliver powerful, reliable vibrations, not only to the clit but also to the entire external vulva. While the Magic Wand really is great for using on the whole body to relax, Hitachi won't admit that its massive sales figures appear to add up to a lot more than the demand for back massages.

If you like the Hitachi but its vibrations are just too strong, masturbation guru Betty Dodson recommends placing a sheet between you and the vibe, or using the Hitachi over your underwear. When using the Hitachi Magic Wand in the traditional lying-down position, tilt it at a 45-degree angle for maximum pleasuring potential. Try lying on your stomach with the Hitachi firmly placed below your groin, and grind away on its vibrating head. Or try using it standing up, with the flat of the head directly on your entire vulva: Clench your ass cheeks and ride away. You can focus the Magic Wand with a lot of pressure on just one spot, or move it around rhythmically to cover all your bases.

THE RABBIT

Originating in Japan, the Rabbit Pearl vibrator has achieved cult status among those of us who like to have it every which way to Sunday. The Rabbit Pearl has rotating pearls in the middle of a gyrating shaft, along with a pair of shimmying ears that extend from the base. The key to the Rabbit's success is that it stimulates you internally and externally in multiple motions. Finally you don't have to choose internal or external—you can have it both ways. In a word: INTENSE!

Why a rabbit, you ask? The manufacture of objects shaped like genitalia is strictly forbidden in Japan. Luckily for us, Japanese designers exploited a loophole in the law and used animal figures for inspiration instead. Thus the Rabbit was born, legal and lovable.

One of the main reasons the Rabbit has become so popular are those ears! Carrie (25) loves to use the lowest setting at first and then gradually increase the vibration as she gets closer to coming. After her first orgasm, she takes a short break and then goes back and uses the ears directly on her clit.

IMAGINING THE CAKE VIBE

The perfect vibrator has yet to be made, but its components are no mystery.

Style. When it comes to sex, where's the fashion? The majority of vibrators are still designed and packaged as novelty items, like the fly in the fake ice, the disappearing dollar, and the pretend dog poo. The CAKE vibe would be designed to make you look and feel sexy, like your special-for-a-date camouflage underwear, your rad beaded belt, or your roommate's silver studded sneaks. You would want to bring it on a date to show it off with the lights on.

Quality. All day long, you've been waiting to get home and get off. As soon as you're in the door, you pull off your clothes, plop down in bed, and reach for your vibe. Head back, eyes closed, fantasy ready, you switch it on . . . and, to your dismay, nothing happens! That's it, kaput, it's done—and after just three months! If this was your toaster, you'd send it back and insist on a replacement, but alas, sex toy companies don't have that sort of accountability. A few gems are built to last, but most vibrators seem built to break. As sexual consumers, we deserve more! How about a warranty?

Versatility. Goodbye, power cords and battery packs. This baby would charge up like the rest of your electronics. No more unwieldy orgasms! The CAKE vibe would fit in the palm of your hand but deliver as much power as the Hitachi. It'd be unobtrusive, made to feel like an extension of your hand, with a near-silent and simple vibration and a curved shape perfect for external stimulation or a little G-spotting.

CHAPTER 5

Scream If You Want To

After my first orgasm, I thought, "Hell, yeah! Now, this is something I need to learn more about!" Over the last couple of years I've learned a lot, though all my orgasms have been while flying solo, so I still have a lot to figure out. The most amazing thing I figured out recently is that I can have a hands-free orgasm. I never knew you could orgasm alone, clothes on, at your desk, without even touching yourself . . . but I did!

—LILLY, 25

If you've got a good technique, female orgasms are no grand miracle. But, in all their expressive, animated, pulsating, and, yes, explosive glory, they are still a sight to see. Plus, they last about twice as long as the male orgasm. We can orgasm on our own, with a partner, multiple times, with and without squirting, in our sleep, and at a moment's notice. The strength, length, depth, intensity, sound, and feeling of our orgasms vary each time. Choice of toy, skill of partner, or vibrancy of fantasy might all lead you to experiencing a stronger and, yes, better orgasm. But rather than rate one over the other, let's just go for the full catalog, shall we?

SWEET DREAMS

In the midst of a peaceful slumber, your dreams turn very erotic and your new crush appears at your side in a field of flowers, pouring water over your thin white camisole. As your breasts become erect and cold, he delicately cups them, radiating warmth from his hands, and you wake up all hot and bothered. The next night, it's more X-rated. A very strong manly-man enters and overpowers you, having his way with you. The dream begins with a forceful kiss that shocks you all over, and leads to a hot and heated sexual session that has you screaming. In your dream, you begin to orgasm so strongly you wake up in the midst of the heavenly feeling. Just a few rubs against your sheets complete the experience and you fall back asleep, spent and content.

Though the term "wet dream" traditionally refers to the male experience of waking up in a little self-made puddle, women can also have nocturnal orgasms. And get this: Whereas wet dreams mark the beginning of puberty for boys and end shortly thereafter, we experience these nocturnal lovefests throughout our lives. We are capable of having a wet dream and waking up both mid- and post-orgasm with our hands still wrapped around our pillows. The wetness and throbbing between our legs lets us know that it wasn't just in our minds.

These orgasmic dreams may have strange sex scenarios your waking mind would never indulge. The fantasy man might be someone you've never thought of as attractive, or the situation might not be altogether sexual. You may even get off on things your waking self would consider out of the question to try. Oh . . . where your mind will go without its conscious boundaries!

Pleasure Tip: While there is no way to ensure a midnight's orgasmic dream, there are a few ways to up the odds. Before bed, get the flow going with some quality sex reading. Or better yet, try having some hot sex or self-loving before you hit the pillow. Alternatively, your sweet dreams might occur as a natural solution to sexual frustration when you've been neglecting your orgasm, in which case you can just enjoy the surprise.

LOOK, MA—NO HANDS

It is also possible to have a hands-free orgasm when we are awake. Sometimes you get so turned on that just the slightest bit of physical attention can be enough to make you come. Like an ancient martial artist, combine your mental and muscle power with a little rub against the chair or a whole lot of leg squeezing, and you're off!

Once you've achieved a no-hands orgasm, the true challenge is to disguise your response so as to not turn off—or turn on—the unsuspecting people around you!

PEARL THONG UNDERWEAR

Some women like to use vibrators. Others like to use their own hands. But for a no-hands approach, nothing beats a pair of Pearl Thong panties. These undies come specially equipped with a thong made entirely of a string of faux pearls. Pearls, you say? Absolutely! The slinky beaded string on these lacy thongs hits all the right spots, massaging you every which way while you're walking, talking, or just sitting pretty.

HIT LIST OF
NO-HANDS ORGASMS

Where: Rock show at the side of the stage
Initial arousal: Vibrations from the speakers
In your mind: Imagine fucking someone in the band
How: Rubbing back and forth against the seam of your jeans in your seat

Where: On the bus
Initial arousal: Vibrations from the bumpy road
In your mind: The memory and image of a sexual encounter you once had in a place you just passed
How: Bouncing along—leaving you clutching the seat in front of you

Where: At your desk at work
Initial arousal: A dirty IM chat with your new beau
In your mind: The words of your lover describing what he wants to do to you
How: Rocking back and forth in your chair

Where: In bed
Initial arousal: Nipple stimulation or a good spanking
In your mind: The sensation of the stimulation
How: A clench against the pillow

Where: At a strip club
Initial arousal: The sensual, rocking, gyrating moves of a dancer
In your mind: The look in his eye
How: Rhythmically pressing your thighs together while getting a lap dance

REPRODUCE AND MULTIPLY

After your partner has brought you to a full orgasm with vigorous curved finger motions and an earful of dirty talk, he moves his mouth over your clit for Round 2. Changing speeds, he licks your clitoris ever so slowly with a long wet tongue and you breathe deeply into the sensation, coming again, this time sharply and loudly. He continues on with lighter motion, squeezing your butt cheeks tightly, and you have *another* sharp climax, leaving you so sensitive you have to pull him up for a thankful kiss. The very best things come in threes.

Some women enjoy multiple orgasms as a result of stimulation continued immediately after the first orgasm. For guys, all the blood rushes out of the penis after one orgasm. Poor boys! Women don't have an on/off valve, so one orgasm doesn't flush all the blood out right away. As a result, our erections come and go less abruptly. It can take us more than five minutes without stimulation to return to a pre-aroused state, which means that anytime before that, we may still be primed and ready to jump back in for some more action. Rather than coming down after one orgasm, the hard-on you just had contributes to the next.

Some lucky girls report that they have multiple orgasms easily and frequently and that one orgasm means more will follow, as long as their hands, vibrator, or partner keeps up the work and follows the program. The only downside to this function is that there may be no reason to stop. Our orgasms can often go on and on until other priorities, like sleep or work, take over!

Pleasure Tip: The key to multiple orgasms is . . . *keep going!* Repeat the same stimulation used for the first orgasm, like continued vibration on the external clitoris, but with harder pressure at a slightly different angle. If the clitoris is very sensitive after an orgasm, wait 30 seconds to a minute before trying again, or pat it with your fingers ever so lightly to calm the nerves. Also, stimulate the clitoris in just a small spot, or with very little pressure, while tightly squeezing your vaginal muscles and focusing on your trigger image. Experiment with switching gears from external to internal stimulation—for instance, change from penetration to a vibrator or a finger.

THE G–MONEY SHOT
Ejaculate if you want to

It's the night you've been dreaming about. You're all ready—you've done your research and let go of your preoccupations. You lay down a towel on your bed so you don't have to bother with washing the sheets. You've already peed, so you know your bladder's empty and you're ready to get down to business. Starting out with a vibrator on your clitoris, you have an absolutely slammin' orgasm followed by lots of post-come stroking and nipple tweaks so that you stay hot and bothered. Then you start in on the G-spot but continue some light external rubbing. Working hard with your fingers, you think about some of your favorite dirty-talk phrases as you massage yourself from the inside out with the come-hither motion, hard and consistent. Sure enough, you feel a rising sensation, sort of like you have to pee. You let loose, and *wham*—you ejaculate all over the towel and your fingers. With practice, you retrain your mind to accept this new sort of pleasure. Now you love to focus on the way your whole body shakes and pulses as your vaginal walls slam together.

Female ejaculation is a natural part of female sexual functioning. In recent years, sexologists and scientists have confirmed that all women have a prostate that produces fluid, and all women possess the capability to ejaculate this fluid. This new information validates the ex-

78

perience of ejaculation many of us have had and allows us to enjoy it, knowing that it is a healthy and normal part of our sex lives.

> The first time I ejaculated was so confusing. I was 17 years old. My boyfriend at the time was performing oral sex on me. I was freaked out and I thought it was pee. I soaked the sheets. I was really embarrassed and I did not ejaculate again for five years. The second time it happened I was masturbating with the Rabbit. I brought myself to orgasm and a split second after, my orgasm fluid started shooting out of me. It felt so good. About a month later I was masturbating, hoping to get that rushing come sensation, and I did. This time when I ejaculated it went on a little longer. I realized that the way I was squeezing my pelvis forward was causing it to last longer. Eventually I got the mechanics and I can now bring myself to ejaculation. Today I have a boyfriend and I want to ejaculate with him, but somehow I can't overcome the fear of rejection even though I know he would be cool with it.
>
> —CAREN, 23

Female ejaculate is distinct from urine. It is clear and colorless, has no pee-like smell, and has different chemical components. Multiple tests of female ejaculate have confirmed the presence of prostate-specific antigen, or PSA, which is also produced by the male prostate and found in semen.

Orgasm and ejaculation can occur at the same time, but they are not one and the same. You can orgasm without ejaculating, and ejaculate without having an orgasm. Of course, this is true for men too, and Tantra as well as other spiritual sexual philosophies encourage men to learn to control their sexual response so that they can orgasm without emitting semen.

Don't worry, boys, we know that your come is for makin' the babies. But just because women don't *have* to ejaculate to reproduce, we shouldn't think the experience is inconsequential. Unfortunately, because ejaculation has become such a part of defining manhood, its female face hasn't gotten much attention outside of porn. The explosion of spam e-mail promising "gushing, squirting hotties" just seconds away has promoted female ejaculation exclusively as male entertainment; consequently, female ejaculation is seen as merely a thrill or a fetish, and not as a functional part of women's sexual physiology.

Ironically, though the porn world actually comes closer to uncovering ejaculation than any other source out there, its "porn star only" status cheapens the act in many people's eyes. Some sex activists believe that ejaculation is overhyped, something women feel pressure to do in an attempt to satisfy a male fantasy. Oh, please!

There's nothing like watching for yourself as a girl squirts in full-on living color. If you haven't seen it before, all you need to do is rent a few DVDs. The instructional-style movies work for the real deal, but there are also straight-up sex tapes that will provide you with gushing gals galore.

Anyone interested in ejaculation would love to have the most thorough medical explanation possible. While we do have the anatomical basics down, there are still a lot of unanswered questions. Women can ejaculate anywhere from an unnoticeable amount to an amount that could never be ignored, and we're not sure why. The quantity may be affected by the time of month, your muscle strength, whether you've had kids, or whether you are pre- or post-menopausal.

To judge by you squirters out there, it seems that ejaculate can easily and quickly be replenished. This may be because once you get the prostate really active, it just keeps on producing fluid. If you find that you want to keep on coming, keep on coming! Don't stop till you get enough. While the link between the prostate, prostatic fluid, and ejaculation is a sure thing, the prostate may not be responsible for every drop of the fluid that comes out.

Some of us know the nitty-gritty bodily details of what ejaculation looks and feels like, thanks to sex educators, a handful of sexuality researchers, and, yes, porn makers. While it is not a necessity that all of us explore and experience the warm release of a good squirt, we all have the choice to do so if we please. Let frequent fountains, tentative squirters, bashful gushers, "I thought it was pee"–ers, and seasoned masturbators unite around the G–money shot: the form, function, experience and pleasure of female ejaculation.

TIPS, TRICKS, AND TECHNIQUES

Go overboard

Use any and every method of arousal you've got—your partner, your fantasies, and every sex toy in the box! Some women report that they ejaculate only after about two or three clitoral orgasms, at which point their erectile tissue has engorged to its peak limit and they are extremely turned on. Extreme stimulation—almost to the point of excess—can be good for inducing ejaculation.

Target the G-spot (female prostate)

Since the G-spot is directly responsible for ejaculation, a good way to start exploring is by giving it some direct lovin'. The female prostate is easily accessible through the vaginal opening. The urethra runs parallel to the top wall of the vagina, so the most basic way to get to it is to enter through the vaginal opening and press up and through the top wall. Fingers, dicks, or dildos can hit the spot.

Kisha (31) always got to her orgasm by stimulating herself with her fingers. She'd make wide circles with her fingers on the outside of her vagina and then increase the pressure around the top of her clitoris. The circles would get smaller and more intense and quicker, she'd shake, her body temperature would rise, her heart would race, and then a sweet shock would turn to a pulsing orgasm. But upon riding her lover, positioning herself so that his dick was curved up against the roof of her vagina, she discovered she could ejaculate. His dick was sliding back and forth, putting pressure on an area she doesn't normally pay attention to when she's alone. They kept going until— *splash!*—and they both cried out—"Oooooooohhhhh"—and jumped to

81

look at the bed and count how many layers she had penetrated with her wetness. Since then they go for "Niagara Falls" by starting with oral sex until Kisha comes, after which she rides him until she splashes. And they keep going until her G-spot acts up something fierce. . . . She whimpers, she shouts. . . . She smacks him; he smacks her; there is possible crying; until he puts her on her back and lets the weight of his whole body rhythmically and deliciously fall into her.

THE CRYSTAL WAND

Check out a toy made just for G-spot stimulation. We recommend the Crystal Wand, a clear curved toy shaped specifically for targeting the upper wall of the vagina. Forceful rubbing back and forth with a hard object is better than the buzz at the tip of a vibrator. You are going to be more responsible for the movement, and the toy is just like an extended finger. Just like your back scratcher, your Swiffer, or an extension cord, tools like the wand help you get where you want to go. Get one and try it out!

Push it

Just like male ejaculation, female ejaculation is characterized by two stages: the buildup of fluid, and then the release of this fluid. On the basis of tests of urine samples, Dr. Francisco Santamaria Cabello theorizes that some women build up this fluid but don't release it from the body directly after it builds up. Instead, he suggests, women ejaculate "retrograde," back up through the urethra and into the bladder, so that the fluid is expelled with urine later on. If you empty your bladder before you masturbate or have sex, and you feel the urge to urinate during stimulation, don't feel like you need to hold back. Experiment with that feeling and push out the fluid you feel as opposed to shutting it off.

Female ejaculation is like going out to a fancy restaurant and after your meal you end up getting dessert for free. It's the extra topping of whipped cream on your cake that makes the whole experience absolutely divine. If you didn't know you could have the whipped cream, then you would never ask for it, but if you did, you wouldn't be able to live without it, especially if the cream was fat-free. Okay, enough of my silly analogies. You want to know how I ejaculate, otherwise I wouldn't be writing this. First, I need to get really relaxed by taking a nap or getting a massage. I can't really ejaculate when I come home all stressed from work. I start by using my wand and then my dildo. It's almost the same during clitoral stimulation, but I try to focus on my pussy more by pressing the dildo upward, creating a little pressure at my G-spot. The trick for me is to pull in and out faster than I would when stimulating the other spots. As I'm doing that I try and actually "pull" out the ejaculation so that when I do come, it all comes out. Think of it as preparing your body as you would if you were having anal sex: If your body isn't relaxed, then it won't work. What I hope to accomplish in the future is to ejaculate every time I orgasm, but I haven't advanced that far yet.

—NANCY, 25

Some serious clit stimulation can be just what you need to fill the prostate with ejaculate and expel it. Emma (27) finds that after massaging her prostate with the Crystal Wand, she can apply the strong vibrations of the Hitachi to her external clitoris, push out, and squirt. Beth (23) has never ejaculated, but she has made another woman ejaculate by applying firm circular motions, while alternately sucking and licking her clit for about five minutes of constant stimulation. There might be other combinations or orders of stimulus that work best for you—so don't be afraid to try and try again.

RECOMMENDED VIEWING

Okay—so we all know that porn is generally overdramatized and is going to highlight squirting across the room, loud grunts and screams, and orgasmic revelations. Porn movies are made for the sake of sexual theater and entertainment, and they are going to be action-packed. While they are great inspirational material, don't assume that they represent a performance standard for real-life sex sessions. Then again, don't let the fact that porn tends to exaggerate for the purpose of entertainment take away from the realization that women absolutely can and do squirt, gush, and pour massive amounts as well as little puddles.

FEMALE EJACULATION FOR COUPLES

Deborah Sundahl's sequel video to her best-selling *How to Female Ejaculate* is an intimate journey into the sex lives of three different couples, all of whom enjoy female ejaculation and want to share their experiences with the world. She includes a mixture of somewhat random interviews, scientific research, personal commentary, and most important, the experiences and techniques exhibited by the three couples.

For people seeking information regarding female ejaculation, especially in the context of couples and relationships, Sundahl's video is the definitive source. It is motivating and educational, once you make it through the very first segment, in which Sundahl interviews people at what appears to be a sex industry expo. Why are we at a porn convention? Because Corey Feldman is there, and his date is wearing a huge furry hat. Feel free to fast-forward through the less-than-enticing interviews conducted in this session, and go straight to the good stuff. If your stomach is strong enough to ignore her eerily soothing comments as she personally stimulates another woman's G-spot ("Yummy, you like that, don't you?"), not to mention the spooky chimes that accompany each flash of a G-spot on the screen, this will be a revolutionary viewing experience.

SQUIRTERS 2

The charmingly svelte ejaculation impresario Seymore Butts (otherwise known as Adam Glaser) appears genuinely dedicated to making women squirt as much and as long as possible. In *Squirters 2,* we get to the good stuff when Butts's trophy girl Alisha Klass wanders into the bedroom looking for her pants so that she can go out shopping. Lucky for us, she has time to show the viewers what an ejaculation looks like before her intended excursion. There is something refreshingly un-porno-like in watching Klass and Butts on the screen together. In their attempt to relay a message about female pleasure, Klass's giggles and interjections and Butts's straightforward approach to sex and pleasure are both informational and entertaining.

Instructions soon go by the wayside as the winning ejaculation shots take over the video. A great montage of squirting females gives new meaning to the term "come shot." Try not to let the unmatched voiceovers of screams and moans from women who are obviously not making them distract your vision from the amazing shots Butts manages to capture. Klass is certainly in a class of her own when it comes to female ejaculation, and Butts has the magic touch, as is demonstrated in the end when a supposed ejaculation virgin enters the picture to experience the fun for herself. Klass squeals with joy to Butts, "You made her squirt in, like, two minutes!"

The final word

Ejaculation is a big, wet, and bold sign of female pleasure. Sure, moans, groans, grabs, and squeezes also indicate a girl is being rubbed the right way—but with female ejaculation, the proof is in the pudding (or puddle, if you like). Ejaculating for the first time can completely change your perspective on your sexuality, and your body.

Pleasure Tip: If you haven't ejaculated, don't feel like you are missing out, or like you absolutely have to experience it to achieve a higher level of pleasure. The purpose of this analysis is not to set some arbitrary new standard that we all have to achieve to be considered sexually complete or fulfilled—rather, it's about making sure all women know about our choices and our bodies.

On Your Own

HIT LIST

Tried-and-true combinations of toys, props,
and techniques that get you off.

What: The mirror
Where: On the edge of your bed with your legs wide open
How: Turn yourself on by watching your body change as it gets aroused
When: After or before a shower
Imagine: Having sex with a beautiful woman who looks just like you

What: The bathtub faucet
Where: Wherever there's great water pressure
How: Pull yourself close to the faucet with your legs up over your shoulders and allow the water pressure to splash onto you
When: After a long day at the beach
Imagine: A hot couple who were at the beach too; you get swept over to them by some strong current—to find their inviting hands waiting for you

What: *Behind the Green Door* and the Rabbit
Where: On the couch in front of the TV/VCR
How: Combine the visual of the porn with the stimulation of the Rabbit
When: Anytime you're home alone
Imagine: How amazing the woman in the movie feels, being rubbed the right way by so many skilled hands!

What: Your fingers
Where: On the airplane
How: Concentrated clit action under the blanket
When: On stressful business trips
Imagine: Getting caught by the person next to you

What: The Crystal Wand
Where: Your water bed
How: Adding it to your Hitachi on high
When: Until you ejaculate, for heaven's sake
Imagine: Gushing like "Old Faithful"!

And when I get that feeling
I want sexual healing

—MARVIN GAYE

Let's Get It On

Tiered Engagement Cake

Difficulty: Intermediate

Yield: One Happy Girl

Ingredients:

3 solid anytime, anywhere positions

1 innie or outie vibrator on standby

A mirror, a digital camera, or a window

A pleated skirt, a tie, or a red shiny apple

1 or more one-night stands

Directions: Pick and choose from the above ingredients and mix together to your taste. Try out combinations more than once and replace recommended ingredients with comparable ones of your own devising.

CHAPTER 6

Beyond the Missionary

> My biggest challenge along my journey of sexual development
> was to orgasm while in the missionary position. Ironically,
> the position most readily associated with sex was the most
> challenging for me. For a while, I wasn't too sexually confident
> or adventurous. I'd mostly just lie there, and I didn't enjoy sex
> because I never orgasmed. Lo and behold, I found that the issue
> wasn't the position itself, but my level of involvement—if you
> want it, you have to work for it.
>
> **—TARAH, 24**

All right, girls, now that you have the ABCs of self-lovin' down, it's time
to share all that good stuff with some lucky, lucky boys. Since sexual
equality is played out in the bedroom (literally!), we can advance the
cause by insisting that our orgasm is a critical part of the sexual dynamic.
Real sexual satisfaction includes both *giving* pleasure and *receiving* it.

Alas, many women still don't speak up in bed, either because we
don't know what to ask for, or we have trouble asking for it. It is nothing less than a national scandal! There is a serious epidemic of women
not orgasming during sex. Instead, we propose a new standard for all
women who like to get down. Our motto is equal pleasure in the bedroom, every time. Exchange the tired cliché that "men are hornballs

and women need romance" for the essential techniques and kick-ass strategies of pleasure and we are on our way.

NOTE

Oops, not so fast, ladies—we know, we know, we promised some great advice, but not before we say something about STDs and safer sex. Not to bum you out or anything, but STDs are a reality for all of us. The best way to avoid the mess, hassle, and gloom of getting one is to use a condom each and every time you have sex—and yes, that means oral sex and anal, and vaginal intercourse. Now, we know a lot of you out there hate condoms, but unless you are in a monogamous, committed relationship in which you both get tested regularly for STDs, you really have no choice in the matter. There—now that we got that off our chests, we can get on to the good stuff.

YOU COME FIRST!

Some days, great sex comes easy. You stumble through the door together, your clothes have been peeled off before you enter the living room, and you're fucking before you get to the bed. You're screaming, moaning, sweating, and coming as soon as you hit the sheets. Despite the social pressure suggesting that the more sex you have, the better, we think quality counts over quantity. But let's face it, most great sex doesn't just miraculously happen on its own. It can take lots of know-how to make sure both players are satisfied.

You know the scenario—it's hot, it's heavy, you are both feeling it, but then boom, he gets off and it's all over, and us girls are left hanging. Think about it—there is not even a name for this state. "Blue ovaries"? When we end up high and dry, we feel that our pleasure just isn't as important; that we're not equal. And that makes us mad.

What's worse is lying there, knowing you're just never going to get off on what's going on. In desperation, you give up and start to . . . fake it! Why do we do this to ourselves? Probably because it's not feeling so hot and we have no idea how to tell our partners the truth. Maybe it's because we put our partners' pleasure above our own. Perhaps it's because some of us don't know what we're missing. Or maybe we don't want the men to feel so inadequate that they will quit trying.

This one is in our hands completely, ladies. You simply do not have to fake it. Don't get us wrong—it is possible for both men and women to engage in sexual activity without having an orgasm, but that is different from pretending to do so. It is okay to give pleasure and not receive every now and then, but only if the favor is reciprocated. No more faking it!

Pleasure Tip: How does a good girl get what she wants in bed without feeling like a bad girl? We say you must simply ask for it. If your partner is not willing to go the distance, then he's a bad boy! If establishing equality in the bedroom is a challenge for you, try laying down a new rule for a while: You come first. Make sure you get off before he starts down his well-traveled path to pleasure. Once equal footing has been achieved, you can go back to whenever, however, just as long as you're confident you'll get what you need in the end.

THE GREAT EQUALIZER
The joint benefits of mutual masturbation

Intercourse is great, but really, why place it on a pedestal so far above all other sex acts? Who ever said that penetration is the be-all and end-all? If you want to establish a new pleasure dynamic with your partner, take a step back to third base to find mutual—and possibly even synchronized—orgasm.

A nice and easy way to start exploring equal pleasure in the bedroom and to show your partner how you please yourself is through mutual masturbation, which we like to call the Great Equalizer. Before you start to get all tricky and super explorative, you've got to review the simple facts: If you know how to please yourself better than he does, show him how it's done. That's hot! These techniques are personal, so you can't expect them all to be in place without a lesson or two.

After you have diligently practiced your masturbation techniques, side by side, you can take the next step and see what you've learned from each other. Your partner may also be able to add tricks that you haven't already discovered yourself. Lie back and relax while your partner experiments with his newly acquired skills. Also try stroking him while you touch yourself, or while you vibrate away, and to turn yourself on, check out the way he looks. With good timing, you can both come at once! (Which, by the way, happens more often in the movies than in any real-life intercourse session, but can indeed occur with mutual wanking sessions.)

The Great Equalizer assures that your partner knows how to get you off in a pinch, and that you've got the technique under your belt to make him feel good. After all that personal instruction, giving a good hand job is no problem. Watch his movements and expressions, ask what new tricks you can try, and finally, enjoy the intensity of his climax—a direct result of your manual efforts.

Pleasure Tip: Try mutual masturbation as the main sexual attraction, rather than simply a precursor to intercourse. While you're workin' it, tell him what you like about watching him jerk off. Then move on to describe the technique you are using on yourself. Tell him how much pressure you are using, what motion your fingers use, how deep you like to go, when you like to slow down, and when you know you are about to come.

LET HIM EAT CAKE

Just as most men wouldn't turn down a blow job, most of us girls will happily accept some lip-to-lip service. The mouth is the perfect tool to stimulate the clitoris—it's not too hard and not too soft, and with just a flick of the tongue and a purse of the lips, it can move quickly but gently.

Okay, we know it must be daunting for the boys. Think about it: Where can a good man go to get training? Even though his mother has the answers, we don't advise a 101 cunnilingus session with Mommie

94

Dearest. Forget about junior high school anatomy class—does anyone even recall the clitoris being included in the biology diagrams?

If you've watched some porn, hopefully you know not to take very many pointers from the pros on this subject. Why? Because in skin flicks, it's all about showing the "pink," so performers are prompted to move their faces, and sometimes their tongues, to the side of where they really want to be. That's why you often find yourself thinking, "What is he doing?" or "That can't feel good; he's nowhere near her clit." So, given the lack of information out there, it's up to us to tell our partners how to lick it good.

However, if truth be told, many women are not totally comfortable when their partners get busy. Are you turned on enough? When did you shower last? How stubbly are you? What do you smell like? Is he going to get bored down there? Will he really enjoy it? The only way you are going to dispel your own personal discomfort is to quite simply *get over it*. When we are truly aroused, our scent is "so fresh and so clean." Embrace your scent! You deserve the pleasure.

> The best experiences for me are always after a long hot bath with my man. I sit in front of him between his legs while he washes my body with my favorite oils, massaging my breasts and inner thighs but never actually touching my pussy. My head is lying back on his shoulder and he is gently whispering dirty thoughts into my ear. After I am dripping wet in every place possible, he tells me to get on the bed and wait for him. I get on the bed still wet and oily from the bath; he comes in and sometimes blindfolds me, and at other times just goes straight down. I love it when he flicks his tongue just over my clitoris while reaching both hands up and playing with my nipples at the same time. I love the sensation of my nipples and clit being played with at the same time while nothing else is touching anywhere on my body—it concentrates the sensation completely on those spots.
>
> —KIMMY, 25

TIPS FOR THE GUYS

Every coochie is unique, and so is the way it likes to be licked. The best tip of all is to simply tell your partner what you like—not one time, but every time. What rocks you might change daily and even in the moment. Ask your partner to touch you and lick you where you like it. If you want your partner to suck instead of lick, tell him. If your partner is too hard, tell him to be gentler. Talking to your partner about what you like will turn him on too, and make him feel great each time you moan louder. Now go heed our advice and practice, practice, practice.

DOUBLE UP

- Begin with soft kisses on the head of the clitoris that get firmer (but not too firm) and faster (but not too fast) as you go.

- After you've licked all over the pussy area, stick your tongue inside, and then replace your tongue with one finger.

- Stimulate the G-spot while you suck on the clit using the "vacuum technique": Put the clit smack dab in the middle of your lips and alternate sucking pressure. Change up to making circles around the clit with your tongue, nibble a bit, and then go back to the vacuum.

- Go for a second finger and increase pressure all around. Use both come-hither and around-the-world motions.

- Up-and-downsies are usually the most effective, but your tongue will get less tired if you throw in a few side-to-sides. Alternate between sucking and fingering, with relentless up-and-down licking.

- Consistency of speed, motion, and pressure works best. It may take some time to find the right combination. Ask her to signal you when you've got it going on, and stick with it until she explodes on your tongue.

GO WITH THE EBBS AND FLOWS

- Get it wet, with broad thick strokes, and put your mouth over the entire vulva.

- Explore everywhere with your tongue, paying attention to the inner thighs.

- Use your fingers to stroke side to side over the head of the clit, and your tongue to stroke side to side over the inner and outer lips.

96

- Move down to lick side to side over the urethra and the vaginal opening until everything is totally wet and firm.
- Come up for a big kiss and then go back down.
- Grab hold of her whole cake, with your thumb on one side and your index finger on the other, and pinch all the lips together. Rub up and down as if you were giving yourself a hand job, while you lick up and down the skin between your fingers.
- While the sensation of a wet tongue is among the finer pleasures in life, a vibrator assist yields tremendous results. When your tongue gets a little tired, break out the vibrator.
- Keep your mouth over the clit and the vibe over the lips.
- Hold steady until she's arching her back and bucking into your face.

ROME—NOT BUILT IN A DAY

- Tell her how much you are dying to eat her and how passionate you are about going down. Tell her you're going to go down on her for at least 30 minutes and that she should just lie back and relax. There is no time limit to oral loving.
- Tease her and let some anticipation build up. Don't take off her underwear or her stockings. Begin by covering her crotch with your warm breath and your warm tongue.
- Massage her whole body with your hands.
- Wait until she's begging for it, and then wait a little longer.
- Now get down to it, applying your most creative techniques, never concentrating on one area for too long.
- Include licks below the vagina, and turn her over for some ass licking, including long, slow strokes to the cheeks.
- When slow moans begin and the heat starts to build, go back to the clit, choose the motion that has worked the best, and stick with it. Creativity isn't always a plus once you are already in the groove. Consistency and concentration are virtues at this juncture, which will surely get you over the hump and into the promised land of pleasure.

SEX CURES HEADACHES
(and blowjobs are good for you)

The old line "Not tonight, honey, I have a headache" is simply a joke these days. Giving pleasure to our partners is less a chore than an excuse for us to get turned on. You reach into a man's boxer shorts, lick your lips with your jaw dropping open slightly, and put into motion a power dynamic that immediately fuels desire in your crotch. Forget bondage—giving head is pure power exchange. Your mouth on a cock is being used for pleasure. On the other hand (and often the hand is involved), it's the giver who holds all the power.

Stacey (29) has found that guys like it best when she uses one hand to pump the base of the penis while she varies her sucking technique at the tip—long and slow or swirling it around the head. She then takes as much of the penis in her mouth as she can and goes upward, sucking the entire time while she twirls her tongue and twists her head back and forth. To make him come, she speeds up this technique, pumping with her hand and sucking up and down until *boom!*

Blow jobs—my favorite! The way I love to give head is with a glass of sorbet and a cup of hot tea nearby. This way I can make my mouth cold and hot. So I suck it a few times with the sorbet in my mouth. This makes him crazy, and then I have a sip of tea and give him some heat. Try massaging about a thumb's length from the back of the balls, where you can usually feel a tiny indentation.

—CHARLENE, 33

The more Jeanna (28) knows her partner, the better the blow job. She finds the ice-cream-cone-licking technique works well for her for the tip of the penis, the shaft, and the zone underneath. Depending on the size of the penis, she'll sometimes go for some deep-throating, taking as much in her mouth as she can, then letting it back out for a few licks. She likes to grab the base and the testicles with her hand while she licks, looking her partner in the eye from time to time.

Pleasure Tip: If you and your partner are "fluid bound," to swallow or not to swallow is a question only you can answer. The taste, amount, and texture of semen vary from man to man. A man with a sweet tooth is said to have sweeter semen. Helen Gurley Brown recommends semen for facials! (We do not.) Taste aside, swallowing is an intimate act, but spitting out the come means more mess. Spit at will, or finish off with your hands instead if you are at all uncomfortable. The hand job also offers an extremely safe alternative to oral. We recommend a little dab of cocoa butter as a substitute for traditional lotions, although almost any skin lotion will do. Any guy will tell you what he learned from years of teenage attempts, that there's nothing worse then a dry hand job, so keep some type of lubrication on hand at all times.

KAMA CAKE
Get the hang of positioning

Righty-o. So now that you've totally figured out your body on your own, and even figured out orgasm through manual and oral stimulation, how, oh, how do we incorporate those lessons into . . . drumroll, please . . . *intercourse?*

The big myth here is that during intercourse, women orgasm from stimulation that is different from what makes us orgasm on our own. *No, no, no!* The techniques that we have discovered masturbating on our own and exploring mutual masturbation and oral sex with our partners are the same techniques that work during intercourse. In particular, if you get off on clitoral stimulation on your own, you must incorporate this with your partner. Because your partner can't tell what is going on inside you, only you can make sure that the position you are in is hitting the right spot. A slight twist of the legs or a tilt of the hips may be all you need to get more on-point lovin'. What's more, different partners require different techniques.

This means you have to take control. While her partner may excite her in other positions, when it comes right down to it, Madison (30) needs to be on top to get off easily. For fear of being beaten to the punch, she hops on top to position everything right where she needs it to be, and to control the pressure and speed she desires. She's found that if she doesn't take that opportunity, orgasm will most likely pass her by. As she sees it, she's not a selfish lover, it's just that she's not engaging in sex solely to satisfy the needs of her partner. What would be the point in that?

"LIKE A FRESH LOTUS BED"

The *Kama Sutra*—an Indian text from the third century—wins the prize for its exhaustive attention to a woman's pleasurable experience during sex. Among its other attributes, the *Kama Sutra*—the title means "Pleasure Treatise"—is a step-by-step guide packed with detailed instructions for being in the moment with a partner. Along with practical suggestions—she cups and lifts her buttocks with her palms while you, the male partner, wrap your ankles around her back—the *Kama Sutra* demonstrates how Indian culture integrated sexuality into everyday life, right alongside religion, spirituality, and all else that is beautiful in the ordinary world. It is unique in the way it discusses sexual pleasure without any hint of shyness or shame: We could learn a lot from that philosophy today.

To illustrate the exquisite detail of each position in the *Kama Sutra*, follow along with us on just one of the hundred—"The Lovemaking of the Crow":

> With delicate fingertips,
> pinch the arched lips of her house of love
> very very slowly together,
> and kiss them as though you kissed her lower lip:
> this is "Adhara-sphuritam" (the Quivering Kiss).

> Now spread, indeed cleave asunder,
> that archway with your nose and let your tongue
> gently probe her "yoni" (vagina)
> with your nose, lips and chin slowly circling:
> it becomes "Jihva-bhramanaka" (the Circling Tongue).

> Let your tongue rest for a moment
> in the archway to the flower-bowed Lord's temple
> before entering to worship vigorously,
> causing her seed to flow:
> this is "Jihva-mardita" (the Tongue Massage).

Next, fasten your lips to hers
and take deep kisses
from this lovely one, your beloved,
nibbling at her and sucking hard at her clitoris:
this is called "Chushita" (Sucked).

Flower-bowed Lord's temple? And we thought we knew all the euphemisms for the female genitalia! Leave it to the *Kama Sutra* . . . where else can you find such detailed instructions for paths to mutual bliss? Start with the Crow, move on to the Monkey, then the Cobra, and get your CAKE on!

Pleasure Tip: May we suggest trying the "upside-down CAKE" before you leap into one-on-one penetrative action? In this setup, he lies on his back while you lie inverted (head at his feet) on your side next to him with your leg resting across his chest. This manual 69ing position allows for easy access and optimal hand positioning direct to all areas of your cake, while you can amuse yourself by stroking his penis. Play it back and forth by touching him with the pressure and speed he's using to touch you, and then take the lead by using the pressure and speed he should follow. When he's at your clit, just touch the top of his penis, and when you want him to touch more of your vulva, stroke all along his shaft.

REACH UP, DOWN, OR AROUND
Hand to clit

Some sex positions leave the external clitoris, the most sensitive part of your body, without direct stimulation. As good as penetration can feel, there are times, most times, in fact, when you need more than just penetration to get off. If you usually masturbate and orgasm with external rubbing, positions that leave room around the vulva can be quickly made more pleasurable by adding your hands to the mix.

There are many opportunities for hand-to-clit action. Whenever you are on top, sitting up, it's easy to reach down and use your fingers to help things along. In the starfish position—he's on his side facing you, and you are on your back, almost perpendicular to him, with your legs draped over his hip—you've got full access to the whole top of your vulva.

The reach-down also works when he's on top. With her partner kneeling between her legs, and either with her legs around his waist or with her ankles resting on his shoulders, Cate (22) can finger herself to orgasm while he penetrates her and watches. Or he can reach down and stimulate her clit for her. After she gets off this way, they move into regular missionary position for round two with some deeper penetration. Rebecca (30) also goes for the reach-down when her partner is on top—he's spreading her legs and holding her knees down with his hands, coming down almost vertically. She rubs her clit while she looks at his face, and while she often comes before he does, watching him come this way can trigger her orgasm.

Just as you may hold on to his balls or touch his ass to put him over the edge, he can reach down while he's on top, or reach up when he's on the bottom. Don't forget reach-around during doggie style. A thumb pressed firmly on your clit while you rock away on his cock can complete the action.

Pleasure Tip: First show off your finger techniques when you are on top to let him know exactly what works. Then, while you're in the position that suits you best, lead his hand to the right spot and let him work it out. Also try meeting halfway: Have him place his hand just above his pelvis with his palm and fingers pointing up, like another little appendage, and rock against them when you are on top.

THE GRIND
Body to body

Think of a pleasure circle, in which external stimulation makes the internal tissue hard and more responsive, and internal pressure makes the external clitoris even more sensitive. Any way you can get this circle rolling is legit. While some positions have the advantage of leaving room for your hands, other positions have other advantages. With either partner on top, lying flat up against each other can easily provide external clitoral stimulation. Pushing your partner's body down on top of you or pushing yourself down on top of him means your faces closer for kissing, your ears closer for sweet nothings, you can smell each other's sweat, and you can grind away.

With her man flat on his back, Sacha (23) gets on top and wraps her legs around his for stability. Then she puts her hands on the wall about a foot above his head, so her whole lower body rests against his. This creates a lot of pelvis-to-clitoris friction, and for Sacha the combination of internal and external stimulation is 100 percent guaranteed. At first it took her a while, and she moved slowly and built up speed, but now, when she pops into this position, she comes almost instantly. When he's on top, she shifts his weight with her hands so that his pelvis grinds against the entire surface area of her vulva.

Rocking it from above, even when your chests aren't touching, can still lend itself to the grind. If you sit up with your shoulders back, your back arched, and your hips thrust forward, the front of your vulva can come down onto your partner's body, and your insides and outsides can get rubbed at the same time. If you can't position yourself quite right, ask for some help from your partner. He can be 50 percent responsible for the grind, even when he's on the bottom, by holding your thighs down and pushing his pelvis up against you while you move on top of him. You can hold on too, for more leverage.

Pleasure Tip: Even though it feels damn good for both of you, the grind may be better for your orgasm than your partner's, since it lacks some of the straight-up thrusting many guys enjoy. When you are on top, take the time you need for yourself in the grind, and then finish him off with some in-and-out action.

STIFF AS A BOARD
Get your legs to do the trick

While you've got to spread 'em to start the action, keeping your legs open isn't always the way to go. Squeezing your legs together instead creates some quick and easy thigh/cake friction and makes good use of your vaginal muscles. Go with stiff as a board when you are on the bottom; standing up, facing the wall, and pressed up against it; on the end of a high bed or table with your legs sticking 90 degrees up; or leaning over a couch with your feet on the floor.

LOCATION, LOCATION, LOCATION!
Hit the G-spot

Generally speaking, women like positions that target the front wall of the vagina and thereby massage the prostate. Even if clitoral stimulation is what gets you over the edge to orgasm, you want to be sure your pleasure is optimally supported from inside out.

Don't go looking for one "spot." Because the erectile tissue follows the urethra from front to back, penetration all along this area can feel good. Though shallower sex stimulates the front of the vagina where a lot of the erectile tissue meets, deep penetration that starts at the front and goes all the way back can work too.

Penetration will feel best when you've got a proper hard-on. Because each woman has different spots that she finds most sensitive, and each man's penis is different, you have to experiment to figure out what works. It might take some time to figure out what position works best when you are with a new partner.

Not to put pressure on the guys, but size and shape definitely do make a difference. Luckily, that difference isn't about just one ideal but about getting two people to fit right together. If you have a partner with a penis that's got a slight curve (in the shape of a banana), missionary-position sex can easily stimulate the upper wall of the vagina. When there's no curve to the little fellow, adjustments must be made.

You don't have to be on top to control the angle of penetration. The same sort of back arch that works to get the right external areas when you are sitting up on top can also work to direct your partner's penis to the right area internally in other positions. Sit back and "take it" only when you are positioned in a way that makes penetration optimally pleasurable. Even when you are the less active one, you can still tilt to your advantage.

When getting fucked from behind, Karin (21) gets the right angle on her knees with her back arched and her head on the bed. She likes to have a mirror in front of her so she can see his face and see how his body is moving. Add some clit or breast stimulation and a little spanking, and she's good to go. Beth (33) also finds that doggie-style entry gives her deep and shallow strokes in the right spots. She also gets excited by not being able to see her husband while they have sex, as a sort of handover of power.

Sallie (32) likes the closeness and visual connection of the missionary position, so she positions her legs over her partner's shoulders to target her G-spot, while getting down with some good dirty talk and watching her partner's facial expressions. Amy (28) likes to lie on her back with her man kneeling in front of her. She tilts her pelvis up and wraps her legs around his torso, and he pulls her toward him. Using the wall as leverage, she pushes into him to pressure her G-spot.

Another little gem we've picked up from other women is the "reverse cowgirl," where you get on top with your ass to his face and control all the ins and outs. Thank God the penis is flexible. Dana (24) finds that in this position the tip of his penis rubs her G-spot and the base rubs up against the back vaginal wall. When her partner puts his finger into her asshole, it rubs up against the base of his penis through her skin, and she likes knowing he's watching her ass rock back and forth on top of him. Plus, when she looks down, she can watch the penetration.

Pleasure Tip: Brand your own method. Give it a fun name like the Vulcan Grip, the Secret Handshake, or the Twist and Turn. Develop your own sexual vocabulary: one that focuses on how you get off. Then you and your partner can secretly use these terms at any point—even in front of other people—as your own secret language to turn each other on.

Cake Bite

DON'T DRY OUT

Dear CAKE,

I am a 28-year-old woman who has never had an orgasm while having sex. I get wet and, depending on how aroused I am, I can stay wet for a long time, but when I am not, I dry up and it hurts. This is frustrating because it makes my partner upset that he cannot please me, which makes me feel worse.

Signed, High and Dry

Dear High and Dry,

To deal with your wetness issue head-on, you should try lube. Lube is designed to enhance any sexual experience, for both men and women. We will automatically self-lubricate when turned on, but maintaining wetness through intercourse (especially when using condoms) can be a challenge. It is perfectly natural to get a little dry, especially during an extended session. It has nothing to do with not being pleased—it's nature, and as we all know, nature is undependable. We recommend water-based lubes because they are safe to use with condoms. You can pick up a bottle of K-Y liquid at any drugstore, or go for something a little more exotic from a sex or condom shop.

Good ol' intercourse should never be painful. If you are using condoms, you might want to change brands. The pain you are experiencing could be a reaction to Nonoxynol-9, a spermicide that comes on some condoms. You may also be allergic to the latex, so try a condom made out of polyurethane instead.

HOT CROSS BUNS
Anal sex, "Ooohhh!" or "Ouch!"?

You're messing around with your beau and, while fingering your clit, he starts touching your ass at the same time. Slightly surprised, you go with it, and have a nice orgasm. From there your anal play progresses, until he proposes anal sex. Curious and turned on, you cooperate with him, knowing you can trust him to be the tender lover that he is. After he applies some lube and warms you up with his fingers, you lie on your back, with your legs around his neck, and he penetrates you while you continue to stimulate your clit. You discover the delicious truth behind a taboo: a feeling of fullness you've never had before, massive nerve sensitivity, a distinctly intense orgasm, and a new faith in your partner.

That's right, lots (and we mean *lots*) of women enjoy the bottomless pleasures of anal play. For those of you already playing at home as well as for those potential first-timers, a few words of advice:

One word: *Lube!* Keep it slippery so it goes in easy.

Two words: *Clit action,* for maximum pleasurable distraction.

Three words: *Get on top.* Control how much you can take.

Once you get over the initial shock of the slight pain—things are supposed to come out of the anus, not go in—you will be surprised how accomodating your butt can be to the penis. It is ultra-important to warm up your ass before going for the whole enchilada. Try the tip of a finger first and gradually work your way in. Patience is definitely a virtue when it comes to anal pleasure, so go slow, but steady. Make sure you are totally relaxed and you are comfortably accommodating your partner's penis before you start any major thrusting whatsoever. Go for slow, steady, and firm penetration until he's in all the way, and then hang out there for a while before you start to rock.

My fantasy is to take a naughty shower with my lover because he knows that I am a very dirty girl. The water is hot; the bathroom is steamy; and my lover is looking very sexy. He starts to lather my tits with the sponge. . . . Mmmm, his touch is just what I need . . . my very Naughty Boy. He licks and nibbles my nipples as he lathers my dirty pussy with the sponge. My Naughty Boy massages my clit with the sponge; he sticks his middle finger into my soapy pussy and his thumb into my ass and finger-fucks me gently, slowly, because he knows exactly how his dirty little girl likes it. Naughty Boy presses me against the shower door, then lathers up his hard cock and slowly slides it into my ass. The water is hot; the bathroom is steamy; and Naughty Boy is fucking me up the ass. He is no longer gentle. . . . At first I feel the pain, the discomfort, but then I start moaning for my Naughty Boy to fuck me hard. He feels so good . . . he bites my back as we both start to come. The water is cold; the bathroom is still steamy; and my Naughty Boy has made his sweet little girl dirty again.

—SARAH, 29

Most of us don't just jump into bed and spread our cheeks right away. It's beneficial to have the entire system as aroused as possible before anal sex. The anal canal is totally different from the vaginal canal, which means that different types of penetration need to be applied. But although it's a different entrance altogether, anal stimulation and penetration can put pressure on the prostate and the perineal sponge as well as, of course, on all the nerves of the anal canal.

If you've ever tried anal sex without a bucketful of lube, you have probably never gone "back" since. If you didn't exactly have the best of luck the first time around, we suggest trying again with a bottle of lube on hand for the squeezing. Keep some by your bed so you don't have to break the flow.

THE ULTIMATE GUIDE TO ANAL SEX FOR WOMEN BY TRISTAN TAORMINO

No one knows the ins and outs of anal sex better than Tristan, who has put together the only book and video companion guide out there for women who want to explore their asses. She covers all the bases, including safety, hygiene, anatomy, toys, and communication. If you have generally shied away from experimenting, you can check out the face of a woman who's beside herself with anal pleasure before (or while) you get down!

My mission was to penetrate a willing male friend with a strap-on we purchased together. Well, we went shopping and actually bought a strap-on of reasonable size. That night, after much mutual foreplay, I got to fulfill the fantasy. My partner was very motivated and enthusiastic about it. I prepared him with a lot of oral attention, sucking his cock and balls and licking his virgin ass. Gently, I prodded him with a well-lubed finger (something I've done to him before, but this night, I guess, since he knew more was coming, he was 1,000 percent more receptive to it). His moans were fierce and we engaged in raunchy dirty talk, really getting into it. I turned him over and, with a greased-up strap-on cock poised and ready, I fucked him: slow and easy at first, but deeper and harder the more he relaxed into it. What a rush. He was so open to it, and so accepting. It was the sexiest thing I've ever done. He didn't come that way, though, which was okay. We had accomplished something we had set out to do, and enjoyed the exploration just for the pleasure of it.

—NINA, 33

Pleasure Tip: Got a bend-over boyfriend like Nina? Some guys love a little anal action, because they have a prostate too, and it's reached through the back door. From fingers to toys to strap-ons—give it a whirl. For inspiration, check out Carol Queen as she rocks her lover Robert to orgasm in the classic instructional video *Bend Over Boyfriend*.

110

ALL TOGETHER NOW

Oh, yes indeedy, the very best of sex is when all your parts are stimulated in the right way at the same time. While knowing your anatomy is crucial, the goal is not to have a certain type of orgasm, or to find pleasure in a standard or predefined way. When Johanna (22) has her partner sitting on a chair or a couch, his mouth is level with her nipples so he can suck on them while they fuck. That position also incorporates good vaginal and clitoral stimulation, leaving her partner's hands free for anal stimulation.

Ideally, you figure out your body and your partner and what positions work best so that you can stop thinking about the anatomical details and enjoy the whole experience. Jessica (27) likes being fucked from behind, on her knees with back arched, head down, and ass in the air. Her partner holds her hips and thrusts his cock into her while she tightens herself around it, holding its base with her hand and then releasing him again and again. She concentrates completely on the feelings under her hand and around his cock. In this position, he can touch her ass, and sometimes he'll lube himself up and push into her asshole.

It's dark in my room, so dark, as I reach over to caress my boyfriend's naked back. His skin feels so soft and his muscles feel so strong. I start to rub his beautiful ass and he rolls toward me. I can't see his face, but I know he's smiling at me. I begin kissing his lips, tantalizing him with my tongue, and then start to lightly suck on his nipples. He groans as I move from one to the other, back and forth, driving him nuts. I reach my hand down to gently cup his balls and tease the tip of his hard dick. I ask him, "Do you want me?" "Of course," he groans. I straddle him with my breasts in his face. He wraps his hands around them, teasing me the way I teased him. Sucking my whole nipple into his mouth, he growls deep in his throat, sending shivers down my back. He grabs my waist and slides me up until I'm sitting on his face. His tongue is so soft. He sucks at

111

my clit, then returns to licking up and down, around and around. I grasp his head with my hands; my hips buck as I start to come. Once I can breathe again, I look down to see him smiling at me. I want his dick so bad now, so I slide my body down his. My pussy is so wet that I can slip him right in. I put my hands against his chest, riding him harder and harder. His fingers rub against my clit while I ride him faster and faster. I feel him start to pulse, which sets off an explosive orgasm deep within me. I lie on his chest, satiated and full of him. He kisses my face and holds me close.

—MELANIE, 24

Mirta (48) most enjoys being on all fours, entered from behind, up against a wall, so she has leverage to push against her partner while he's thrusting into her. In that position, her partner's penis strokes her anus and G-spot at the same time, while his hand rubs her clit. All that pushing and stroking and thrusting makes her want to explode. Being taken and filled makes her feel animalistic.

Pleasure Tip: Are you on the Pill? For some of us, the Pill is a safe and effective way to enjoy sex without the fear of pregnancy. For others, the Pill and other hormonal methods can supremely mess with our bodies, and especially our libido, mood, and overall desire to get it on. There is a complete lack of options for men besides the condom—which, let's be honest, many of you privately admit to hating. Even with less than satisfactory options, a modern, heterosexually active girl has to pick one to work with.

For a comprehensive discussion of all the contraceptive methods available to you, check out *Contraceptive Technology* by Robert A. Hatcher and/or Planned Parenthood's website, www.ppfa.org. Both cover everything you need to know about oral contraception, barrier methods, and fertility awareness.

ALWAYS HAVE A PLAN B

You know the scenario—it's Friday night, and you just had incredible, mind-blowing sex with your favorite beau, but at the moment of orgasm, the super-silky, lubed-up condom slips out of place and the dreadful inevitability happens—you just had unprotected intercourse. For the moment, let's pretend that you and this beau of yours have been adequately and appropriately tested for every STD in the book, so the one and only fear on your mind is the possibility of an unintended pregnancy. You are not alone; contraceptive methods have failed for the best of us, so we all need a backup.

You decide that there is only one thing to do: Throw on some clothes, hike down to the nearest 24-hour drugstore, and pick up a dose of emergency contraception (EC)—preventive medicine at its best.

But wait! Not so fast. Instead of giving you what you need, the pharmacist notifies you that you cannot get EC without a prescription from your doctor. You will need to wait until Monday to get EC. Since EC works only within 72 hours of unprotected intercourse, and since the sooner it is used, the more effective it is (nearly 100 percent effective when used within the first 12 hours), your chances of becoming pregnant are seriously increased. All because emergency contraception remains one of medicine's best-kept secrets.

There are 60 million U.S. women of reproductive age, and 7 in 10—42 million—are currently sexually active and do not want to become pregnant. Despite the demand, safe, reliable, comfortable, and affordable options are few, at best. Existing hormonal methods of birth control can have unbearable side effects; they are not available over the counter and are not covered by health insurance. Moral opponents of EC think that increased access to reproductive health will make women promiscuous, loose, and downright slutty. Of course, we don't hear anyone complaining about the free samples of Viagra easily available to any man who's looking for a 12-hour boner, now, do we? What a freak-

PLAN B

What is emergency contraception? The "morning-after" pill, or emergency contraception, is a concentrated dose of what we all know of as the birth control pill and can reduce the chance of pregnancy by 89 percent if used within 72 hours of unprotected sex. (So, if you are counting, it is really the "three-mornings-after" pill.) The U.S. Food and Drug Administration classifies it as a contraceptive, not an abortion pill like RU-486. Pregnancy occurs when a fertilized egg is implanted into the lining of the uterus. Emergency contraception prevents ovulation and fertilization, while also changing the environment of the uterus so that implantation of a fertilized egg is unlikely. If you are already pregnant and a fertilized egg is implanted in the uterus, using EC will not dislodge or destroy it. For more information on EC, check out NOT-2-late.com.

ing cliché. Female sexual pleasure, bad, bad, bad. Male sexual appetite, good, good, good. Nice double standard, ain't it?

It's simple. Failed contraception and lack of access to contraceptive methods like EC equals more unintended pregnancies. As a consequence, there are more abortions. The good news is that when there are good sex education and improved access to contraception, the rates of unintended pregnancy and of abortion decrease significantly. Widespread availability of the morning-after pill will contribute to this decline. Just look at the overwhelmingly positive effect in France, where the morning-after pill is widely available: French women have one of the lowest rates of unintended pregnancy in the world. (And what industrialized country has one of the highest? You guessed it—the U.S.!)

Pleasure Tip: EC not available over the counter in your hometown? If you are a smart, savvy girl, you know that two doses of the same old birth control pill that millions of women take every day can be used as emergency contraception. The number of pills per dose depends on the brand, so ask your gynecologist about your pill. And ask for a prescription for EC in advance and leave the pills lying securely next to your box of condoms.

HOT MAMA

Women these days are getting married later, making more money, and delaying reproduction—and we are also experiencing our sexuality more deeply and more pleasurably. Unlike the titles of "Domestic Goddess," which implies a natural female proclivity for household work (yeah, right!) and "Superwoman" (she is omnicompetent and self-sacrificing), "Hot Mama" reflects the uncompromised woman who does not compartmentalize her life, but celebrates the fluidity of femininity.

Motherhood is a clear manifestation of becoming a sexual being, from the act of conceiving itself, to giving birth, breast-feeding, and having swollen breasts and hormones in overdrive. Just as our culture demands that we be either mothers or career women, it also makes an arbitrary decision to cut us off from our sexuality once we become mothers. How absurd! If anything, we as women become more sexual, more sexually confident, and more in tune with our own sexual capacity. We love Hot Mamas!

Unlike the MILF ("mother I'd like to fuck," for you laypeople) dreamed of by sophomoric males and rechronicled in *American Pie,* a Hot Mama embodies a sense of pride, prowess, and a go-get-'em attitude that says, "I am a sexual creature." Now we need our social institutions, cultural expectations, and in some cases our male partners to come up to speed. Instead of silly headlines fitting babies against careers, we need to hear news flashes like "First Female President Strips for a Cause, Pregnant!—and Has Baby While in Office!"

CODA: AND FINALLY,
YES, SIZE MATTERS

Yes, "size" does matter, but when it comes to our pleasure, stroke and technique put the cherry on the cake. When we talk about "size," we're thinking not only of the length of his member but also of the magnitude of his pleasure-inducing skill set, the extent of his sexual repertoire, and the proportions of his lovemaking genius. That's right, the size that matters is the size of his capacity to give us girls pleasure.

> He grinned up at me again and then buried his face between my legs, his wide tongue easing between the folds and making me feel hot and liquid, like sliding into a warm milky bath. His tanned hand settled down my white belly, teasing and expertly pressing the button that drives me wild. I felt his other hand slide beneath me and cup my ass, and my eyes flew open in shock as he slid a finger in. I was about to protest when his tongue and both hands starting moving hard and fast, so hard and fast that I lost control and fell off the edge. The world spun as I thrashed my head from side to side and cried out loud for the first time. He continued to stroke me softly while my heart pumped furiously and I tried to remember where I was. I looked down and saw his cheek on my glistening belly, his blue-black curls falling over my waist. He looked quite pleased with himself. When I could breathe and talk at the same time again, I asked him why he still had his jeans on. After all, I'd never been with a guy who didn't seem to have his own orgasm first and foremost on his mind. He shrugged and rather unapologetically told me that he wasn't very well endowed and knew he could make me smile best with his mouth. I laughed, thinking of all the 7-inch-plus men I'd been with who thought size was all that mattered. How lucky I was to have found a guy with a small dick.

> —GENA, 25

Okay, now that we've got that out of the way, let's talk some specifics.

What is the average penis size, anyway? Most men fall between 5 and 7 inches when erect, and 3 to 5 inches when relaxed. Is bigger really better? Not necessarily. No matter how big a man is, we girls can accommodate only so much girth and length. Since the average length of the vaginal canal when aroused is approximately 5 inches, a man who's bigger than, say, 7 inches is likely to bump up against the cervix with a full thrust. This can be damn painful, thus answering the question "How big is too big?"

Even though a good fit helps, more important is what a man does with the equipment he's got. The key here is girth, not length, which allows all men the opportunity to use unique techniques to stroke us right. The female anatomy is surprisingly resilient and pliant. We, too, come in all different sizes. Size is all relative.

What is the largest erection on record? Eleven inches, baby!

So what is the big secret of making a girl come? After you've read this chapter, it should be perfectly clear that *there is no secret!*

Maybe the new "what matters" question should be about how a man's technique, style, and strokes measure up. Instead of "Does size matter?" we should be asking . . . **"Does making my girl come matter?"** To that we answer simply, "Like nothing else."

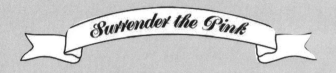

LAYLA, 27 I want to go to his house in nothing but heels, a thong, and a long thin sweater. I would like him to be resting in the bed, and when I walk in, I want his mouth to drop. I want him to tell me how sexy I am while trying to unbutton my sweater. I'll push him away and tell him if he wants anything under that sweater, he's going to have to strip for it. I can see his dick grow hard in his pants as he tries to find some music to dance to. Then the music is playing and he starts his show, grinding his dick in my face, knowing how bad I want it. Every time he brings it closer to my face, I lick it through his pants.

Pulling me off the bed, he makes me a part of his little show. He does a lot of grabbing and caressing and then he slides his fingers between my legs, checking to see how wet I am. Playing with my clit, he tells me how bad he wants to suck it. Then he turns to his imaginary audience and asks if he should eat my pussy. He drops to his knees and I tell him, "Eat my fucking cake" (he loves it when I talk dirty). He goes to work, sucking and moaning, grabbing my ass. I manage to stand him up and tell him that I want to be tied up and tortured. He has been dying to do this and rushes to find something to tie me up with.

He lays me on my stomach and ties my hands to the bedpost. Sensing that I'm a little worried, he tells me to relax. He starts to lick my back slowly until he reaches my ass. Then he loses control and starts to eat my ass out. He spreads my legs to get his tongue further in and turns into this wild animal that hasn't eaten in days. Then he sits up and I can feel him rubbing his dick up and down the crack of my ass. I start to tense up because I know what he wants to do. He slowly licks my ear to distract me and I feel him start to enter me. He sticks his tongue deeper in my ear and I start to moan loudly and he's turned on instantly. He goes deeper and deeper until he's all the way in my ass. My screams get louder and louder and he loses control again. He's pumping harder, and because my screams turn him on, he covers my mouth with his hands and tells me to shut the fuck up, but I can't. I start calling him "daddy" and tell him that I want to be his little slut, and that does it. He waits until I come and he quickly pulls out and I can feel his warm come on my ass. He tells me I'm the best and we fall asleep in each other's arms. When we wake up, I take this fantasy out and let him read it, just to let him know that he was never in charge and he was playing my game all along. Mean, aren't I?

LEINANI, 34 My husband works the late shift, which really puts a damper on our sex life. The other night, he came to bed at around 1 A.M. and started whispering in my ear, telling me how horny he was. He softly caressed my bare breasts, but I was so tired from taking care of our son, I told him to buzz off and rolled over. He kissed me tenderly and rolled over to his side of the bed.

A few moments later, I felt more gentle kisses on the back of my neck and a raging hard-on against my ass. Again, I told him that he had to let me sleep. Moments later, he quietly went to my underwear drawer and pulled out one of my satin thongs. I secretly watched him wrap it around his cock, whispering and moaning my name as he jerked himself off to an amazing orgasm. The next morning, I found my thong was filled with come from the night before. When he woke up, I told him that I'd actually watched him jack off and gotten turned on watching him. When he asked me why I didn't join in, I told him I'd kinda liked watching him get off to the thought of me.

That night he came home just as horny as the night before. As he whispered in my ear and caressed my breasts, I pretended to be fast asleep. But he knew I was up and willing to let him have his way with me. He continued to kiss my breasts, licking my now rock-hard nipples and slipping his hands down my body. He found me wearing the very thong he had used the night before to jack off with (washed, of course), which made his dick even harder. Slowly he moved his fingers through the folds of my pussy, each touch making me more and more excited.

At first, I found it hard to pretend I was still sleeping, but as he worked my body into a sexual frenzy, it got very easy to keep my eyes closed. He then turned me on my side and kissed the base of my neck and used his two hands to rub my nipples between his fingers. He kissed and licked every inch of my neck and shoulder area, paying close attention to all the places that drive me crazy. I wanted to reach down to finger myself, but I waited to see what he would do next. He laid me on my back and, while he kissed and played with my breasts, his free hand made its way down to my now soaking-wet pussy to stroke my clit. As I began to get closer to an orgasm, he pulled out his finger and moved his head between my legs. Thank God I have a man who loves to eat my pussy. He began licking in small circles over my soaked thong. Then, pulling it off with his thumbs, he spread my legs and, with great and delicate precision, he traced the outer folds of my pussy with his tongue and slid a finger into my slit. As he licked me, his fingers slowly slipped in and out, getting deeper and deeper each time.

Flicking my clit with his finger, he started to tongue-fuck me to orgasm. He switched back to licking my clit and fingering me, using two and then three fingers. I was on the verge of the most amazing orgasm that I have ever had when his fingers reached up and hit my G-spot. I came, bucking and shaking like a wild horse, and he continued to finger me through my orgasm. When I finished, he pulled his fingers out and licked them, savoring the taste of my pussy. He kissed me on the cheek and said, "I love you, sweetheart. I hope you enjoyed that!" Then he rolled over and lay down to go to sleep.

I opened my eyes, grabbed him, and told him to get on me and fuck me hard until he came. In seconds, his cock was sliding in, inch by inch. I just wanted it all, and I grabbed his hips and pulled him completely into me, filling every bit of my pussy. Rolling over on top of him, I rode him rhythmically, feeling every bit of his dick slide in and out. He grabbed my breasts and I saw his eyes start to roll into the back of his head and I knew he was ready to explode. I changed to a bouncing motion, allowing him to feel every bit of my pussy walls on his cock. He grabbed my hips and came inside me and I collapsed on top of him. "Honey," I whispered, "I'd do this any night you wake me up like that." Needless to say, he rouses me awake like this three or four times a week. Thank goodness for the "night shift"!

CHAPTER 7

A Little Help from Our Friends

My boyfriend and I just bought our first vibrator. We went to a sex boutique and picked out one with four different textured attachments. That night we used one and it was a very, very pleasurable experience. I've never been so turned on in my life as I was while watching my boyfriend kneel before me, my legs spread open as he circled the vibrator around my clit. As he was glancing between my eyes and my crotch, he began to straighten his back and come closer to me so that the tip of his penis was kissing my vagina. I wanted him inside me so bad, but the sensation on my clitoris was so strong I wanted to stay like that forever.

—AMY, 27

What's a girl to do when a sex position that's good for our partner's pleasure does little for our own? A lot of positions simply don't give the clitoris any of the direct contact that some women need. If this is the case for you, it's time to bring in a pinch hitter, like the Silver Bullet, Strawberry Kiss, or Pocket Rocket, and give your clit the attention it deserves. If external stimulation is important to you, using a vibrator during sex can help assure that the clitoris won't be left behind!

Introducing a vibe with your partner can be a sticky issue. Some men worry that they will be replaced by our vibrating buddies. *Au contraire, mon frère!* Although we don't always need to use a vibrator during intercourse in order to get off, incorporating a vibrator into your sexual interactions *is* the best way to absolutely, 100 percent ensure that you do indeed have an orgasm. Nice! We like!

MEN LIKE GADGETS TOO

All you want is a little kink in your straitlaced boyfriend. He's an investment banker—very suit-and-tie, very missionary-position, and usually you're his well-behaved girlfriend, taking it as he gives it, letting him take the lead. But tonight things are different. You've been in the bath, and you've already come once from the stream of water in the tub. Leading him into the bedroom, you undress him and request that he eat your pussy. As he starts licking gently between the folds and sucking on your clit, you interrupt him to pull out a large, clear pink dildo from the nightstand. He's shocked, as he would never expect you to have a sex toy on hand, but you ask him to stick it in your pussy and fuck you with it while he eats you. Just saying the words makes you more turned on, and he follows your directions, pumping the dildo in and out while he licks and teases you. You want to scream, and you squeeze your breasts as the orgasm rocks over your body.

This only inspires you further, and you tell him you want his cock. Your dirty talk surprises him, but he plays along, telling you how much he loves your wet pussy. Penetrating you, he takes the lead and blindfolds you with a scarf he grabs from the bedside chair. He flips you over to fuck you from behind, and his cock feels so good as it slides in and out of your pussy. Pushing him down, you straddle him, and he begins to play with your clit, rotating his thumb on it and pulling at it with his fingers. When he comes, he pushes you back and eats you again until you are writhing on the bed, screaming and coming, happy that you've finally gotten what you wanted.

Sounds like a fantasy come to life! If you've got two playthings—a partner and a sex toy—there's nothing stopping you from putting the two together.

What I love to do now is lie on my bed on my stomach with my hands on my Honey Bear vibrator. The vibrator is, of course, positioned on my clit. My hands are over it, directing it. I have my boyfriend lie on top of me on his stomach, in some sort of bearlike hug. For some reason the feeling of his weight on me and his body around mine feels really good. He whispers dirty things in my ear, which I love. The best part is when my body starts to spasm in orgasm and my butt moves up and my waist twists. I can feel my boyfriend laughing sexily and enjoying himself, being able to be that close to me and feel my body moving in orgasm. It is a really close primal experience for me.

—JESSICA, 24

The trick in introducing the vibe with your partner is to make it sexy. There must be open communication between the two (or three, or four . . .) of you. Something like "I think it would be really hot to use a vibrator while we have sex." Or "Can I introduce you to my friend the Rabbit?" Hell, you can always blame it on us: "CAKE told me the Hitachi Magic Wand will gives us both amazing orgasms—wanna try it?" And our all-time fave is "Listen, honey, making me happy will make you happy—now, where are the batteries?" Just be direct, and if that doesn't convince him, then try telling him to use a vibe when his tongue needs a break. That ought to work. That said, if your boyfriend can't get with the program, it might be time for a new boyfriend.

Pleasure Tip: Sometimes a man with a new toy can get confused. Help him along in the process and you will both be big winners. Take control: Start an evening by putting on a little show of your masturbatory skills, and see how quickly he'll want to join in the fun. Try directing your partner, just as you direct your vibrator. Let him know how he can combine vibration with the stimulation a warm live body has to offer. Our rule of thumb is to use an outie vibe to stimulate the clitoris during intercourse and to use an innie vibe during mutual masturbation. But there are hundreds of different combinations to try out, which only add to the fun! Follow Grace's lead:

I emerge from the bathroom with my vibrator and you smile gorgeously. "I can't wait to watch you make yourself come," you say, and I laugh. I wet my fingers and rub them around the opening of my labia. I massage the tip of my vibrator against myself until it is wet enough to slip in. I move it up to my clit, rubbing gently at first, finding my spot, and bending my knees up against you. You want to touch yourself and you do. You're cradling my foot and I am beautiful and so are you and I lean in for a moment and take your balls into my hands and nuzzle my face into you, and you moan. I lean back again; this time the sensations are deeper and I put the vibrator aside, just using my fingers swishing back and forth against my clit until I feel that heat start to rise, and then I stop; I want to do this again, and I want you to help me.

I slip the tip of my vibrator inside me and I ask you to hold it and you do willingly, and I bend my knees again and move my hips close to you. You are gently sliding the vibrator in and out of me and I clench my cunt around it and feel its movement throughout me and I move my fingers against my clit in time with you and I look at the way you look at me—a little scared and a little in awe, with your hard cock moving slightly in front of you—and you say you want to be inside me. I laugh and I think it's absolutely perfect and you move to rub your cock against me and I push you back and say no. I am down again, one hand in my hair and one hand just lightly rubbing my clit, so much sensation at this point I am very much on the edge and

I tell you to push harder, push the vibrator as far into me as you can till you think it's too far, and then go farther, and I move my fingers against my clit, faster and faster, and then give myself one more moment; the heat rises and recedes and suddenly it's here all at once and your hand moves, holding on to the vibrator as my vaginal muscles clench and suck at it as I come and you touch yourself and I lie back and watch you, my body tingling and my pussy still pulsing like a heartbeat.

—GRACE, 28

We wanted to hear from the men—"How do you feel about using a sex toy with your partner?" Maybe, just maybe, all the supposedly insecure guys might be a bit, well, freaked out by our buzzing friends. Well, well, weren't we just so pleasantly surprised to hear that lots of guys are graciously and winningly incorporating sex toys into lovemaking? In fact, it seems that you all downright love the results of equal pleasuring. Moreover, thank you for providing an evolved vision of male sexuality.

Welcome to the new, new kind of guy. Let's call him a CAKE Boy.

Here are some of our favorite responses, out of a deluge of responses, to the vibe question:

On a whim, I bought my wife a classic-style vibrator 3 months ago as a surprise. My plan was to secretly introduce it to her that night while going down on her. Once she was nice and wet, I started to rub her with it and then finally use it for penetration. Since then, we have used it each and every time we have made love, and she has incorporated it into her self-pleasuring sessions. Just hearing her describe how she gets off with it sends shivers through my body. And when we are together, watching her use it to climax has got to be the ultimate turn-on. I don't know how any guy can be intimidated by their partner using a vibe. Quite honestly, this new level of sexual pleasure and intimacy we have discovered makes me feel like I'm the luckiest guy in the world.

—JACOB, 32

127

Score!

I have to highly recommend the wearable vibrator during sex. When I first looked at the combo cock ring–vibrator gizmos, available at just about every sex shop for peanuts, I wasn't sure if this tiny piece of gel would really add much, but then I put it on and surprised my girlfriend with it and wow!! We had a hit!! Now any time she wants to go the distance, she puts my ring on and revs me up and off we both go. A mutual benefit. There is some technique involved . . . a little extra grinding on the boy's part helps. Lingering in the fully inserted position, sometimes for an extended period of time, puts the vibe in full contact with its target. And there is the added benefit for the boy of having a vibrating cock ring: feels good and tightens things at the same time.

—STEPHEN, 30

Rockin'!

Pleasure Tip: Check out a vibrating cock ring, or a small vibrator that you can strap on around your hips and wear during sex. Its effectiveness is dependent on its position on your clit, though, so make sure it sits just right.

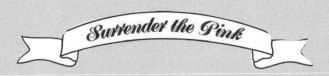

SUSAN, 35 We have just finished dinner at a French restaurant located downtown. It is a beautiful night in San Diego and we are enjoying the walk back to Louis's loft. I begin to feel warm and relaxed from the two bottles of Pouilly Fumé that we shared over dinner. We hold hands as we stroll down Fourth Avenue, walking past the coffee shop where we've had breakfast every weekend since we began dating one month ago. The shop next door to it is always closed in the mornings. This evening, however, the "Adults Only" sign is blinking in neon red. Louis pulls me inside, where it is quite bright and there are only a few customers. Porn videos and magazines line the walls.

He leads me to the center, where various sex toys line the shelves. "How about this one?" he asks, pointing toward a pink vibrator with a curved head. I nod and he picks it up off the shelf and walks toward the counter. I hear him ask for batteries and I am quite impressed with his attention to detail. As he is about to pay, he sees me across the store examining the cock rings. He places his credit card down on the counter and asks the guy behind the counter to give him a minute. He returns to me and kisses the back of my neck, as he runs his hands over the front of my shirt, slowly fondling my nipples, making them erect in the process. The guy in the next aisle is watching us intently, but we don't care. I press my ass backward into Louis's cock and feel how hard he is.

I tell him to select a cock ring and he quickly picks one from the shelf. The guy cannot keep his eyes off us and is obviously eavesdropping. The cock ring he has chosen cannot possibly be big enough for him and so I tell Louis to get the largest size possible. He whispers in my ear, telling me that I am being naughty, and that he will punish me later for my bad behavior. This leads us to the handcuffs and whips, where we select a small black leather whip, a blindfold, and a pair of handcuffs. We finish with some incense candles, bubble bath, and Kama Sutra oils.

As we head for the counter, Louis spies a two-headed dildo. He tells me that he wants to buy it and use it to fuck me with triple penetration, using the dildo in my pussy and my ass while fucking me in my mouth with his cock until he comes. His plan makes me so wet that he could do it right then and there, under the bright lights of the store, with the nosy guy and cashier looking on. I lean in to Louis and whisper that I would love it if he fucked me like that.

He pulls my hand over his pants and guides it over the outline of his cock, which is now rock-hard. We work our way to the cash register, where he pays. The cashier tells us to have a very nice night, giving us both a lewd smile as we exit. "That perv watching us obviously wanted to fuck you," says Louis as we continue our walk toward his place, taking a shortcut through a side street. I tell him the guy was pretty hot (he wasn't) and ask him if he is jealous. There is nothing I love more than making him jealous. He ignores me and slips his hand up underneath my skirt, pushing my underwear to the side. He comments on how wet I am as he slides two of his fingers into me.

I try several times to stop walking, in order to kiss him, but he refuses. He orders me to keep walking and keeps his fingers inside of me. My skirt is hiked up over my bare ass, for anyone to see, and my pussy is soaking wet. Fortunately, it is late and the streets are practically deserted. I can't wait any longer and pull him over to the wall of a building, lean up against the wall, unzip his pants, and wrap one leg around him, forcefully pulling him into me. Some late-night revelers pass the street perpendicular to us and whistle, but we ignore them. They eventually walk on.

Louis drops our bag of goodies on the ground and gets down on his knees. He shoves my skirt farther up and rips my underwear off, tossing them to the side. He licks my clit over and over until I am about to climax, when he abruptly stops and asks me to tell him again how hot the guy in the store was. I explain that I was just kidding and ask him to please continue, but he refuses me. Then I start to beg him and he tells me maybe that guy will finish the job. I start to worry that he is really upset with me when he suddenly turns me around and starts fucking me from behind. I push my hands into the wall, in order to steady myself. As he thrusts his amazing cock in and out of me, I beg him to do it harder and harder. All too soon, we both climax. As I cry out, I see the bag from the store lying on the ground and realize the best is yet to come.

CHAPTER 8

Dirty Talkin'

Dear CAKE,

I fantasize every time I have sex but am too scared to tell my
husband in case he feels hurt and rejected. I've read that many
women fantasize—not really about things they'd actually like to
happen but rather about things that turn them on. Because I
don't feel I can share these fantasies, we have a fairly dull sex life
and I masturbate a lot without him. My last relationship was
quite the opposite and I loved the sex as a result, but my ex
always took the lead in our dirty talk and was unshockable, so I
felt comfortable talking about anything and experimenting
with all sorts of things. Dare I tell him my filthy thoughts?!

—Emily, 27

Yes! Revealing your dirty thoughts might be just the kick in the ass your
sex life with your husband needs. You can talk about your fantasies in
fun but diplomatic ways. Sometimes what turns you on is what is happening right there between the sheets, and your thoughts are con-
sumed by accentuating the dirty, hot parts in your mind. Of course,
you're not always just thinking about the moment. Some fantasies can
include images and stories that turn you on but that you wouldn't want
to realize, and these can be good ones to share too.

GET TALKIN'

I've always wanted to fuck you up against this table. Sometimes when I'm alone, I masturbate thinking of you standing behind me, ramming me hard, making me come hard. Why don't you come over here and try it out with me? Why don't you start by touching my clit while you put it in? That's right, your cock feels so good, and my pussy feels so wet. I need it so bad, please fucking give it to me. Fuck me harder. You feel so good in my pussy . . . oh, goddamn. Fuck! Smack my ass, please, please, I'm begging for it. You're making my cunt wet and sticky and I can feel the juice running down over my ass. Take some of that juice and rub my ass with it. Imagine another woman licking your balls while I fuck you. I'm touching my nipples and squeezing them, and when you make me come, I'm going to turn around and suck your dick to thank you for fucking me. Turn around and get down on the couch, please. That's good; lie back and show me your beautiful dick. Oh, you're very hard now. Keep your arms to the side. That's right, good boy. Now what do you want, baby? Tell me. Whisper it to me in my ear. Does that feel good? I'm fingering my clit while I'm sucking you. Oh, no, don't even try to come yet. You're going to have to wait until I'm ready.

—ELIZABETH, 32

A description of what's in your mind can turn quickly to talk of the dirtiest kind. Too bad no one teaches this stuff, writes it down, or, for that matter, tape-records it for future reference! Oh, the things they never told you in etiquette class. Dirty talking is all about giving it raw. Doing it well. Getting your fuck on. There's no attention to grammar, no punctuation to hold you back, no ifs, ands, or buts, no predicates, nominates, or conjunctions. This is not about the ins and outs of Schoolhouse Rock—it's just you and your lover letting your inner nasty freak soar in a moment of unbridled passion.

Ever since childhood, Robin (34) has had swashbuckling fantasies, Blackbeard epics with Captain Hook at his finest, if you will. They tie her up, take her away aboard their black-masted schooner, and sail her off into the unknown. Now, she likes to tell her lover that he's a pirate and she's his captive. She relays the naughty high jinks with her band of pirates and tells him that he, with his eye patch and peg leg, is the dirtiest rat of all. "Oh, baby . . . take out that cutlass and make me walk that plank."

The words—the simple sound of them, or the way they feel coming out of your mouth—can supercharge sex. But dirty talk can be a touchy topic. Certain words, like "cunt," "dick," "pussy," "fuck," "daddy," "slut," "whore," can be one person's On button and another's Abort All Activity switch. Someone asking you to come might make you come, or might just make you feel he's impatient.

Not all dirty talk is created equal. One guy used to tell Judy (50), "You're going to love it when I do this," or "You're going to love it when I do that," until she finally said she'd rather hear him say that *he* was going to love it when he did this or that. He never said another word. Another guy used to hum in her ear after sex, which she thought was pretty cute.

The hottest sex Fiona (25) has with her lover is when she refers to him as "Daddy." Their sessions start out with nice, gentle foreplay and quickly progress into rough, balls-out sex as soon as they start talking. He likes to grab her tits hard when he's fucking her from behind, saying stuff like "Come on, you little slut, come for Daddy. You know you want to. You love my hard cock inside your tight little pussy, don't you,

you little whore?" And she says things back to him like "Oh, Daddy, you know I'm your little slut. I love the way you feel inside of me—please, give me more. I want more. Please, Daddy."

But really, the main goal of dirty talkin' is to tell him what you want—or, rather, what he can do for you in a sexy, uncompromised manner. Our favorites include the demure and coy "I want you inside of me," "Do me from behind," and "Fuck my brains out." On the flip side, there's nothing better then when your lover can reciprocate in kind! Even the most prudish of prudes will feel the temperature in her loins rise when she hears "I'm going to eat your pussy till the cows come home." He said, she said . . . all of a sudden, you are flying back and forth with more naughty verbiage than you ever knew existed. The subliminal takes over, and everything you've seen, read, heard, and fantasized about comes to the tip of your tongue and beyond.

Pleasure Tip: Are you a screamer, or do you like to whisper? Are salacious groans and moans your gig? Or are sweet nothings for you? Start by developing your dirty-talking techniques over the phone, using your favorite phrases and images to heat up the conversation. If you feel a little shy about breaking out the dirty talk when you're together, start by describing what you are feeling, and giving his body compliments. Work up to describing a fantasy that you have and that you think he'd enjoy imagining you both in. Move on to using explicit phrases to direct the action. If you just can't get your tongue untied, call a phone sex line and pay up for some dirty talk on speakerphone.

PLAYING IT UP

Bianca (21) and her boyfriend were rolling around on her bed one night, making out in their undies. All of a sudden he started to make doggy noises, in a flirtatious way, of course. They proceeded to growl a little at each other, which quickly changed to race-car noises as they got warmed up. Teasing her with his cock, he slipped it into her panties at the side of her crotch, and all the way up and out the top of her panties, so it was resting on her stomach. It looked like she had a penis!

She started jerking it off as if it were hers, asking him, "Do you like my big dick? I'm going to fuck you with it, you know that?"

They continued this way all night long, and she loved playing the dominant role that he usually takes in bed. During sex, she made the same noises he makes and said the same things he says, while he played her role, saying: "Please fuck my pussy, I'm so wet for you, I want your cock inside me right now, and I love how you're fucking me, I can feel your huge dick deep inside me." This role-reversal play ended up being a huge turn-on, as well as a glimpse of how they saw each other during sex.

While experiments like this usually work best when they happen spontaneously, there's no reason not to plan out a fantasy you have in your head and make it happen. A big fan of wearing costumes since playing dress-up as a little girl, Rose (35) finds it easier to change her demeanor when she's dressed for someone else. As soon as she gets dressed up for sex, she gets completely turned on in anticipation of what will happen, not knowing how the episode will turn out, or how her partner will react to a new side of her. She's always seen role-playing not as fantasy becoming reality, but as an opportunity to act on a part of her sexual self that truly exists, and then fantasize about it later.

With careful planning, she once surprised her husband with a modified Japanese tea ceremony. Tightly wrapped and fully covered in a kimono, with pale face and red lips, playing traditional Japanese music on the stereo, she performed as much as she remembered from her studies in Japan. The ceremony is a lengthy process, and after every few steps, she would stop to take off a piece of his clothing, kiss him, and suck on his fingers, always very subserviently, on her knees at his feet. When the tea was finally made, he was completely naked and very aroused.

Still dressed, she let him sip the tea while she held the cup for him, thereafter taking a drink herself, letting the hot liquid warm her lips, tongue, and throat. She wrapped her lips and tongue around his cock and let it slide into her hot mouth. Of course, her Western addition to the ceremony was the ice water to cool his cock and her mouth after all the heat. She let him unwrap the kimono—untying intricate knots and unraveling layers of heavy fabric is also painstakingly slow—and when he finally got to her very hot, wet skin, they practically devoured each other.

Role-play scenes can add a new dimension to a sexual relationship, by bringing out a different side of yourself and your partner that you may never have seen otherwise. When you experiment with different roles or personalities during sex, the options for your sexual identity become endless, and the potential for living out some of your more hard-to-realize fantasies becomes greater.

Whatever props you decide on—Kate (22) like to be tied up in pretty pink ribbons, wearing roller skates and a skimpy camisole, while being led around on a pink studded leash—both partners have to get turned on by the script. At the risk of sounding clichéd, if you are the boss at work, you might like to be a servant at home. If you fantasize about ripping open your boss's button-down, you might ask your partner to make you the misbehaving secretary. Who said you should never take your work home?

Role-playing is the power dynamics of domination and submission, and exhibitionism and voyeurism, all rolled up in one game. It is the ultimate fantasy, directed through and through by the active participation of both partners. Is he your pool boy, even though you don't have a pool? Stories and plots are often based on distinct roles. Sometimes they are clichéd because that's the whole point. You might try out these fun roles: teacher/student, boss/assistant, master/servant, doctor/patient, sports star/cheerleader, or "sugar mama"/escort.

Pleasure Tip: Indulge some of your dirty thoughts and use them to experiment with your partner. Sure, asking him to put on a suit and play professor may not be the same as getting to fuck the philosophy instructor you've fantasized about, but perhaps you can play a more naive student than you ever would have wanted to be in reality. Be armed and ready with some new gear. Props and costumes can set you up for a performance you can enjoy acting in and watching at the same time.

CHRISTINA, 25 It is late and I am working on the computer. My husband, Steve, is downstairs working on his music. The phone rings. "Hello?"

The male voice on the other end says, "Hey—what are you up to?"

"Not much," I reply, but I don't recognize the voice. "Who is this?" He laughs.

I feel bad, thinking I've offended one of Steve's friends. "Is this Chris? Do you want to speak to Steve?" I ask.

"Hmmmm . . . I'd really like to talk to you. You can call me Chris, if you'd like. The truth is, you don't know me. I just dialed this number randomly. Your voice is so sexy, though. Won't you talk to me for a while?"

Now, this is unexpected. I've been looking forward to seducing Steve, but he's probably lost to musical inspiration for the rest of the night. So I close the door to the office.

"I don't want to call you Chris," I tell him. "I am going to call you Antonio. And you are going to do everything I tell you to do. You will call me Mistress or Ma'am. Understand?"

"Yes, ma'am." His breathing is getting heavier.

"That's good. Antonio, how old are you? Tell me about yourself. You sound like a baby." I mean, who else would be making prank calls on a Wednesday night?

"I'm a senior in high school. I run track and play soccer. I'm planning on going to Duke next year. I'm tall, six-three. I work out a lot. It helps me clear my mind. I'm half French and half Italian, so I have dark hair and eyes, but my skin is fair. I think about sex all the time. God, I can't believe you're talking to me. What do you want me to do, Mistress?"

"I've hit the jackpot," I think. Here is this kid, bursting with hormones, hot as hell (in my mind, at least), putting himself in my hands to do whatever I want him to do. Oh, if only he were really here, I'd show him what to do, all right. I sit on the edge of the guest bed and twirl my hair, trying to think of what to say next. I close my eyes and imagine this Adonis standing before me awaiting instructions.

"Antonio, come stand in front of me and slowly take off your clothes. When I tell you to do something, I want you to really do it and then to tell me how it feels."

"Mistress, I'm in front of you now. I'm kneeling to remove my shoes and socks and now I'm taking off my shirt . . . I'm unbuckling my leather belt . . . unbuttoning my pants . . . and pushing them down. I'm only wearing black boxer briefs and I have the biggest hard-on. I'm taking off my underwear, and now I'm naked. I'm shivering, even though my room is warm, because you're making me nervous. I want you to touch my cock, but I'm waiting for you to tell me it's okay."

"Antonio, find some lubricant—Vaseline or hand cream will do just fine—a candle, or a hairbrush with a long handle, or anything else equally phallic."

I am really going to have some fun. The thought of the panic-stricken look he must have on his face gets me wet, and I let my hand wander under my blouse to start caressing my breasts. "Um, yes, ma'am—I'll be right back." I hear him put the phone down and start rummaging through his room. It takes a few minutes, but then he returns. "Mistress, I have a long, thick candle and some Vaseline. I am really shaking now because I know what you want me to do and I've never done it before."

"Well, if you know what I want you to do, then do it, and tell me all about it. If you turn me on, by the time you're through, I will be rubbing my fingers all over my wet pussy. Would you like that?"

"Yes, Mistress! . . . Well, I've opened up the Vaseline and I'm rubbing it around my asshole. I'm sticking a finger in and trying to work it around some. My cock is getting harder, and it's starting to throb. I am taking some more Vaseline and coating the candle with it . . . and now I'm propping one leg up on the bed and bending over. Ahhh, ah, ahh, I'm pushing it inside my ass—it hurts—but God, it feels so fucking good. I can feel all the ridges on the candle and I'm trying so hard to keep it in. Fuck! Oh fuck! I'm pushing it in and pulling it out, I've got a rhythm now. Please, Mistress, please touch me."

"Good, good, Antonio. You're doing very well. So well, in fact, that I've gone to find my own vibrator. It's thick and feels tight inside me. I want you to kneel down—keeping the candle in your ass—and work me with my vibrator while you eat me. Do you like cake?" I am fucking myself with my vibrator, but the room is dark and his voice is so desperate and husky that I have no trouble imagining he is licking me—slowly at first, tapping my clit with his tongue, and then faster, increasing his pressure and ramming the vibrator into me with a twisting motion. I'm breathing very heavily now.

"Antonio, pull out the vibrator and put your hand in me. Push it in. Yes, I want your whole fucking hand inside me. Hurt me, fuck me, make me come!" I'm trying to keep my voice down, remembering that Steve is downstairs. I really don't think that I could stop right now even if he walked into the room. "Antonio, I'm coming! I'm coming all over you, can you feel it? Oh, you're so fucking good! Grab your cock and jerk off onto me. I want you to come all over me too."

"Ohhh, yes, I feel like I'm on fire, I'm going to explode. Mistress, I'm going to come, Mistress, I'm so close, I'm going to come all over you. Fuck! Shit! Fuuuucccck!" I hear him gasp and drop the phone. His moaning is muffled, but I'm barely listening anymore because I hear footsteps coming up the stairs. Quickly, I press the Off button on the phone and toss it off the bed. Steve walks in the room and finds me all sprawled out—vibrator inside me, face flushed—and says with a mischievous smile, "I've been neglecting you. How can I make it up to you, darling?"

CHAPTER 9

Express Yourself

I love to be watched when I'm enjoying myself—whether it's during sex, or masturbating for someone, or when I'm receiving oral sex. My partner always insists on keeping the lights on when we make love, and for me that's a huge turn-on. I love the fact that he gets off when he sees me in all my glory. I also like knowing I'm being watched when I give oral sex—that's so hot! I feel the sexiest when I'm dancing, too, so when I'm being watched as I dance (whether it's at a lounge or performing a private show), I feel powerful and beautiful because I'm doing something I love to do.

—FRANCES, 26

"My milkshake brings all the boys to the yard." "Shake it like a Polaroid picture." "Express yourself." Exhibitionism is hot—at least in the musical realm—but what about for us girls? Do you like to play the sex object or are you a behind-the-scenes kind of girl? When it comes to playing out exhibitionist tendencies, would you rather watch or be watched?

THE CAKE GAZE
Subject *and* object

The idea of the "male gaze" originated in feminist film theory, to describe how female characters are objects of a male, predatory perspective. This theory expanded to women in advertising, TV, and other media, and before we knew it, the male gaze ruled the world. As useful as this theory may be in unveiling the power and prevalence of male fantasy, we are not stuck in a passive position of a sex object for men's pleasure. In our nonglossy lives, we have our own perspective, and even when we are being looked at as sexual, we are looking right back.

> Women are in a bind. According to one kind of feminist sensibility, we must demand to be subjects and avoid identification as sexual objects. Fine. However, women are brought up with our sexuality tied deeply to our experience as objects. Our ability to feel sexy in many ways is rooted in our ability to be desirable, i.e., to play the object role. It is important for us feminists not to condemn women for enjoying this role, because doing so stands in the way of women's sexual fulfillment.
>
> —ERIN, 22

We like to call this the CAKE Gaze: women choosing to be subjects, objects, or both at the same time. We get to be watched, adored, ogled, and above all in control. We can derive a lot of pleasure and power from playing the role of "object of desire." The crucial point is that we knowingly choose this role as part of an equal sexual interaction. From dressing up for a date to stripping in the bedroom, women's exhibitionism can be playful and positive.

Dressing sexy, dancing sexy, or otherwise being sexually provocative can be a fun and powerful act. We don't discourage rock stars or movie stars from doing it, so what's wrong with living out your own sexual stardom? Just because someone else enjoys your sexual expression does not mean he owns that expression.

The thrill of playing the sex object is that your unbridled sexual energy is in control of turning someone on to the point of madness. You own your body, and every action you choose to perform with that body is yours. Our interest in exhibitionism should not be discouraged simply because it also serves the male desire to watch. At the end of the day, you are defined by how you feel, not by what someone else thinks of you.

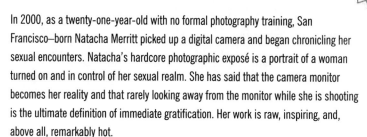

DIGITAL DIARIES

In 2000, as a twenty-one-year-old with no formal photography training, San Francisco–born Natacha Merritt picked up a digital camera and began chronicling her sexual encounters. Natacha's hardcore photographic exposé is a portrait of a woman turned on and in control of her sexual realm. She has said that the camera monitor becomes her reality and that rarely looking away from the monitor while she is shooting is the ultimate definition of immediate gratification. Her work is raw, inspiring, and, above all, remarkably hot.

"SHAKE THAT ASS . . ."

Showing off your body and demanding and enjoying sexual attention do not limit your ability to define what that power means to you. While you may be playing the role of a sexual object, you have complete control over the power dynamic. In fact, part of what a performer gets off on is the reaction of the audience. If everyone is turning everyone else on, who's to say who's who? Object? Subject? It all quickly becomes irrelevant.

Traditionally, a stripper's job is to play strictly into the patron's fantasy. Even this position can be arguably powerful, since at the end of the day the money flows from guest to dancer, and the dancer also gets what she's there for: exhibitionism along with financial compensation. But not all exhibition is structured by money, and experimenting with different roles can be sexually empowering.

Ashley (22), while not a professional dancer, calls herself an unapologetic and powerful exhibitionist and rejects the interpretation that this makes her a victim. On the contrary, she feels liberated by it. First, she likes being watched, plain and simple. She is an exhibitionist and a voyeur and a woman who believes in defining her fantasies however she chooses. (And by the way, why do we judge the women who choose to strip more negatively than we judge the men who choose to watch?) Telling Ashley that the men watching have all the power and she is just a victim is *demeaning*.

Second, she is a feminist who prioritizes choice. While she fights for women's right to choose across the board, she chooses to fuck however she likes. When Ashley dances for someone, she demands they watch her. She wants to be looked at, admired. This gets her off. She makes the rules. She is the "object," but she is defining how to dance, what to wear, how much to charge, when to stop, when to go further. A very active subject, indeed.

When I give a lap dance, I am an ambassador of the erotic. I am strong, fearless, in control, and so damn sexy. I am a fantasy, a mystical urban nymphet. But anyone can wear glittery makeup, tall boots, and skimpy skivvies. What makes me so different? I started giving a lap dance to an attractive, shy woman. "I've never done this before," she said, "I don't know what to do." I told her, "Just go with it. Trust your instincts." And she did. We started moving together and fell into a groove. Both of us enjoyed the ride. I am a Superhero of Sexuality. I trust my instincts. In fierce go-go boots and sexy finery, I help women trust their gut and feel it in their bones . . . one lap dance at a time.

—AMY, 29

Fonder of voyeurism, Missi (21) enjoys frequenting strip clubs, especially since she knows she'll usually be the only woman there who isn't working. The dancers always touch her more than the typical male customer and usually kiss her face and neck. Missi loves having a beautiful semi-naked woman in her lap, and loves watching a dance performed just for her. Even more, she gets turned on knowing the men around them are getting hard under the tables, and she images that they go home and masturbate to the image of her with the dancer. When she takes her husband along, she gets hot watching him receive a dance—and she knows that when she watches, he gets even hotter.

Pleasure Tip: Plan your own CAKE Party. "I want to be a sex object!" proclaimed a CAKE Girl recently. "But," she continued slyly, "I want the men in the room to be objects also . . . you know, eye candy for everyone."

But sadly enough, when was the last time you were given a space, a reason, and an audience to take it up a notch? You don't have to rely on strip clubs made for men, wanky Chippendales, or scary swingers clubs. Create your own event where women are in control and feeling good while a combination of guys and girls are the sex objects for our pleasure. Pick a theme, a fun costume, and an interactive activity so you can get your funk on. Striptease-a-thon anyone? How about a masquerade or an all-amateur male lap dance party for girls only? If you are in New York City, check out a real-life CAKE event.

"I'M YOUR PRIVATE DANCER : . ."

You are an exotic performer hired by a group of men who want to see you masturbate for them. The rules are that they cannot touch you, which makes it all the more arousing, since you are making yourself come for real. You situate yourself on a bed with pillows under your hips so that you are totally exposed for them. They are silently aching as they watch you rub your wet pussy in the sexiest way imaginable. You can see them getting aroused by the sight of you, their cocks swelling through their jeans. They are not allowed to expose themselves or masturbate during the act, though some cannot help but rub themselves and stroke themselves as they watch. You can hear their soft groans as you arch your hips up toward them and grind wildly against your hand. You let them know you are going to come soon. None of them dares break the rules by touching you, but they get very close and can't keep their eyes off your soaked pussy. You tell them you are coming and watch their expressions as you do so.

As with all things sexual, what we see and do in public has an effect on what we experience in private. Enjoying watching and being looked at is an essential part of what happens in the bedroom. While you might not be one to get up onstage in front of a crowd, performing for a lover at home might be just up your alley.

After a great date, you rush home together. You want to show him just how beautiful you are, and you know he wants to see you. Already, your low-cut blouse, sitting perfectly on your breasts, reveals a lot of skin. You've worn this particular blouse because it's a special occasion . . . you want to seal the deal. Once you're home, you begin to undress each other with anticipation, leaving the lights on to enjoy the pleasures of seeing and being seen.

While it's fun to strut around in some new lingerie and heels in the living room while you make your partner watch, it's even more fun to tease by putting your pleasure on exhibit. Masturbating for a partner not only shows him what we like but also displays how important our pleasure is to us. Your partner can watch you and learn your moves, your strokes, and your techniques so he can please you better in the future.

Exhibitionist-style mutual masturbation can bring out the voyeur and performer in us all, and playing with these roles can be a big turn-on. Watching your partner giving himself the ultimate pleasure is like having your very own live peep show.

From ogling and fawning over the Rolling Stones to going to a movie just to catch a glimpse of Brad Pitt's ass, we love to see a little eye candy, a little skin, and lots of action, every day of our waking (and sleeping) lives. So why not ask for it in the privacy of your own bedroom? Part of the fun is switching up roles and trading places. If you're willing to go all-out for your partner and be a sex object for his eyes only, how about being in control and feeling good while he is the sex object for your pleasure?

As an exhibitionist, you can flaunt your best assets and cause a commotion. The power Jennifer (26) gets from being desired fuels her active imagination. She dreams about having a really hot guy at her mercy, totally digging her. With one fierce look in his direction, she forces him to go down on her. She acts like a queen basking in the sun, watching him do magic with his tongue. She then imagines demanding that he get totally naked and pleasure himself in front of her while she watches, turning the tables on objectification.

Pleasure Tip: Integrate your masturbation rituals with your partners. There's no better way to feel sexy than pleasing yourself in front of your partner—you may even want to take the spotlight for yourself. Make a whole show of it—get all dressed up and strip for him, then get downright dirty and uninhibited with yourself. Try tying your partner's hands up and masturbate for him until he begs you to let him go.

Cake Bite

STRUT YOUR STUFF

Practice, practice, practice—turn up the tunes, strike a pose, and move and groove it—use a mirror, tell a friend. Don't forget to bring your pasties, your Wonder Woman and Spider-Man costumes, your days-of-the-week knickers, your props and feathers, Bob Mackie showgirl outfits, spiked heels, Adidas kicks, and so on.

Need some inspiration? Here's your mission:

Tune in to reruns of *Dance Fever,* the fast-driving dance series that served up some of the best amateur disco dancers from around the country with an unforgettable host, Deney Terrio.

Pick up some styling moves from John Travolta in back-to-back viewings of *Saturday Night Fever* followed up with its precious sequel, *Stayin' Alive,* directed by none other than Sly Stallone's brother.

Get in the mood and get your hands on Madonna videos—"Express Yourself" and "Vogue."

Rent Nina Hartley's *Guide to Private Dancing* and/or *Dirty Dancing* with special appearance by our main man Patrick Swayze—whatever your pleasure.

Bust out your moves this weekend for an audience of one.

Your boyfriend and you go out to dinner, but you decide not to wear any underwear. The whole time, you can't wait to get home to tear each other's clothes off and get to what is so accessible underneath. When you get home, the lights are off, but the blinds are open, and his shoulders and chest look so hot on top of you. You imagine you are in an office, after all your coworkers have gone home, naughtily fucking on top of a desk, while everyone in the building across from you can see.

These sorts of voyeurism and exhibitionism fantasies are just what get Carrie (33) hottest—in particular, being seen by others, whether she is undressing in front of an open window, skinny-dipping, or getting it on in public. Occasionally she "forgets" to close her blinds after she gets out of the shower, or when she's peeling off her sweaty workout clothes, or while checking out different hot outfits in the mirror. Even though she doesn't know if she's been seen, the idea totally turns her on. Steaming things up in public is still just a fantasy, but she'd like to play it out.

Pleasure Tip: Videotaping your sexual interactions with a partner is one surefire way to act on all of your exhibitionist tendencies. Be the star of your own one-act play and watch yourself get down over and over and over again.

GET YOUR GROOVE ON

While sometimes the best music is just the ohhs and ahhs of your own hot pleasure, we all have our favorite tracks for switching up the sex vibe. Every girl can tell you the exact song she lost her virginity to, and her favorite "sex compilation" CD. There are as many genres of sex as there are genres of music. Appropriately, we break it down for you, specially formatted by category for every occasion.

Smooth Operators. Great for heavy petting, juicy kissing, lots of touching and ahhhh . . . making love. Favorites include Miles Davis, Norah Jones, and Nina Simone for the jazz lovers among us; Lenny Kravitz, John Legend, and Jack Johnson for their smooth, velvety sounds; Sade, the ultimate smooth operator; and, for the old-school lovemakers, Marvin Gaye and Barry White.

Heavyweights. Jeff Buckley, Massive Attack, Mazzy Star, Morcheeba, Radiohead, Portishead, and Coldplay are especially good for sex with mood-making intensity, deep, long, tear-wrenching pleasure, and a brooding partner. Great for make-up sex.

Booty Callers. It's 3 A.M.; you're drunk, looking to get laid, and sex is like an extension of your dance moves, fun, energetic, and provocative. Try Outkast, "I like the way you move"; N.E.R.D., "You can have a lap dance here for free"; the Beastie Boys, Jay-Z, and Prince. For disco fever flavor, check into Kool and the Gang, Earth, Wind & Fire, Donna Summer, Blondie, Gloria Gaynor, and Chaka Khan.

Straight Shooters. You know, the kind of music for fucking like you've never fucked before—is that Mick screaming, or is that you? You are *feeling* it with the Rolling Stones, Hole, Supergrass, Sex Pistols, the Cult, Led Zeppelin, Nine Inch Nails, and the Clash.

Female Invigorators. An official shout-out to the ladies who grant us some egocentric sex. When it's all about being a woman, favorites include the Yeah Yeah Yeahs, Erykah Badu, Jill Scott, Bjork, Kelis, Gwen Stefani, and of course Madonna, "Like a Virgin."

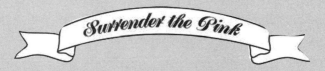
Surrender the Pink

ANNA, 29 One of my favorite sexual fantasies is being onstage. This probably has something to do with the fact that I'm a singer and I love the electric energy in the room when I'm performing. I am in an old theater, with crimson velvet curtains and drapes. The auditorium is shrouded in darkness, with a single spotlight centered on a big plush red velvet chaise longue in the middle of the stage. I enter the stage, naked and beautiful, wearing only six-inch black stilettos.

My lover, a woman in a sequined, fringed, old-fashioned magician's-assistant costume, leads me to the chaise and sits me down. She starts to demonstrate her skills to the audience, showing them how I respond to her touch. Kissing me and sucking my nipples, she stands behind me and runs her fingers all over, leaning down to pull open my legs. She spreads my labia apart so the audience can see my pussy. I'm completely high on the energy; the attention is a total adrenaline rush. She slides her fingers into me, getting me really wet and open, and then gets down to kneel between my legs and lick my pussy. I feel her licking and sucking and focus on feeling her mouth on me. I am close to coming, when she stops abruptly.

I sit upright on my haunches, legs splayed open, forming a V. I begin to touch myself slowly, exploring my pussy, my folds of soft skin, and the wetness now over my fingers. I arch my back, becoming increasingly aroused, and I move backward and forward, as if in a rocking chair. I begin to moan, constantly watching my audience, which now shows signs of visible torment at being so close to the object of their desire.

My assistant goes to find a willing man from the audience (in my fantasy, everyone is willing!) to come up onstage and help me come. I love imagining a stranger's fingers and mouth on me, and a whole roomful of people watching. He crawls onstage between my knees,

153

placing his mouth over my pussy, lapping my juices, using his tongue inside me before standing to bend me over and fuck me.

My magician's assistant helps out too, playing with my nipples and kissing me. I feel beautiful and relaxed. They work on me, my whole body and my pussy, until I come in hot, gushing waves rolling through my pelvis and down through my legs. The audience's energy feeds my orgasm. I lie there for a minute and just bliss out, and then I take a gracious bow, kiss my helpers, and walk offstage.

CHAPTER 10

Casual Encounters

I have always had this fantasy. I am walking down the street, and I see a guy I think is hot. I go up and start kissing him without saying a word. From there we proceed to a discreet (but yet public!) spot and start screwing. After we are both done, we go our separate ways, without ever having said a word. The concept of having sex with a total stranger and never finding out anything about him is just so damn sexy. The whole aspect of simply not giving a fuck, while getting fucked, just doing it for the sole purpose of having some good clean fun is so hot!

—CAROLYN, 25

Ladies, all the ladies, let's talk about the thrill of loving 'em and leaving 'em. While commitment, safety, love, and monogamy sure aren't bad, sex without any of that hubbub can be pretty darn good too. Sex within a relationship is something that both men and women seek and enjoy, but a casual romp in the sack can benefit us girls as well, in ways that are just now becoming accepted. Many of us have fun with partners whom we don't necessarily see as marriage material, and our sexual pleasure is not limited to monogamous relationships.

Casual sex for women made its first public appearance on the cultural scene during our mothers' generation. Erica Jong's sexually motivated female protagonist, Isadora, was one of the first to break the rules. In the 1973 classic *Fear of Flying*, Isadora's willingness to risk her marriage and reputation to explore her sexuality free of constraints was intensely controversial.

Needless to say, women of that era identified with this desire and embraced Isadora's story. At the same time, this new way of thinking was condemned by those who feared that sexually liberated woman would threaten the social status quo. But it was too late, the silence had been broken, and Isadora's fantasy of the "zipless fuck"—perfect sex unmarred by buttons, zippers, or other forms of attachment—had become a culturally valid female fantasy.

> The zipless fuck is absolutely pure. It is free of ulterior motives. There is no power game. The man is not "taking" and the woman is not "giving." No one is attempting to cuckold a husband or humiliate a wife. No one is trying to prove anything or get anything out of anyone. A zipless fuck is the purest thing there is. —Erica Jong, *Fear of Flying*

Over thirty years have passed; today women are exploring casual encounters with enthusiasm and following Isadora's lead with increasing success. We have more opportunities to enjoy this option without stigma, and progress has been made: This generation's "zipless fuck" just happens to be part of our overall sexual repertoire.

MYTH: Women cannot separate sex from love and are inherently monogomous.

TRUTH: Women and men choose monogamy when they want to, but both sexes may have a need to explore their sexuality independent of any commitment. This depends on the individual, not the gender.

Although women can and do enjoy sex for sex's sake, our culture is very protective of the myth that men would be happy with a lifetime of one-night stands, whereas women are looking to tie the knot. A woman who steps outside these cultural boundaries, even in this post-Madonna era, is *still* a "bad girl." But our real sex lives aren't divided into following the rules or breaking them. The virgin/whore divide is an obsolete idea, because there's not just one set of rules anymore. We're deciding what we want, and we can have a whole spectrum of fantasies and experiences with sex outside of socially recognized relationships. The one-night stand is not inherently negative or male, and it's possible for women to have a pleasurable, responsible, and safe one-night stand.

The old "one woman, one egg" versus "one man, millions of sperm" idea has been shoved down our throats so much it's become one of those things we blindly accept. It goes something like this: Because women have just one egg per reproductive cycle, it is to women's reproductive advantage to be selective about who gets access to that one egg. We "naturally" want to bond with that one male partner in order to get child-raising resources out of the deal. Men, in contrast, are wired to spread the millions of sperm they produce every month as far and wide as possible. Thus, this theory supposes, men are inherently and biologically more sexually adventurous than women, and women are, by nature, more monogamous.

Who can argue with biology, right? We can.

The one-egg-vs.-a-million-sperm theory is based on a selective interpretation of facts and a notion of sex as meant for procreation, rather than on a larger unbiased biological picture and a notion of sex as meant for pleasure. Across a majority of species, the female reproductive tract is like a gauntlet that knocks out unwanted sperm. This means that it may be reproductively advantageous for a female to have multiple sperm contributors, so only the very best make it to the top. While theories of human sperm competition and female sperm choice are controversial, cross-species analysis proves that having one egg does not necessarily mean that having just one partner is the most successful reproductive strategy.

On the flip side, men have reasons to be monogamous. The more they invest in their offspring, the better the offspring's chance to survive. Insemination with no follow-up is not necessarily the best way to ensure that your genes persist.

Fast forward to modern times—both men and women have been freed from their reproductive destinies by the advent of contraception and other medical advances. Sex is no longer tied to reproduction, and behavior is not based solely on what is best for offsprings' survival. One could argue that because women ovulate only once a month in contrast to men's 24/7 impregnating potential, it is women, not men, who are more inclined to have sex simply for the pleasure of it all.

The act of sex is no longer simply a biological imperative, and it's well past time to end the classic "virgin (if you hold out for the perfect man)/whore (if you sleep with multiple partners)" dichotomy. Fantasies about finding "the one" can go hand in hand with fantasies about "the one-night stand." Interest in sex for sex's sake does not prohibit us from enjoying sex for love's sake. We've been stuck in the morality swamp for far too long, and it's time to pull the "bad girls" up from the bottom and toss the "good girls" in for a swim.

Let's start with the idea that casual encounters do not necessarily entail sex or intercourse, but can often stop at kissing, grinding, and flirting. Casual sex experiences can benefit a growing girl's sexual evolution in many ways. By exploring what and who turns us on, and defining the how, why, and where, we take ownership of our sexuality and define our own sexual needs as well as our boundaries. Is it a good thing that casual sex for women is now visible? Well, we'd say yes, but actually, all judgment should be left aside, because it's not a moral matter.

To continue the zipless revolution, we are encouraging casual encounters as a choice for women to consider on an individual basis. For the zipless record, we suggest a variety of ways to enjoy fantasies about or experiences with people other than your one true love, based on the true-life stories of women who do. Casual encounters aren't about finding your true love (although you may find him in the process). They are about the pure, unadulterated pursuit of pleasure.

THE RULES
Define your boundaries

Dear CAKE,

My question is a big one and does not have a simple answer—it is about one-night stands. I am relatively new to the world of casual experiences and I wonder whether there's anyone out there who can have them without remorse? I wonder if—for safety and emotional reasons—they are even worth having at all. I am curious to know other women's experiences with them. Samantha, are you out there?

—JULIA, 25

Julia, you are not alone! In the proud tradition of the aforementioned Erica Jong, the writers of *Sex and the City* gave a new generation our Isadora in the form of Samantha, a fictional character who, despite other people's judgments, enjoyed sex when she wanted, where she wanted, how she wanted, and with whomever she wanted. Of course, Samantha's choices, defined by a set script and the right pair of shoes, are somewhat easier than the ones real women have to make. But real-life casual sex can also be controlled by a self-defined set of rules and regulations.

The number-one piece of advice women give to each other is to know yourself and the context, and be sure of what you want. Set boundaries on one-night stands, boundaries that are both emotional and physical. To have a good casual encounter, you have to protect and assert your own needs, along with respecting what your partner wants.

After all, what's the point of getting down if it doesn't feel good? If we could be assured that our orgasm would be a priority, then it would seem that casual sex encounters would look a lot more attractive to a lot more of us. A sexy smile can last only so long, and once the romp begins, we are looking for the skills to match our attraction.

During her first one-night stand, Jennifer (24) hit the jackpot. It was the holidays and most of her college friends were out of town. All alone in the big city, she decided it would be fun to hit one of her favorite wine bars for her first solo bar experience. After a few glasses of wine, she strolled over to a group of five men who had just come in after work. Feeling confident and independent, she decided she would try going home with a stranger for the first time. After about an hour of speaking to one guy whom she was particularly attracted to and felt comfortable with, she asked him if he'd like to leave with her. He responded by grabbing her arm and pulling her out the door.

Without exchanging names or any personal information, they got in a cab and drove uptown to his apartment. Once inside, he slowly undressed her and laid her on his bed, then took his clothes off. He was a very good partner: He was verbal, which she found terribly exciting, and was careful to take his time, making sure she was sated. Jennifer swears he went down on her more than ten times. After their romp had concluded, she got dressed and slipped back into the night, feeling just a bit guilty because he kept asking her to stay. The next morning, she still couldn't believe what had happened. She never would have imagined something like that was within her command.

Unfortunately, we may not all be lucky enough to come upon a partner with mad skills. Frankly speaking, many men do not know their way around female pleasure, and in the case of an unfamiliar body are either clueless or careless. This is when we have to take matters into our own hands. It's up to us to let the new boy on the block know exactly what we need, even if he's going to be around for just one night. Casual sex can be an opportunity to demand that male partners get with the equality program by putting our orgasm on the same level as theirs.

This philosophy extends to taking full control over the physical dynamic, down to how many bases you want to cover in one night. For example, Bianca (21) decided that setting the limit at vaginal intercourse was arbitrary, and she ended up rethinking her views on her own physical boundaries. Until recently, the concept of casual sex was very foreign to her. But she decided to change that: She had been sexually active for some time, and there was no reason to stop just because she was single. Moreover, if she was already at the point where she was with a guy and clothes were falling to the floor, why shouldn't she be able to continue the action?

Bianca's last casual experience had been with her ex, before he was her boyfriend, and she had been so stuck on not having sex outside of a monogamous relationship, she asked him to have anal sex instead of vaginal sex! And she had no qualms about sucking his cock and letting him eat her pussy. Once she thought about it, that didn't really make sense—if he was fucking her ass, he might as well be fucking her pussy! It's not as if one counts more or less than the other. After splitting up with this same boy, Bianca set her mind firmly in the other direction: She decided to have another casual sex experience. When she did, she felt in control of her sexuality, simply because she knew that when she wanted to have sex, she could.

It's up to you to define the physical parameters, just as it was up to Bianca to set hers. Whoever said that you have to go "all the way"? What was once considered only foreplay can now very satisfyingly be the whole shebang; it's up to you to find your own comfort level. If pleasure is the end goal, you can get there by a number of routes.

While Laura was up late one night at her office, her boss, a dead ringer for Bruce Willis, approached her desk to make sure she had the keys to lock up. She'd been procrastinating by reading dirty stories online, and she showed him an article about a woman on a mission to fulfill her fantasies. He was older than she by 15 years, and they began to chat about what 25-year-olds do now to get off, compared with what he did when he was 25. The conversation became very erotic very quickly, and they became engrossed in personal details about sex and masturbation. Laura told her boss how she loves the female body, especially her own, and said she would never deny herself an orgasm when that was what she wanted.

Sitting across from him, she hiked up her skirt and started touching herself, and he followed her lead. What began a bit awkwardly became easy to get into, and they both got off. The next day, they joked casually together about what they would tackle next. In this case, mutual masturbation kept things casual, erotic though it may have been.

New sexual encounters always leave open the possibility for you to experiment with your sexual personae in a way you never have before. Long-term monogamous relationships or long periods of sex with a vibrator may be cozy and comfortable, but it can be difficult to change your sexual persona once someone already sees you in a specific way. Part of what is attractive about the idea of casual sex is an interest in the newness of it all—a new body, a new experience.

Pleasure Tip: A one-night stand gives us complete license to flex our creative muscles, which makes it a great opportunity to use new techniques, positions, or fantasies you've been dying to try out. Make sure you know what you want in the morning before you jump into bed. If all you want is to get laid, you'll find that a casual encounter can precisely fit the bill.

I had a hot stone massage once that was, beyond a shadow of doubt, the best massage I have ever had. First, my masseuse rhythmically rubbed the smooth, hot rocks into my muscles. The heat penetrated really deeply into my body. It felt like four smoldering hot hands were touching me all over at the same time. Then, without warning, she would massage with a frozen stone. It was absolutely excruciating . . . excruciatingly pleasurable! The roller coaster of hot and cold, the anticipation, and the deep relaxation were so intense. It was like having sex! For the finale, she did some type of vibration therapy with crystals. She would hold a crystal at the base of my skull and slowly travel to my butt cheeks. It felt like a small vibrator tickling me all the way down. An hour and a half later, when she left me facedown on the table to relax, I was so horny that I had to do myself right then and there! I came immediately! I can only imagine how incredibly hot it would be to have a hot stone massage from a sensual male masseur and have him "finish" for me. I'd pay extra, no problem. Legal or not, am I alone here?

—MADISON, 27

BANG, BANG
Choose your target

While it's still a serious matter, and maybe the most important choice you will make all day, choosing a casual-encounter partner is, well, more casual than choosing a long-term lover. You don't have to worry about whether you'd want his toothbrush on your sink, whether you'd have to bring him home to meet your parents, or whether he'd get along with your girlfriends. More important, if we always practice safer sex, we do not have to worry about whether our sex partner will be a good dad. A casual-sex partner does not have to fill your every expectation, but there is one basic requirement: attraction.

Acting on a feeling of instantaneous attraction can be very exciting; in turn, the feeling that you're so sexy that a stranger is overwhelmed by his attraction to you can be equally mind-blowing. From both perspectives, the possibility of being so passionate with someone we don't know but have a spontaneous sexual connection with is enough to make our heads (or bodies) spin. A perfectly common reaction to physical attraction is sexual excitement, and we can get turned on, often and easily, by people we don't know.

Of course, a hot body and good looks can always whet our palates for some lovin'. But above and beyond simple attraction, anonymity, in particular, plays a big role in female fantasy. The exciting part for some of us is particularly that which is *not* connected to a relationship: the freedom of indulging in attraction without ever having to know someone's name. Pure physical pleasure can be heightened when we are freed from having to consider what will happen when the moment is over. Anonymity resolves the issues of consequences. There are no sacrifices. No one gets hurt.

Pleasure Tip: The next time you see a hottie on the street, imagine you can stop time and make a move right then and there. Always be on the lookout for who makes you hot.

Physical attraction can go hand in hand with emotional attraction, and some of us can get turned on only by a sexual partner who is a potential friend as well. Luckily, we have friends, neighbors, and coworkers as candidates!

Lily (24) found herself getting hot while dishing with a friend at work about the first time they thought about sex. He was fascinated to learn that she masturbated regularly. After their conversation, she fantasized about a casual encounter between them, wherein he caught her in the act of getting herself off. She had a completely hands-free total mind-fuck orgasm, on the spot. Just ten minutes later she found herself sitting in the bathroom with her back up against the cold tiles, getting herself off with her fingers, even though usually she needs a small vibrator. Later on that night, she got off again, in the shower. The entire day, Lily felt as if everything around her were trying to caress and seduce her in some way; her clothes, the breeze against her hair and skin, and even the food she ate were infused with sexual energy.

Pleasure Tip: Safer sex is also about picking a partner who feels safe to you. Decide who would feel right to make your current casual sex fantasies come true. Maybe it's a good friend to romp around with at your will, a slightly mysterious acquaintance, a totally anonymous encounter, or just a fantasy man.

PICK YOUR SPOT

Unattached, exciting sex can take place anytime and anywhere. It's not just about the boyfriend in the bedroom anymore, but also about the bartender in the bathroom, the stranger on the street corner, or the ex in the elevator. Roam the open road for pleasure, and seize the opportunity to enjoy sexuality wherever you please.

Workin' it at the office

You've been exchanging incredible e-mails since the first day at your job. One afternoon, while everyone else is gone and you are attempting to work quietly, you end up at his desk with some papers to file. You take advantage of the moment, and while he's on the phone and can't verbally resist, you turn his chair and move down to your knees. His shock turns to a smile, and you begin to unzip . . .

Checkin' it out at the gym

While relaxing in your gym's coed sauna, you eye a beautiful man lounging beside you. Moments later another hottie walks in, sitting next to you, so close you can feel his body heat even through the thick air. It sure is your lucky day: The man beside you offers you a back rub. You accept, and he turns you around gently and starts to rub your shoulders; you close your eyes and feel your muscles loosen as you relax completely. When you open your eyes, the other man is sitting at your feet. He asks you if he can rub them.

You say yes, and as one pair of hands moves down the front of your chest and the other moves up your calves to your thighs, your towel loosens around you. Totally naked now, in the hands of two strangers, you allow one to bend over you and caress your breasts and stomach. The other has his one hand on your ass and his fingers inside of you. As your back arches and you yearn for more, the man on top slips his huge penis inside your mouth and the other licks and sucks your clit. Together, they tag-team you to orgasm, only moments before the sauna door opens.

Acting out at the movies

It's a weekend and the theater is packed, so you and your best friend are sitting up close to the screen. The cute young stranger on your right keeps giving you sideways glances, and refuses to give you space on the armrest, so you decide to give him the attention he is asking for. While the movie plays, you let your hand slip over to rest on his thigh. He starts breathing faster, but he doesn't turn his head from the screen. Your hand goes farther up his thigh, and he covers it with his jacket. Under the jacket, you unzip his pants and start slowly sliding your hand up to the top of his dick . . .

Hitting the books at the library

He enters the library and starts looking for books but sees you instead. He sends you a piercing look that's so sexual you almost come in that instant. While you move your gaze to the top shelf of books, he kneels down within inches of you and whispers, "I'm very good on my knees," without looking up at you. You suddenly feel weak and wet. Quickly glancing around, he runs his hands up your leg and just touches your pussy gently through your knickers. "Let's go," he says, and you do. He takes a staff key-card and opens a door to a flight of steps behind the stacks. Pushing you up against the wall, he rubs your hardened nipples with his thumbs and says, "This is for you, not me. You will have whatever you want."

Groovin' it in da club

It's been a rough couple of weeks: You got dumped, you had a million exams, and you feel frustrated and unsexy. Deciding to change your mood, you head out alone for the first time to dance with a few men and get your self-esteem back in gear. You get more attention than you expected and, feeling confident, you eye a tall muscular guy across the floor. Without a word, he wraps his arms around your waist and pulls you in to him. His big hands slide down your thighs and cup your butt, making you lose all your inhibitions and forget your usual shy manners.

166

Gyrating down his leg, you touch the floor with your ass and stare at the bulge in his pants that's in front of your face.

"Wanna get out of here?" he asks. You nod. Back at his apartment, he hastily introduces you to his roommate before he leads you to his bedroom. To your dismay, he pulls out a guitar and performs a touching yet slightly out-of-tune rendition of "Lightning Crashes." Thankfully, as soon as the song is over, he reaches over to kiss you tenderly. Moments later, your top is off and your pants are close behind. In an uncharacteristic moment of boldness, you lay him down and unbutton his shirt with your teeth, working your way down to his pants. Leaning over the bed, you grab a condom from your bag, slipping it on quickly before he penetrates you. The box spring lets out a squeaky, sexy rhythm as you rock against each other. He picks you up with his impossibly muscular arms and, still inside you, slams you on your back against the pillows. Nearly out of breath, you somehow manage to pulse back as he pushes against you. In one last effort, he stops to prop you up on your hands and knees and comes at you from behind. The box spring sings its song and you moan along. Soon moans turn to screams and he yells too, as you feel him come, your body shaking violently at the same time. Your arms give out and your face falls into the pillows as he crashes on top of you, kissing the back of your neck and groping your body. You sleep the night in his arms, against his rock-hard body, with a new sense of security. You feel sexy again.

Planes, trains, and automobiles

You're on the road and there are two handsome young men in the car next to you. You acknowledge their presence with a little wink. Rolling down your window, you begin to shout a conversation with them as you drive. You take the next exit, they follow, and from then on it's a complete adventure. They take the lead, and you follow them to their destination, a vacation cabin. After no more than five minutes inside, you start to kiss both of them, your panties saturated from the arousal and excitement of these two strangers. You all get naked and you are the absolute center of attention . . . you experience double penetration for the first time and your orgasms are countless. After this experience, you never see them again.

Maxin' and relaxin' on vacation

You're out salsa dancing with your girlfriend one night of your vacation in Geneva. You meet some nice boys from Andorra, in town for a slalom ski championship in neighboring Chamonix, and you end up dancing with one until you are both pouring sweat and the place closes. It's raining heavily outside when you walk out to where your car is parked. He hardly speaks English and you know you'll never see him again, so when you reach your car, you bend back against the hood, lifting your soaking-wet dress up above your knees. You have incredible sex, unaware whether anyone was watching, not caring if they were, and it's an experience that turns you on for years after.

DROP THE JUDGMENTS
Get over yourself

Despite what may be going on in our active minds and restless bodies, we can still feel fear being judged for our sexual behavior. Pangs of criticism creep in and taint the mind-blowing orgasms Kay (35) has from casual sex. She remembers casual sex as rampant when she was a teen in southern California during the '80s. Sex was just what you did when you went out on a good date, despite her parents' attempts to steer her in the good-girl direction by reminding her that boys only want to marry virgins. Now that Kay is an adult, she feels a new moralism in the air; casual sex seems wrong by today's standards, leaving her to wonder what people think of her, even as she lies on her back enjoying the best sex of her life. Sometimes we are our own harshest critics.

During a hot, sweaty summertime blackout, Alexandra (22) did what her mother would have thought of as a very bad-girl thing. She was stranded at the beach in the company of a sumptuous lifeguard. They had very intense sex, and she experienced a simultaneous climax with a partner for the first time—and the second: a very good thing, in her book. Like many women, Alexandra was raised to think that she should be able to count her sex partners on the fingers of one hand, since of course no man would marry her if her partners outnumbered his. The lights-out, sand-filled tryst drew her all the more strongly to the learning experience of casual sex, and now she can't imagine not being exposed to lots of different flavors of men.

Pleasure Tip: Ditch the double standards—have no fear, cultural norms will catch up with us if we give them no choice.

LANA, 33 I see him and he sees me. I don't want to know his name, where he gets his hair cut, his first pet, or whether he's angry at his dad or mom for stuff they did in the past. I just want him. Pure. Intimate. Clean. He starts to speak, but I stop him with a kiss. His lips are thinner than mine and finely etched. I want to kiss away the years on his mouth until he is a boy again. I step back. Everything about him is elegant—his jawline, his long, slim fingers, his neck, his wavy poet's hair. I unbutton his shirt and there is the finely knit rib cage I had hoped for, nipples the color of pomegranate seeds, and chest hair both dark and light that I want to sink my teeth into. His hands are buried in my hair as I lick his collarbone, gently tug his chest hair, and flick my tongue across his nipples. Another kiss, and he is mine.

I slide my hands down his pants to feel his ass and trace the shape of his cock. His beautiful pale skin flushes as I unzip his pants and remove them and his socks until he stands naked before me. His cock is as beautiful as the rest of him. He starts to pull at my clothes, but I shake my head no. The contrast is just too luscious—his white skin against my black suit, his flesh against the soft fabric. I run my lapels over his nipples and he shivers. We slowly slip to the floor, our lips touching, my suit tight against his body. My black jacket has slipped off and his mouth is on my shirt, kissing my breasts until my nipples stiffen and he sucks them through the fabric. They are hard, like blueberries, in his mouth. His mouth is at my throat as his fingertips move toward my panties.

By now he has the rhythm of our game down, and his fingers stroke my clit through the cotton. His fingertips dent the fabric as he presses a little bit harder until my clit is plump and insistent. My black-stockinged legs are wrapped around his naked body and those elegant fingers dance and stroke, dance and stroke, until I am all clit and pounding blood. I utter the first words we've said to each other: "Your cock. Now." I take off my panties and he slides his cock into my pussy, high and tight. All I can feel is him inside me, moving with such elegance and purpose that I feel faint. The sight of us is so gorgeous—his naked ass and back clasped between my legs, the spiked heels of my black shoes digging into his spine as his fingers circle my clit.

Our breath quickens as I tighten my pussy around his cock. I can feel him pulsing inside me as he moves higher and faster and harder. The heat and the friction are just too much, and I start coming. My pussy quakes and I am panting and purring as he comes with a deep, lonely moan. We lie still for a moment, our bodies resting against each other's, until he rises from me. I lie back smiling as I watch him dress. He looks a lot like me—a serious urban type all in black. I rise and my skirt slides to the floor. I toss off my jacket, shirt, and bra until nothing remains but stockings and shoes. "Those too," he says. His arm slips around my naked waist. We begin again.

ROSE, 34 When I go to visit my parents, I always take a long bike ride through some beautiful trails near their house. I get up early, before anyone is awake, and take off. My favorite place to stop and rest is a beautiful pine barren, near a small lake. The trails are pretty strenuous, and by the time I arrive there, I've usually worked up quite a sweat. The friction of the bike seat on my pussy arouses me as well, especially in the morning (I always wake up wet and very eager for sex). Sometimes I'll leave my bike and walk to the water's edge, take off my clothes, and wade in, letting the clear water lap at my inner thighs. Every once in a while this turns me on to the point that I will masturbate right there, unable to make it back home without a release.

It was a morning just like that. I emerged from the water in only my white tank top, and sat on a huge fallen tree, the bark grating pleasurably into my ass. I spread my legs wide and let the cool early air graze my open pussy lips. I just sat for a moment, clenching my pelvic muscles tight, then letting them rest, massaging my insides and becoming so turned on; I thought that if the breeze blew any harder, it would get me off before I even touched myself. Looking at my pristine surroundings, I was surprised by a flash of unnatural white just ahead of me. My gut instinct was to cover myself, but then fear turned to curiosity when I realized that it was a man, standing in the water with wet waders on, fishing gear in hand. He was adorable, with messy bedroom hair, tan skin, a rugged chiseled face, and a beautiful body. He looked young, and his cheeks flamed with embarrassment or excitement . . . probably both, from seeing me in such a state.

My eyes locked onto his and neither of us moved or spoke. Hardly missing a beat, I smiled and continued. Pushing my tank up, I showed him my full brown breasts, nipples hard from the shock of air. He came over, padding across the bed of pine needles that would be our mattress. Taking my wrist, he put my palm to his mouth and licked it with a strong, wide, rough tongue. He liked what he tasted, and dropped to his knees to taste some more from between my legs. I had plenty to give; as he ran his tongue over all of me, and then thrust it far inside me, it felt almost like a cock.

My whole body began to quiver, and I pulled my legs up to spread wider for his gorgeous face. I lifted his head away for a moment so that I could lie on the ground and be more comfortable. He smiled as he undid his waders and let them drop, kneeling down in front of me. What a perfect cock I was about to take in, not too long but very thick. He slid it into me soooooo slowly, making me gasp and beg for every inch. When it was fully engulfed in my pussy, he began the most deliberate but gentle thrusting. I looked up to watch this absolute angel fucking me under a ceiling of pine trees and blue sky—this was truly heaven.

Every time he thrust, he pressed my clit, and it wasn't long before I was arching my back and pressing my head back into the ground, riding wave after wave of orgasm, smelling our mingling sweat and the pine surrounding us. He came immediately after me, under the pressure of my tightening pussy. I stayed there for only one perfect moment before brushing the needles off my butt and dressing. Not even looking at him, I put on my helmet and got back on my bike. I couldn't resist one last glance, though. He was grinning from ear to ear, with his waders around his knees. That was the last I saw of my fisherman.

EMMA, 24 Last night, as I was coming in late, a guy in a terry-cloth robe and slippers was paying for takeout in the lobby. He was a total dish, but I didn't recognize him from the building. New owner? Visiting relative? Guest? He held the door for me and we got in the elevator. It was awkward and he was making some lame remarks about the weather when I turned to him and said, "Female curiosity compels me to ask. Do you have anything on under that robe?" He blushed and I could see that he had a lot under his robe, but none of it was clothing. Busted!

I moved to stand right in front of him and raised my eyebrows quizzically, biting my lip and grinning. He mumbled something about expecting the coast to be clear at such a late hour as I put one hand on the elevator wall over his shoulder and reached into his robe with the other, never taking my eyes off of his. I heard his bag drop to the floor as my hand found his cock and gave it a rough squeeze. The look on his face was priceless! Released from the confines of his robe, he stiffened quickly in my hand as I rubbed the velvet underside appreciatively.

He was beautifully built so this was going to be a lot of fun! Never taking my eyes off of his, I spat into my hand and started jerking him off. His knees buckled, but he steadied himself, hands braced on the railing, leaning back into it as I stroked him quickly and hard. He was like a rock as my fist pumped up and down, polishing his shapely head, stroking his length, and circling his small, tight balls in a wet blur of slippery motion. With a deep groan, he leaned forward slightly and shot off with such intensity that it felt like a power surge in my hand. I saw that his come was all over his beautiful chest and belly as I wiped my hand on the inside of his robe. I sweetly drew it back around him, tied the belt around his waist, and told him to enjoy his dinner as I stepped out on my floor and disappeared down the hall, trying really hard not to laugh so loud that he could hear me.

Let's Get It On

PLEASURE MISSION

Take a few minutes to mark a "yes" or "no" next to each statement below. Then write down one thing that you have not done, but have fantasized about doing, as your Pleasure Mission for the week—an under-the-covers assignment to get off in a new, hot way. You have one week to complete the task. Any challenge set out and attempted will be considered a success. There is no failure. Use all resources available to make it happen. Report your successes back to us at www.cakenyc.com.

I have dressed up for my partner.   _____

I have videotaped myself having sex.   _____

I have had anal sex.   _____

I have taught my partner how to give me better oral sex.   _____

I have strapped it on for my partner. _____

I have bought a vibrator for my male partner. _____

I have used a vibrator with a partner. _____

I have acted out my favorite fantasy. _____

I have fantasized about someone at work. _____

I have had a casual encounter. _____

I have had anonymous sex. _____

I have had a lap dance. _____

I have given a lap dance. _____

I have performed a striptease. _____

I have gotten a happy-ending massage. _____

I have described my favorite fantasy to my partner. _____

My Pleasure Mission for the week is: _____

_____

_____

_____

_____

_____

Oooh baby you want me?
Well, you can get this lap dance here for free.

—N.E.R.D.

PART III

On the Road

Layered Coconut Key Lime Pie

Difficulty: Advanced

Yield: One Complete Woman

Ingredients:

A growing collection of visual images   Nipple clamps, whips, and a blindfold
A reliable girl-toy   An explorative couple

Directions: Blend these ingredients together, adding more of one when you please. Take a taste of the raw batter, and continue to blend. Refrigerate and eat cool.

CHAPTER 11

The Porn Myth

Several girlfriends and I think that women are at least as visual
as men. The male image has to look beautiful, naughty, sexy,
strong, vulnerable, and arousing at the same time, and I think,
to date, this combination has sadly not been represented in
visual imagery for us girls.

—ANGELA, 23

You're browsing around the back room of your local video store, looking for a hot title to go home with. Hmmm . . . *Teahouse Twats, The So-
pornos, Meet the Fluffers, I Cream on Genie, Big Titted Super Sluts, Teen
Fuck Holes, Young Girls' Fantasies #28* . . . *Phat Azz White Girls #12*,
ohhh, *White Hot Nurses* . . . that could be watchable. More than 100,000
porno films have been made; there must be *something* here that suits
you. Should you just go home empty-handed and flip through this
month's *Penthouse,* or replay the sex tapes you and your honey made a
while back? Finally you settle on the latest Jenna Jameson title—since
you just read her best-selling book—and scoot out before the gentle-
man browsing next to you asks for a recommendation.

    When we're trying to find a little visual inspiration to wank off to,
we'll find a wretched selection of unsatisfactory options. On one hand,
we have *Lifetime* movies in which romantic satisfaction is offered in lieu
of sexual satisfaction. Movie stars are hot enough, for sure, but we rarely
get to see them in the buff, or in the act of pleasuring women the way

we know (or, at least, would like to think) they can. On the other hand, we have a wide range of porn in which female satisfaction is often ignored altogether. Even though we are desperately seeking visual imagery to aspire to and learn from, our choices are still pulled from La-La Land, and we get *fucked* in the process.

That's right, the good stuff arouses us, but there's simply a lack of it tailored to the female eye. We want to see ourselves on-screen and identify with the subject. We haven't been catered to as sexual viewers, but we should be!

Whether we ultimately decide that we love it or hate it, in our search for sexual entertainment, some of us—in fact, many of us—watch porn. Ladies: We rent almost one third of all porn movies. On our own. This invites a question: In an industry made for men, what's in it for women, and why are we consuming it? Our intent is not to analyze how the porn industry operates. Nor is it to discuss whether women working in porn are happy and are treated fairly, or whether porn is a healthy way to make a living. We look at how and why visual imagery turns us on.

JUST THE VISUAL

I love erotic art from all periods in any medium—explicit drawings, paintings, engravings, photography, and illustrations. I like to see solitary depictions of men and women I find attractive, men and women coupling, women with women, and men with men, probably in that order of preference. I think I lean toward images that include women getting off in some way. It's important to me that something is strong and beautiful as a piece of art as well as a sexual depiction. I like seeing things that taste of reality . . . or rather, that are produced in such a way that I can suspend disbelief. I find some Japanimation very arousing. Sometimes I draw my own weird little kinky fantasies—it's a habit that goes back to scribbling dirty pics in the margins of textbooks in grade school. They might be penetration shots or typical images of figures arranged in love scenes.

—URSULA, 25

While visual imagery turns on the majority of women—over 92 percent, according to the CAKE Report—the scope of exactly what we like to see is extremely diverse. We respond to all sorts of visuals, from those we see every day—like the hot trainer at the gym or a cute couple kissing on the street—to directly pornographic images meant to turn us on, like erotic photography, nude illustrations, or amateur videos on the Web. As long as we are not distracted by content that specifically turns us off (one woman's favorite fingering technique is another woman's worst sexual pet peeve), there's nothing to stop a woman's positive response to visual imagery.

Sometimes leaving most of the visual up to the imagination can be more erotic than having every piece of the puzzle explicitly laid out and connected for you. Slivers of nudity obscured by shadows, clothing falling off, long, slow body shots, and hands on skin can be just the right touch. Then again, sometimes we like it raw and explicit. Some girls are all about the hard core, and God bless them.

What turns us off is also diverse. Tastes vary, and one woman's trash is another woman's treasure. Many of us can't stand fake female orgasms and fake nails. For some, busty and lusty is just our speed. Some women don't dig the male come shot. Other girls tell us they are all about the money shot—the G–money shot, that is. To each her own.

GOIN' TO THE MOVIES
When plot counts

It is assumed that men are stimulated by visual images and women are stimulated more by context—that we would rather *read* a story about sex than actually see it. Who came up with this black-and-white dichotomy? Guess what? We like to do both!

Women are visual creatures who respond to sexually explicit material. While we may respond sympathetically to the fantasy portrayal of love in the classic chick flicks, we're usually a lot happier when that romance is paired with some fantastic sex. However, this combination is scarcer than natural breasts in Hollywood (or the Valley).

181

You remember it like it was yesterday—"Now . . . I've had . . . the time of my life and I owe it all to you." That's right, a little flashback to 1987, when Patrick Swayze suavely taught us teenage girls what really good deflowering sex was supposed to be like. You may have hated *Dirty Dancing*, or you may have loved it, but if you saw it during your virgin years, we know it had an impact on the way you viewed sex and losing your virginity. Don't get us wrong, we still love to watch it from time to time, but as one of the very few representations of a woman's first sexual experience, it sets one's expectations in a total fantasy realm.

> I was 15 and *Dirty Dancing* was my obsession. I loved it!! I must have intimidated the 15-year-old boys when I grabbed them at school parties and started riding their thighs. And yes, it indeed portrayed sex in a different light, romantic, easy, reciprocal, long, and sumptuous. I must have cheated myself for a while, thinking that the right look and dance moves would get me off as well.
>
> —BARBARA, 31

The illusion of romance aside, Baby (the main female character) wanted her dance teacher so bad because of what she first saw when she carried those watermelons up the stairs. Her big eyes originally widened at the sight of the misbehaving staff getting down late at night with moves that turned her on. Oh, Patrick, Patrick . . . what would it feel like to have just one dirty dance with you?

We want to see things that turn us on alongside things that make us think. Is that too much to ask for? When we get wrapped up in a movie character, we want to see her having a grand old sexy time so we can fantasize about being in her place.

BODY DOUBLE

Here are some scenes in which CAKE Girls wish they could be the body double. We are sure you've seen many of these, but a second viewing with sex on the brain couldn't hurt. They are all good places to start. A warm-up, if you will, before we get into the hard stuff. Ladies, start your engines.

- The sun-kissed heaven in the Mediterranean of *Sex and Lucia*

- Pierce and Renee doing it up the stairs and on the desk with body shots of whiskey in *The Thomas Crown Affair*

- The threesome with two hot, young, nubile boys and one experienced woman in the Mexican countryside in *Y Tu Mamá También*

- Tough girl Gina Gershon schooling the innocent Jennifer Tilly on the ins and outs of juicy lipstick-lesbian sex in *Bound*

- Hot mama Frances McDormand lounging in bed with her young beau, enjoying a striptease by her son's fiancée in *Laurel Canyon*

- Tom Cruise having stand-up sex in front of the refrigerator with Kelly Preston screaming "Never stop fucking me!" in *Jerry Maguire*

- Halle Berry's Oscar-winning performance with Billy Bob Thornton all over the couch in *Monster's Ball*

- Rain pouring down all over Kim Basinger and Mickey Rourke on the stairwell in *9½ Weeks*

- The ritualized spankings for misspelled words in *Secretary*

- The throng of people passing by while the French schoolgirl and an older Asian businessman have hot, sweaty sex on the floor in *The Lover*

- The way David Duchovny says, "Yeah, baby, what?" while fingering Brigitte Bako in the bathtub in the original *Red Shoe Diaries* movie

- Naomi Watts making out with the buxom brunette version of herself in *Mulholland Drive*

- Nicole Kidman losing it to Jude Law up in the mountains, after waiting four long years in *Cold Mountain*

- Mark Ruffalo talking dirty over the phone to Meg Ryan and then eating her out with skill in *In the Cut*

- Naked politics in the bath, between two men in *The Dreamers*

TRIPLE X
All plot aside

I have always been curious about porn on the Internet. When men I have dated raved to me about the wonders of it, I felt fiercely jealous that they can indulge and please themselves so easily and without any guilt. I have always avoided Internet porn, and porn in general, for moral reasons—somehow it just felt wrong . . . and too easy. Porn surfing was also a tough task for me because I have recently been saddled with a well-meaning but obtrusive and sorority-esque roommate. I worried about what she might think of me if she ever found out. Many thoughts were running through my head, like "I am so dirty for looking at this stuff" and "If she knew, she would surely think I am a freak." Well, I mustered up the courage, logged on, and immediately went to one of those sites with the free, pirated passwords and browsed, timidly at first. While surfing, I became so turned on that I touched myself with a vibrator on a low setting. I came in seconds because I was so visually stimulated. I am shocked at being so turned on by many of the sites, including the "barely legal" ones. In my rational mind, I know that these are the most exploitative of all. I think I am attracted to them because I identify with the bodies of the girls. Like them, I am slim and smaller-chested. I am happy now that I have crossed this psychological barrier. That I am not afraid anymore of the unknown world of adult sites. And that I can get myself off in a matter of seconds.

—JULIE, 25

As a whole, the genre known as porn is produced by men, to get men off. As we have been told by those in the industry, this is a 10-minute project. Max! Inspiring, huh? Porn is all about the "money shot." You know how it goes. A little sucky, sucky, fucky, fucky, and then more sucky and then the grand finale—the doughy, shady-looking guy pulls out for the come shot! Has anyone heard of female pleasure? Female orgasms? We would like to think that seeing women being properly pleasured would also turn men on, but it seems that may not be the case. To be honest, we are simply not sure what's going on here.

We have a mandate to actively seek out and promote material that is attuned to our specific tastes. Despite the scarcity of options, women are actively searching for anything and everything that may turn us on. Fortunately, the search is under way, and women are both creators and consumers of a new generation of entertainment made for the ladies. With Carol Queen's educational videos on the G-spot, Candida Royalle's housewife fantasies, the Suicide Girls' modern pinups, *Sweet Action* magazine's real-boy naked pics, Playgirl TV's new take on what women want to see on the telly, and even Harvard University's erotic magazine for students, women are taking back the visual imagery domain from the boys and making some porn intended for women!

Today, though some feminists decry the dehumanizing products of this male-dominated industry, many women unabashedly declare their love of the stuff. For the first time, women are taking a real look at the porn phenomenon (from outside the business and from within) and uncovering its mystery for themselves. Though we *critique* the majority of porn, which slights female pleasure, we can't *ignore* that women can get pleasure out of it.

Porn can be visually exciting; it can inspire sexual interactions with a partner or provide stimulation for solo sessions. Porn also affects the female perspective on what sex should be and look like, while also turning us on to sexy images, not just as partners of porn watchers but also as porn watchers ourselves. For the purposes of this discussion, let's presume that the porn we are referring to is the 1 percent that may have some value in stimulating or educating women. At the real heart of the matter: Where else can we *see* sex? No matter how negligent it can be toward female pleasure and orgasm, porn can be instructional in its own way.

While watching porn, we are more likely to imagine being the woman in the film than the man fucking her. In order for us to enjoy

THE JACKPOT

The golden age of porn might be over, but the gold rush is still on. The porn industry just keeps on getting bigger and bigger; it is one of America's most profitable sectors. Let's take a brief look at the hard facts. According to Frank Rich in *The New York Times Magazine,* the U.S. porn industry takes in between $10 billion and $15 billion each year, which should come as no surprise given the copious daily renting, viewing, purchasing, and surfing of it. *Deep Throat* alone has made over $600 million in sales, subsequent to its theatrical release. That's a lot of porno dollars. More than 10,000 porn films are made each year, about 30 a day. Americans buy or rent $4 billion a year worth of graphic sex videos. One in four Internet users visits at least one of the 60,000 sex sites on the Web a month. Surf that porn, people! Sex sites generate $1 billion a year in revenue. Americans spend as much on porn as they spend attending professional sporting events, buying music, and going out to the movies combined.

Despite the marginal quality of the content, porn is going mainstream. While it remains taboo in much of the country, millions of Americans regularly enjoy porn in private. And who is the largest distributor of porn? Whether they want to admit it or not, General Motors, America's largest corporation, distributes more porn in a year than does Larry Flynt himself. GM, along with some of America's other big-time brand names, like Marriott and Time Warner, is now making millions by silently selling XXX-rated materials via satellite and cable. Now, that's the American way!

this viewing experience, the woman must be having a good time. Her experience is our experience, and if she is genuinely aroused, we can be too. We want to see sympathetic female characters whom we can understand. Karen (27) is tired of all the faking in porn. She wants to see real women and men engaging in real sex for once. More than aware that five licks will not get her off in real life, Karen wants to see how long it takes to achieve a real female orgasm.

Most of all, we want the "money shot" to be the female orgasm in all its glory. If Alexa (27) directed her own porn film, she would have the climax of each clip—each vignette, as they say—to be the woman having an orgasm instead of a man coming all over the woman's face! The woman's orgasm would be the result of the group effort of all the men focusing on getting the woman off. The best porn features women who seem to be enjoying themselves, and men who actually appear to be attracted to the beautiful women with whom they are having sex.

> Porn empowers me. Watching it makes me feel adventurous, courageous, and curious. Porn makes me want to be a better lover. It helps me to appreciate my body and the bodies of all kinds of women. Not only do I have great sex watching it, but I enjoy myself while watching it too.
>
> —TARA, 24

Despite all its flaws, many, many women are looking at porn for their own arousal and entertainment. Plot, character development, and focus on female pleasure aside, in actuality we are capable of responding to explicit visual imagery regardless of its content. While the focus of porn may sometimes be off, we can still enjoy the raw, visceral, and stimulating experience of watching people having sex on camera.

The bottom line is that when women have positive sexual images to look at, our sex lives get better. While porn surely isn't the full formula, it's still a part of the equation.

Pleasure Tip: Think of porn as an education. This content can be a learning tool, a reflection of how sex actually happens, and an inspiration for arousal. Everyone could stand to learn a few new positions. Sit down in front of your television with a pile of pornos, and surprise yourself with the unexpected things that get you hot. When you sample what's out there—amateur couples at home, chic lesbians in bathroom stalls, big-breasted blondes in the boardroom, the mistress and her slave in the dungeon—it's hard not to find a little something that looks good to you.

Let it rev you up and turn you on. Try porn out as a means of comparison shopping without ever having to buy anything. See what you like and figure out what you don't. Porn is like a tasting menu!

And remember, we are not saying that you will find the porn-viewing experience entirely satisfactory. In fact we are asking you to be critical of what this material looks like and to get in touch with how it makes you feel. Don't like what you see? Sign on to the Open Letter to the Porn Industry.

OPEN LETTER TO THE PORN INDUSTRY

Re: More lust, less bust

It's time to lay down the law. No more faking it! Although we have to take our hats off to the select group of women who are hell-bent on making chick porn, on the whole there just isn't enough porn made for women. Or for anyone who cares about female pleasure, for that matter. Despite the smattering of female-produced, female-focused films that are made every year, the overwhelming majority of porn is still made by men for men. The main thrust (pardon our French) of porn portrays women solely as vessels for the fulfillment of male pleasure. We have nothing against male pleasure, that's for sure—but let's not ignore female pleasure altogether! Focusing on female pleasure won't alienate your current market; we think men like to see a woman in the throes of true ecstasy too—it certainly seems to work for them in the bedroom.

Across the board, we want to see real female orgasms from our XXX entertainment. As thoughtful viewers, we protest the lack of female orgasms and pleasure in porn. If there were more accurate images of women in sexual material, we would be more compelled by it, for sure. We'd also like to see you balance the surgically altered, bleached-blond starlets, as cute as they can be, with "real" women. Make some of *us* the stars, and we bet you'd see your numbers rise. Showcasing the diversity of looks and body types among women who enjoy sex would be a better model for all of our sex lives.

Love,
[YOUR NAME]

CAKE-APPROVED PORN
We like it real and diverse

So where to start? The rows and rows of *Dirty Debutantes* and *Rocco Does Whoever* are very hard to sort through. The mass of porn is overwhelming. Taste in porn is subjective. Some like it hot. Some like it wet. Some like it hot *and* wet. Fortunately, we have donated hundreds of hours of screening time to find the tastiest tidbits for your viewing pleasure. After scrupulous analysis, lots of fast-forwarding, several bouts of "Oh, my gosh, what was that?" rewinding, and a few good long pauses, we are pleased to present a detailed compilation of how we like our porn.

Yes, yes, yes—we have to say it again. We want to see real women, experiencing real pleasure and real orgasms, in realistic scenarios. We want to be able to watch and see ourselves in the experience. We want to be treated as the viewer, not only the object.

Face it—the action in porn is mostly fake. You have to ignore the timing of the orgasm, or the fact that the male actors haven't made any effort to build women up or, seemingly, get turned on. They just flip the switch and get right into it. Give them a break: They're working. There are some hot moments when the actors really get into it, the chemistry is there, and the actresses themselves have sworn how turned on they were at the time.

Here are two choice cuts recommended for those of you who like it *real:*

Eyes of Desire, directed and produced by an ex–porn star, Candida Royalle. If you ever thought that female orgasms are silent, polite, or dainty, Royalle proves you wrong. These orgasms are off the hook! The stars in this movie come like it's the apocalypse, and it's so real you have to turn down the volume. Lots of good lovin' where it counts! We recommend watching the film next to a mirror and imitating Chloe's orgasm faces, then trying them out in bed once you're on the right track.

I Dream of Jenna: By her own account, you can watch the number of orgasms Jenna has when her real-life boyfriend goes down on her.

We like to learn

Male-dominated porn seems to be the same stuff warmed over and over and over. All the actors have the same sexual techniques (they all must have had the same teacher in Giving Head 101)—predictable and very boring. I would be so turned on watching women do what they really do during sex—different positions, watching close-ups of women giving and receiving oral sex would be such a turn-on and an education! What they do with their hands, teeth, lips, and tongues. Yum!

—INDIA, 34

There's nothing like a little porno for a quick lesson about the birds and the bees . . . and butt plugs, and strap-ons, and role-playing. A new crop of female directors has merged self-help and porno for the perfect mix of inspiration and instruction. Whether you need the instruction, or your new partner needs a little catch-up session, instructional porn can inspire a new pleasure experience.

Recommended for those of you who like to *learn:*

Fanny Fatale's How to Female Ejaculate. We know you know about female ejaculation, and maybe a lucky few of you have experienced it, but nothing beats being able to rewind and fast-forward a woman shooting it across the room in a smooth arc of pleasure. It's a serious crowd pleaser. Plus, Fanny Fatale gives you all you need to know with her introduction and step-by-step, in-the-moment interviews of her talented female friends. While the style is distinctly '80s (you really have to get past the weird hats and suspenders), the women still blow a gasket the likes of which most of us have never seen.

G Marks the Spot. The smart and amazing Carol Queen shows you all you need to know about the G-spot—where it is, how to find it, and how to touch it. This film is more reality than fantasy, and you're the big star!

We like it retro

The 1970s were the heyday of porn kitsch, the era of disco, cocaine, and, apparently, letting your bush grow out. *Behind the Green Door* and *The Opening of Misty Beethoven* are classics that are becoming masturbation staples for women in need of that totally fluffy, bushy, and doe-eyed look from the good ol' days.

Recommended for those of you who like it *retro:*

The Opening of Misty Beethoven. The making of a sex goddess, '70s style. While the plot is rather dated—Misty's goddess status is dependent on her partner's satisfaction—the scenes are undeniably hot. Don't be fooled by the healthy dose of '70s kitsch and assume that you've seen it all. Midway, Misty straps it on with a cool studded leather harness for a threesome that's sure to inspire. Watch it once and you will be singing the soundtrack for days!

Behind the Green Door. Imagine yourself in an underground sex cabaret where the main attraction is an unassuming woman who will experience real sexual pleasure for the first time. Like the sound of that? We bet you do. The show culminates in an *Eyes Wide Shut*–esque sex romp that includes members of the audience. Based on the concepts of experience, interaction, evolution, and freedom, *Behind the Green Door* makes a sexual statement that continues to butt up against contemporary social boundaries, all the while prioritizing hot and sexy visual stimulation.

Sometimes a little bit of cinematography and style can go a long way. Check out the 1970s chic in jet-setting Marilyn Chambers's *Insatiable,* complete with one of John Holmes's finest performances. Don't pretend you don't know who (or what!) we are talking about.

Emmanuelle is another crowd pleaser. Who can resist the charms of the lovely and ravishing Sylvia Kristel, as she comes to understand the power of her own sexuality with the magic of Thailand as the backdrop. Sylvia Kristel is about as close as porn has ever come to having a traditional Hollywood actress take the plunge, and she is a sight to behold. You can revel in vicarious delight as she seduces and is seduced by really sexy men and women alike.

We like it styled

Women don't like tacky porn any more than we like tacky dresses. While what constitutes a good sense of style is subjective, we still want some thought put into the matter. Only recently have directors started understanding that women don't want to see mustachioed mullet-headed guys with mesh tank tops banging it out on the hood of a two-tone Camaro. Some of us want to see a fashion shoot gone wild with the woman in the center of the action wearing Manolo Blahniks and silk stockings while getting fucked up the ass.

> **Lighting is important. The contrast of darkness with a very
> direct light from one side can be a supremely beautiful way
> to show the body. Candlelight may be a cliché, but it's a cliché
> for a reason. Something about the flickering illumination, I
> guess. Shadows are an intangible extension of the body. I would
> love to see the shadows of people making love; the idea is so
> suggestive and very voyeuristic. It would be a sexy scene.
> Texture is important too. I imagine people with beautiful,
> luminous skin on white sheets, with natural light coming in the
> window. Bedding that looks so good to touch can only
> complement a body.**
>
> **—NICOLE, 26**

There's no one set of rules. Some women want only black-and-white film images, others like high-contrast, full-color, slow-motion video. Some of us want a set with red velvet drapes and lots of candles, while others want to see a tropical fantasy. These specifications are visual elements worth responding to, not "context" in the emotional or romantic sense.

Recommended for those of you who like it *styled:*

Director Andrew Blake is the king of glamour girly porn. Gorgeous, natural-bodied women, cavorting in semi-soft-core bisexual chic, exclusively populate his films. While still far from realistic in many respects, it's hot as hell. Blake's vision pays close attention to the value of style and leaves any sense of context entirely to the viewer's imagination. Sex is what counts here—beautiful girl-on-girl sex, that is.

Justine. We are constantly asked, "Where can a good girl go to see some hot, fun, sexy, girl-on-girl action?" Set in the NYC underground scene, *Justine* is pure eye candy for all you girls out there who love to see hot, hot women getting it on with each other.

House of Dreams. An early item from Andrew Blake, *House of Dreams* features Zara Whites and all of her masturbation fantasies coming true. A definite turn-on; just fast-forward through the bad '80s neon light scene.

We like it all about the boys

One thing that sexual imagery and porn are missing across the board is *hot men.* Now, don't think there's not a logical reason for this. The test of time has shown that men don't want to be intimidated by the men in porn. In fact, they want to participate in a fantasy world where any poor schlub can bang the super-hottie he sees in the Laundromat—and sometimes within minutes of meeting her. That's why the most successful porn stars include the fat and hairy Ron Jeremy (aka the Hedgehog) as well as the very homely Ed Powers. However, what is curious is that the men in porn tend to have enormous sex organs, dwarfing some of the best-endowed men out there. More wishful thinking, we suppose.

Every sexual variant has a decent porn magazine, until you try finding one for straight girls. Though *Playgirl* has been banking on the objectification of the male body for years, its primary audience is gay men—and the idea that women are turned on by pictures of naked men hasn't expanded far beyond this small slice of the porn world.

If we like to look at hot men on the street and hot men naked in our beds—and we do—why wouldn't we want to look at hot, naked men on the big screen? We obviously look at men's bodies for personal enjoyment, and any straight girl can tell you what part of the male body she likes best. Some like the pelvic bones on either side of a six-pack, others the smooth curves of a nice ass, or collarbones leading to broad shoulders and sculpted arms.

We want to see more . . . but more of what we want on the street, and in our beds. Girls say: Go easy on the grease, the fake tan, and the airbrushing, and give us a little of what we really want. Once again, it's impossible to generalize. Some women do like the buff construction worker or the fireman. Others like the scrawny rocker dude. Jess (23) likes her men best when they are ultra-masculine, with body hair and a stubbly jaw, and pleasuring themselves for the camera. Whoever said women don't like to objectify the male genitalia was dead wrong.

You said it, girl. We are over that flaccid penis *Playgirl* action.

We like it kinky:
boys who like boys

Don't *all* women want to see two hot straight men together, just like the guys want to see Jenna and all her pals? For girls who like boys who like boys, watching two men making love is the way to go. The sight of dudes getting it on for their own benefit is a hundred times better than watching the ponytailed guys in straight porn grunt out an orgasm. Two guys together can be intensely sexy even for straight girls.

> I love two men together even more than man-on-woman. A lot of straight women I know feel this way. Seeing two men together is equal to the renowned craving in men for watching two girls get it on. What I love about gay male porn is that the men are okay, looking aroused and intense and into the moment, while in straight porn the guys tend to look vain and absent, like mannequins or dolls. A man stroking his cock with great intensity and arousal is guaranteed spontaneous combustion for me. Can't beat it! And if he's looking directly into my eyes so I can see every sensation, that's even better.
> —ANNE, 32

The taboo against men going at it with such voracity may be the reason why some women can't resist it. When women watch two men get it on, there is a certain reversal of the power dynamic—the woman as the viewer is completely in the driver's seat. We also get to imagine what it might feel like to be smack dab in the middle of a "CAKE Sam'ich."

We like it live

So, you've watched all of our recommendations. Now what? Given that the library of hot porn for chicks is limited, maybe it's time to go out on the hunt for other sources.

Why rely on filmed images when you can watch the real thing? While watching sex up close and personal is pretty hard to arrange, you might just get lucky if your neighbors forget to close the blinds. Then again, some women don't have to rely on others to provide visuals—they just need a partner and a mirror, and voilà—live porn, right at home!

Pleasure Tip: Recipe for a porn party, CAKE style: Get out the popcorn. We know you love it. . . . Go to your local video store, take out a few of our suggestions, and create your own porn party with your friends in the comfort of your living room. Talk about what you like and what you don't—you'll be amazed at all the new things you learn about your girls. Better yet, snuggle up with a DVD and your partner . . . and see where things go from there.

Cake Bite

THE VISUAL IMAGINATION

We are putting you in the director's chair. What would a sexy movie look like if you were in charge? Consider possible themes (hard-core tussling, innocent flirting), characters (male models waiting on you hand and foot, secret admirers writing love letters on your body), soundtrack (heavy moaning, heavy metal), props (ropes, exotic flowers, chocolate sauce), costumes ('50s, glam, rock and roll), and locations (garden party, Cuban bar, lush white loft) . . . then go shoot it yourself!

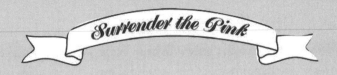

ELLE, 23 This is a scene from my sex life that would make a great porn clip.

You hurriedly open the door, shuffle me into your house ahead of you, and turn to slam and lock the door behind you. Then you shove me against the wall face-first—not violently, just urgently. As my hands clutch at the wall, you press against my ass and I arch back to meet you.

You tousle my hair so it tumbles across my shoulders, and entangle your fingers in my locks. With a quick turn of your wrist, you yank my head back and I arch further, my body now forming a deep curve with my tits flattened against the wall. My hot breath quickens while you slide your middle finger inside me, your thumb brushing against my stomach as you began to make deep, slow beckoning motions inside my cunt. "Oh, God!" The words escape my mouth while your palm circles lazily. I gyrate my ass against your hand and your dick.

You kiss me hard, mouth open, and your tongue wraps around mine. In one deft move, you hoist me up onto your back and carry me up the stairs, while I lick your neck, leaving hot little trails up to your earlobes. In your room, you practically throw me onto your bed, then turn to put on music. Metal: fast and loud, growling out through the speakers. You turn back around with the stolen goods—the black sleeping mask and handcuffs from my bedroom. Sliding my shirt off all the way, you unzip the side of my skirt and pull it over my boots so I'm left wearing nothing but a garter belt, fishnets, black boots, pink tie, and a pair of thoroughly unnecessary and very damp underwear.

You help me shimmy out of my panties and lay me back down on the bed. Looking me in the eye, you tell me you love me before you raise my arms up over my head and snap a cold metal cuff around each wrist and fasten the blindfold around my face. I hear the sound of your clothes dropping to the floor. Interesting. "Hi," I say tentatively. My legs lie splayed open, my wrists locked together over my head, my body bare to your eyes.

You grip the insides of my thighs, hard (there will be thumbprints, I think). Good; I want it rough now, hard and fast. There's something dripping on my clit. Your rough warm tongue slurps upward, ending in one firm lick of my clit. "Oh, God!" I moan and writhe, but the handcuffs keep me in place and you press your shoulders into my thighs to keep me from bucking too hard. You move up to my tits and nibble at them with your teeth, pulling until I squeal out and you massage them to allay the pain.

Your dick presses closer and closer to my pussy and you move your body down against mine, your chest brushing against me as you kiss your way back down my body. "Please, please," I gasp, pushing my feet against the bottom of the bed as my pussy drips onto the sheets.

"What do you want, baby? Do you want me to fuck you in the ass?" you ask.

"Oh, yes," I breathe back. You slip your finger into my pussy hard and fast, and you lean in close to my face. "Do you want me to fuck your pussy instead?" You force your tongue into my mouth before I can answer. "Tell me, tell me," you order. "I want to hear you say it. Tell me what you want and we'll see what you get." You grab my tits and rub your cock up against my clit and I throatily respond, "No, fuck me in the ass."

"You want it in the ass? You want me to ram you from behind? Tell me!"

"Fuck me from behind, please, bend me over the bed and ram your huge cock into me and make me scream." You moan long and loud and unlock my handcuffs, climb off me, and flip me over, grabbing my ankles and roughly pulling me toward the edge of the bed. Gripping my thighs, you order me to spread my legs. "Spread them farther. Fuck, you're so hot. Look at you, like a dream, all wet and open. I want to make you scream."

You bend down and spread my ass cheeks wide open and push your face right in there, going to work with your strong tongue while I writhe against the edge of the mattress. You fumble under the bed as your tongue explores its way to the front of my pussy and you pull out my Rabbit vibrator. "Holy fuck!" I say.

"I'm going to fill you up completely, I want to feel you come, baby." You lube up your cock, spreading the thick goo up and down the shaft, and edge your slick fingers into my asshole. First one, then two. More lube; then you reach for the Rabbit again and turn it on low, and rub it up against the front of my pussy.

"Oh, fuck, I want to feel you fill me up, I wanna make you come all over me!" I say.

"Good, how's that?" you ask as you ease into my ass. I moan in response and nudge the dial up, grinding into the vibrator. In and out, you fuck my cunt with it, and it hits every ridge inside. I push back to help your cock into my asshole. Plunging all the way in, you shout out and raise your hand to spank me. I cry out, "Harder!" and turn the dial all the way up. Fuck, you are about to burst. You are humping me so hard, pulling it almost all the way out and then slamming it back in. With the Rabbit at full power, you grab my hips, pumping faster and faster, and I plunge the vibrator in and out at the same time.

"Oh, God, I'm gonna come, I'm coming so hard!" I scream through gritted teeth, and you smack me again while I come. You pull out, yank me by my shoulders down onto the floor, pull off my blindfold as quickly as you can, and spurt all over my face. You keep coming for about 30 seconds, all over my chest. I lick my lips and massage my pussy while you sink back onto your knees and wipe the palm of your hand over my face before you give me a deep wet kiss.

Your body is trembling, but you look me in the eye and say, "Are you still turned on, baby?" I drop my eyes, suddenly shy, and you tell me not to be. "All right, then," I say, "do you want to watch, or do you want to help?" You grin back—"Now, that's more like it!"—and help me back onto the bed. Your legs are shaking, so I lay you down and put a pillow behind your head. Then I straddle you and let your mouth do the work. After such a workout, I come again in less than a minute, and sigh as I sink back onto the bed. I curl up against you, and you hold my small hands in front of your face, lightly kissing the red jagged lines across my wrists before you kiss my lips and wrap your body around me.

"Thanks." I smile.

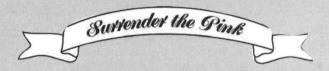

AMANDA, 29 My fantasy porn scene takes place on a big sailboat en route to the Caribbean, and I'm the star. The day is hot, but the winds keep it comfortable. The sun is baking down on us, tanning our skin. I am enjoying the rhythmic motion of the waves as I lie in the sun, relaxing. My skin is starting to turn a little pink, so I take out the suntan oil, which has been warmed by the sun to the perfect temperature. I pour some in my hand and rub it into my legs, starting at my feet and ankles, up my calves, over my knees, and then to my thighs. I am wearing a blue-and-white floral bikini top and a blue sarong around my waist.

You see me rubbing the hot oil into my tanned skin and offer to do it for me instead. Of course I accept. I give you the bottle of oil and you pour a pool into your palm. You rub your hands together to make sure they are covered in the coconut-scented elixir. I turn around so my back is toward you, and you start at my shoulders, moving my hair to one side. You work your hands down my spine to the small of my back, knowing I love to be touched there with very light hands. I can feel the electricity flowing through my spine as you move to my sides and back up to my shoulders and arms. You put more oil on your hands and begin to kiss my neck as your hands move around me and start rubbing oil into my stomach, my chest, and the front of my neck.

You can't neglect the parts of my skin that are not getting any sun, for fear that they would be jealous of all the skin that is getting your attention. You slide your hands under my bikini top and massage my breasts, pinching at my nipples until they are hard. You untie the back of my top and slip it over my head, now nibbling on my left ear. I arch my back, pressing my breasts deeper into your hands, tipping my head back over your shoulder so you can kiss my neck better. I turn around and wrap my legs around your waist, pulling myself into you, kissing you the entire time. I take the bottle of oil and fill my hands with the warm contents. I start rubbing it on your chest and shoulders, on your neck and face. I can feel how hard you are getting, which turns me on even more than your expert touch. I guide your hand under my sarong so you can feel how wet you have gotten me. You slide in one finger, then two . . . playing me, tempting me, teasing me. You move down from my lips to my neck, to my chest, stopping on each breast. Biting playfully on each hard nipple. You kiss your way down my stomach, stopping just short of my pussy, which is aching to be licked. You are teasing me again . . . because you know I can't take it!

You untie my sarong and lightly kiss the inside of my thigh. With a very light tongue, you start to trace the outline of my dripping pussy. I am aching with temptation, wanting you to take me, right here . . . right now. Finally, after what feels like days, you take my clit in your mouth, moving it around with your tongue. Feeling how hard it is, lapping up my hot juices. Unable to hold back, I come over and over while you are darting your tongue back and forth inside me, rubbing my clit with your finger. I am panting with desire . . . I want you to feel all the same pleasures I am feeling, so I sit up and slide down on you. I can see how hard you are through your surf shorts. I take them off, letting them drop at your ankles. I put more oil on my hands and take hold of your hard cock. I slowly slide my hands up and down your shaft until you are all oiled up. I then massage your balls while I tease your cock with my mouth and tongue. I slide my tongue up and down the shaft, massaging you at the same time. I circle the tip of your cock and then take you into my mouth. Slowly at first, then faster and faster. I grab your ass and push you deeper into my mouth as I work your hard cock with my tongue. I massage your ass, gently spreading and kneading your muscles. I take your balls in my mouth and massage them with my tongue.

You say you are about to come and that you want to come in my mouth . . . so I take your hard cock into my mouth and slide up and down, sucking you until you shake with pleasure, coming hard into my mouth. We are both satisfied, for now, so we lie in the sun together, letting the rays fall over our naked bodies. Until we are both hungry again . . .

CHAPTER 12

"Straight" as a Ruler?

Dear CAKE,

I've always felt very sexually attracted to women, and in a way consider myself bisexual, since I am attracted to both sexes. There was, like, a week in college where I struggled with the "Oh, my God, am I gay?" question, but then I got over it and decided that if my feelings toward women qualified as being gay, then probably most women in the world would also qualify. I've never fantasized about having a relationship with a woman, just about having wild, crazy, steamy sex with another sexy and attractive woman like me. So I settled on "bisexual" as a decent definition for me, with probably "normal, straight woman" being an even better one. I definitely think that most women fantasize about being with another woman, not necessarily someone they know, just the idea of being with another woman. Help me out, CAKE—can you confirm or deny?

—ELISABETH, 22

Elisabeth, consider yourself confirmed! Straight up, many self-defined "straight" girls have sexual fantasies about other women, and some even have sexual experiences with other women as well, which invites a question: How "straight" is straight?

Getting turned on by the *idea* of sex with other women has long been a part of the "straight" female sexual repertoire. Nancy Friday's *My Secret Garden* provided the first significant anecdotal evidence about what was then a totally taboo fantasy. Once strictly the realm of the imagination, the girl/girl formula is now a consistent part of the cultural zeitgeist.

Our culture increasingly promotes the specific vision of hot women getting it on with each other. Madonna, a sexual icon and trailblazer for the past twenty years, has boldly experimented with her sexuality while constantly under the public eye. Her makeout performance with Britney Spears at the MTV Video Music Awards in 2003 was more a sign of what's acceptable than a symbol of what is still taboo. Not only did their kiss indicate that it's okay for a married straight woman to kiss another woman, it made the act fashionable and attractive.

It's true that the male fantasy of girls getting it on with each other has played a role in making girl/girl sex culturally acceptable, or even desirable. Men are an integral part of our sexual lives, and our partners are influential when it comes to how we perceive ourselves sexually. So, if the notion of two women together turns our male partner on, that increases our interest in making his fantasy come to life. That said, women's girl-on-girl desires are about much more than pleasing men.

In *Friends, Will and Grace,* and *Sex and the City,* the idea of women with women has made its way into the American mainstream, and not just in the form of a male fantasy. Over the past several decades, films such as *Bound, Basic Instinct, Laurel Canyon,* and *The Hunger* have featured some of the hottest female stars of Hollywood having their way with each other. We respond to these images because they reflect our own lives and desires.

Today we are actively exploring sexual experiences with other women in a host of different combinations, with various methodologies and philosophies. There are women who think about getting it on with another woman while in happy monogamous relationships with men, newly single women who engage in no-strings-attached makeout sessions with female friends, and women who "do" mostly men but have had female sexual partners and would again. Our experiences range from childhood exploration to college experimentation to present-day uninhibited getting it on.

OH, BEHAVE!
Get over labels

If you got 100 percent honest answers from most people, about both their fantasies and their behavior, almost no one would be totally straight or totally gay. A majority of women today are having thoughts and engaging in behavior that qualify them as bisexual by traditional definition, and some women are happy to embrace this term. But there is a lot of diversity in both "straight" and "bisexual" behavior, and there's no clear line between where straight ends and bisexual begins.

Lola breaks it down like this:

I could be called straight just because I prefer to be sexually active with men rather than women. I could be called straight because I haven't had that many encounters with women. I could be called straight because I don't get into relationships with women. But I choose to call myself bisexual because I do worship women with my eyes, lust after a precious few, make out with some on occasion, and have engaged in sexual activities with a handful. I choose to call myself bisexual because loving women, adoring women, and fucking women has been a constant (albeit not all that frequent) in my life.

From experimenting in grade school, to showering with gal pals in high school, to my first kiss in college, and now to the threesomes I have initiated lately, I prefer cock as a sensation. I prefer the broad shoulders of men. I prefer the easier read I get on men in relationships. I prefer dating someone not of my gender, with none of my bleeding, without the similarity in physique and physical traits. But I love the softness of another woman's tongue and lips on mine, the similar thoughts and feelings we can share, the roundness of her hips and thighs, breasts and ass. I am a bisexual because, while I am courting men right now, I don't foresee disqualifying a woman as a partner simply because she is of my gender. Maybe I just haven't met the right one yet.

—LOLA, 27

Leigh Ann (25) is unsure how to classify herself sexually. She likes being with men and ultimately wants to marry one, but she fantasizes about women and has been with women, just for the sexual experience. She finds sex with a woman to be softer, lighter, and more sensual, but also less emotional and more detached. On a continuum, she thinks she is more straight than bi, but neither label adequately describes her sexuality.

What is the purpose of the label "straight" when it no longer refers to women who are attracted only to men? There is not a single point on a scale or a grid that can define our identity, especially not when that identity changes over the course of our lives. How do you account for sexual experiences that you may not want to repeat, or fantasies you have but would never want to act on?

The real-life experiences of "straight" women can be broken down based on a variety of desires. We like to call this the CAKE Scale.

THE CAKE SCALE

This scale is for women who make choices to expand our otherwise "straight" sexuality and venture into unrestricted territory. The categories are just a framework to examine the fluidity of female sexual behavior—feel free to mix and match! Hopeful Benders, anyone?

The Rulers. Those of us who are as straight as the proverbial yardstick and profess to have no attraction whatsoever to other women. Well, here's a news flash for you. According to our current data, the Rulers have just become the minority. Rulers, you are simply too straight for this chapter.

The Minders. Those of us who fantasize about other women regularly as masturbation material but do not intend to act these fantasies out.

The Hopefuls. Those of us who fantasize and actually wish to explore more sexual experiences with other women but have not taken the next step forward.

The Benders. Those of us who have had sexual interactions with other women but still date men and identify as straight.

SAPPHO'S RIDDLE

THE EVOLUTION OF SEXUAL IDENTITY

Sexual identity is a relatively modern concept. The idea of sexual identity—of using labels, such as straight, gay, or lesbian—is a social construct, a way of grouping people based on sexual preference and then assigning social meaning to those groups.

Ancient Greece: Love without labels The word "lesbian" originally referred to a person from the Greek island of Lesbos. The lyric poet Sappho, also known as the Tenth Muse, lived on Lesbos and was a teacher at a school for women. She wrote poetry that, in some translations, addressed the issue of love between women. Today some scholars refer to Sappho as potentially heterosexual, others as bisexual, and yet others as lesbian. Regardless, the term "Sapphism" has become synonymous with lesbianism, and Sappho has become the de facto first historical lesbian.

Early 1900s Heterosexuality first made its formal appearance in the very early 20th century, as an obscure medical term meaning "abnormal or perverted appetite toward the opposite sex." It would be 30 more years before it took on the meaning that we are accustomed to today. In 1934, *Webster's New International Dictionary* explained that heterosexuality is "a manifestation of sexual passion for one of the opposite sex; normal sexuality." Ah, well, isn't that reassuring.

Thus, the roots of sexual identity were grown of a divisive and discriminatory strategy. Sexual identity was conceived to create a boundary by means of which "normality" could be preserved and privileged. In this respect, "straight" was the standard against which all other behavior was judged as abnormal and deviant. In particular, the conception of sexual identity has been used by political and religious establishments to ostracize or identify individuals who lead "deviant" or undesirable lifestyles, aka gays and lesbians (and, God forbid, orgy-indulging swingers).

1940s Not until the mid-20th century was there a clear advance in thinking. Alfred Kinsey's research marked the first attempt to define a quantitative range of human sexual behavior. The Kinsey scale consists of a horizontal 7-point linear scale, numbered from 0 to 6, with "hetero" at the far left, or 0, and "homo" at 6 on the far right. If the Kinsey scale rates you a 6, you're "totally gay," and if you're a 0, you're "completely straight." At the very least, this system acknowledged that sexual identity could be quantified by behavior on a continuum—with lots of gray areas. In other words, despite people's need for labels, it appears that the way they act tells a different story.

While it represents a step in the right direction, Kinsey's linear system was not without its limitations. In particular, it still allowed for a black-and-white definition of sexuality as straight versus gay, and it identified people depending on what side they weigh in on more heavily.

In the 1960s gay men and women—for instance, participants in the Stonewall Riots—rallied around the issue of sexual identity, fighting the discrimination that came along with the hetero-normal ideology. In the process they succeeded in creating a real sense of community but also reinforced the "us vs. them" mentality.

The translation of sexual behavior into a public and personal sexual identity has multiple purposes—to be in solidarity with others, to send a message to your family and friends, to fit in when you felt that you otherwise didn't, to form a social group, and, most important, to end discrimination based on personal sexual choice. The political activism of the gay community has proved that a clear definition of sexual identity makes sexual behavior culturally visible, and that if enough people stick up for their right to sexual freedom, behavior and identity can eventually become acceptable and rightfully explored. Oh, what a wonderful world it could be.

In the 1980s along came Fritz Klein, who brought some clarity to the identity picture. In his book *The Bisexual Option,* he took the Kinsey scale and blew it out into full Technicolor. He transformed the horizontal line into a complex three-dimensional grid, and added categories like fantasy, behavior, attraction, emotional and social preference, and self-identification and lifestyle on the X axis and a time line with past, present, and ideal on the Y axis. While bisexuality never really came into vogue, Klein certainly theorized a new option.

2005 The CAKE Scale. Today we favor action over words. With all our gender-bending, label-crushing, category-defying sex, the future of sexual identity is in our hands.

THE RULES OF ATTRACTION
Explore your gender

We've established that the concept of sexual identity is complex. Now let's go deeper and look at the ways that we describe our attraction to each other. Straight from the source we see what advantages or alternatives this experience offers us outside of our interaction with men.

Women love women like men love women—as sexual creatures to desire. Some of us think that other women will have a better understanding of the female anatomy, some are looking to experience soft, sweet, compassionate sex, and others simply enjoy the excitement of exploring and breaking a taboo.

You may be a questioning type of gal who wants to make sure all her bases are covered. Just as a well-rounded student must participate in academics, sports, music, and theater, so might a well-rounded sexual woman cover her bases with men and women. As true equal opportunists, we say: Why discriminate?

Whether admiring our best friend's ass or wanting to get it on with that girl from the bar last night, we are constantly assessing how we feel about the women in our waking and dreaming lives. Aisha (25) loves women. She thinks they are incredibly beautiful, sexy, and amazing, but it stops there for her. She would never want to have sex with another woman. When it comes to sex, she is all about the penis. Her attraction to other women's bodies stems from wanting to look like or be like them, not from desiring to have sex with them. On the other hand, Rachel (28) thinks women are beautiful and indeed finds herself fantasizing about being sexual with another girl. As a self-identified "straight" girl, she once wondered whether it was normal to want to masturbate looking at naked women (instead of men) but still love all the joys of a relationship with a man. After being tormented by this nagging thought, she now believes it is entirely okay to pine for some girl-on-girl action.

If you embrace your sexual desires, there is no contradiction between wanting to sleep with women in your mind and actually sleeping with men in your bed. There can be a distinction between what turns you on to *think* about and what turns you on to *do*. The masturbation fantasy Lilly (25) has strikes her as unusual for her own tastes, but nonetheless irresistible. Her boyfriend's cousin happens to be bisexual, totally into Lilly, beautiful, and blond, and she has a wonderful body. Late at night, alone in bed, Lilly fantasizes that the blonde is naked in bed with her. She moves her lips to Lilly's, kissing her deeply, making her body tingle with pleasure. She slowly wraps her hands around Lilly's body and undresses her. The blonde's soft hands rub her breasts; she pinches Lilly's nipples and rolls them around with her tongue. Next, she slowly moves her head down to Lilly's dripping pussy, licking and sucking at her clit. Lilly's clit begins to throb. Their hands explore each other's bodies, and soon Lilly is at the mercy of the blonde's every desire, switching up the roles and making her come again and again. But this is only her fantasy.

Pleasure Tip: If a girl on the brain does it for you, embrace the full extent of your sexual being and enjoy the fruits of these mental labors. Accept that you enjoy this fantasy in thought alone and use it to the best of your ability to experience pleasure.

There are many of us for whom this fantasy would ideally become a reality—but we haven't quite sealed the deal. Chloe (27) is interested in making love to another woman but has only experimented with kissing other girls. She describes another woman's kiss as soft and gentle, something a man could never imitate. The eroticism of women is not only the admiration of another woman but also the vision of our own qualities in someone else. What could be sexier than that? Chloe got her chance at a downtown performance that involved a great deal of audience interaction. One of the girls in the show came up to her and gave her a good long kiss that astounded her more than kissing a man ever could. The memory of the interaction still excites her.

The thought of translating fantasy into reality is accompanied with so many questions. Where does one start? There is little opportunity for women to test the waters, as it were. Do you start within your circle of friends, or with a total stranger? With or without your partner? Should you try the online W4W personals, or venture into the unfamiliar terrain of a lesbian bar? How do you approach another woman? How do you deal with the potential for rejection and humiliation? Vivianne decided to make her fantasy a reality at an all-women's club. After a long day at work . . .

> I go for a drink at a bar known for its women clients. I sit alone, sipping my cosmopolitan, feeling very sexy. I see this beautiful brunette; her eyes and smile catch my attention right away. She's a little taller than I am, with beautiful deep brown eyes, a perfect shapely and fit figure, big round breasts, long tanned legs, and a beautiful ass. She's sitting on a sofa on her own, in the dark corner, wearing a black skirt, a tight top revealing just enough cleavage, and a great pair of stilettos. Her legs open slightly and I catch a glimpse of her crotch!
>
> When I close my eyes, I can almost taste her skin, breasts, and juices. I walk over to her. She smiles and, without saying a word, I feel her lips on mine. I feel a little awkward because maybe someone will notice us. I thought perhaps we could talk, but she obviously doesn't want to talk. I try to open my mouth to introduce myself, but she slides her finger in my mouth and I slowly start sucking it. I can feel her hand cupping my breasts, squeezing my hard nipples; I can't believe what is going on. I try to resist and keep my legs closed, feeling a little embarrassed, but it feels so good I slowly give in to her. Her lips feel so soft against my skin. She takes my fingers and I start feeling her pussy, it's so wet and hot and I want more. She can sense my innocence and curiosity, and she uses them to her advantage. She lifts my skirt and I move my panties over for her. She pushes me back and wants me to completely relax. I hesitate; she looks up and smiles as she slides her fingers into my pussy, and I completely surrender to her.
>
> —VIVIANNE, 32

Physical attraction and the body beautiful

You can't believe it—you've fucked a woman. You've always loved men, and your truly amazing boyfriend knows how to give you what you want, but you met this girl who just turned you on. Her tits just begged to be sucked, her ass just begged to be slapped, and her cunt, God, her fucking cunt, was amazing. She fucked your pussy like no man ever had, licking your clit gently but quickly, moving from your clit, back to your ass, back to your clit, so that you never knew what to expect. Blowing your mind with her tongue, she moved in and out, giving your clit a blow job of its own. She knew exactly what you wanted, and you ground against her, loving the way her body felt against yours. You 69'd, and she made you come so hard and fast it was unbelievable. Her body, the way she tasted, the way she smelled, the way her slick pussy felt against your fingers . . . you never wanted to stop fucking her.

Curves, hips, breasts, both sets of lips, and perhaps even shaved skin can feel good under our hands. Rose (34) thinks that nothing is sexier than the sight of a woman's head between her legs. As she looks down over her own body, all she can see is the other woman's eyes peering up at her with long, dark eyelashes and flushed cheeks. Everything about her is soft—her skin against her thighs, her touch as her fingers hold her open for her tongue, her breath against her hair, her lips dragging over hers. This image never fails to push Rose over the edge.

Some of us are as obsessed with breasts as straight men are supposed to be. These big or small and mostly soft and rounded symbols of femininity can be a big part of the girl-on-girl equation. When Maggie (33) gets horny (which is pretty damn often), she loves to think about other women. She imagines rubbing her tits against another woman's, lightly to tease at first, and then with more urgency. She also likes to imagine straddling a girl and rubbing against her, clit to clit.

Your fantasies and experiences may not be about the gender you are attracted to, but about how being with a woman makes you feel about yourself. Something about the familiarity of the image is exciting. You have seen yourself being sexual so many times that seeing it in

"Straight" as a Ruler?

another woman is like looking in the mirror. In this way, being with another woman can be like a window into yourself.

Pleasure Tip: Go ahead! Run your hand over your own breasts and imagine what it would be like if they belonged to, say, Angelina Jolie. Feel good?

Women with skills

Nothing is better than going to bed with someone who knows your body really well. Simply the idea that another woman would know her way around the female body is enough to make some of us interested in getting down with girls. While owning the anatomy doesn't give you a license to drive someone else's, a woman who masturbates, has orgasms, and knows her own body may indeed have some trophy-winning skills to share with you. And if you've spent years learning your own body, experimenting with toys and technique until you can orgasm in minutes and then again minutes later, why keep those skills to yourself?

The first time Ursula (25) fooled around with a woman, it was very strange for her, because running her hands over another woman's body felt a lot like masturbation. Though she is more stimulated by sex with men, she finds being with a woman a double kind of pleasure. She gets off almost on the other woman getting off, because she knows exactly how it feels.

Indeed, though an orgasm might not feel the same for everyone, you can still imagine you know exactly how your partner is responding to your touch—how the pressure builds up and the clit starts to tingle and your whole body starts to lift until you know you are breaths away from orgasm. You can follow along, step by step, almost as if you are experiencing it at the same time.

Emotional rescue

Though physical attraction is certainly enough for some, sexual attraction operates on many different levels, and femininity is more than just a pretty face. The idea of women as sensitive and emotional beings of-

214

fers another reason to be curious. For Bree (31), sex with women is always gentler and instantly has an emotional component, whereas with men she finds it easier to feel detached. She finds that women last longer and are more sensuous, but she feels that nothing is more powerful than getting penetrated by a guy.

Being with another woman may also free us from the idealized physical standards that have become the norm. As women, we all have to deal with the inhibiting effects of unrealistic standards for the body beautiful. Some men and women continue to believe that achieving this idealized body is physically possible and desirable, despite the reality of what the average healthy body looks like. You might feel less self-conscious with another woman who understands what an insurmountable challenge physical perfection can be.

Finally, by either nature, nurture, or necessity, women are thought of as intuitive creatures, and some of us hope that a female partner will pay more attention to our pleasure. It's easy to feel turned on by imagining a partner who instinctively knows exactly what you want and how you feel—who will listen to the sound of your breath to know when to go faster or slower or give more or less—who can feel you beginning to orgasm and continue doing just what you need.

Pleasure Tip: When it comes to your emotional needs, use your explorations with women to redefine what you want from sex. Always get what your heart desires, no matter what gender your partner may be.

Taboo, power, and pure sex

All emotions and physicality aside, breaking a taboo is a hot and exciting experience in and of itself. Being with another woman when you identify as straight is like going into forbidden territory, wherein you can act out a new sexual role. Kay (42) gets off on the prospect of pleasing another woman. She likes the thought of dominating another woman, and maybe even strapping on a dildo and fucking her like a man. So much for traditional male/female sex roles!

A fantasy I have had for at least a year now begins with kissing a woman, long and lusciously. Our mouths are wet, tongues licking and kissing in sensual bliss. I undress her and touch her soft, beautiful body. My hands are moving around and over her breasts, her stomach, and the small of her back. Her nipples grow erect. My mouth engulfs them. Licking, sucking. She's moaning as my fingers begin to playfully tease her pussy, her silky clit wetness. She's moaning loudly as I go down on her. My face is in her crotch, my tongue expertly glides up and down, up and down, over her swollen clit. Her pussy is engorged, plump, wet, and juicy. Her pelvis is writhing up and down, her jewel in my face. She's about to come as the pleasure heightens into a frenzy of moaning. I'm so getting off. But delaying her gratification will intensify her orgasm. I kiss her mouth, tasting both her sweetness and her ecstasy. She goes down on me. My clit feels enormous, bulbous; she's sucking and licking it rhythmically—slowly at first, then faster and faster. I'm groaning. It's almost painful as I'm on the verge of coming. I stop and tell her I want to fuck her with my strap-on. I'm dying to penetrate her; I long to be within her, her beautiful silkiness. Her thighs are spread. I'm panting, groaning, thrusting long into her. As I fuck her more deeply, the strap-on doesn't feel strapped on anymore. It's my cock sliding within her, sensually, deeply, my finger caressing her clit. I know what it feels like to be within her. The boundaries lost, merged. As she starts to come, I'm tipped over the edge. She's coming loudly—fuck, she's screaming. Her head is rolling from side to side. She ejaculates all over my cock.

—CLARISSA, 33

We also enjoy the freedom that girl-on-girl action gives us because there is no defined end to the sex. With a traditional male/female sexual experience, the male orgasm is considered the end of the interaction. Because we generally need less "down" time than men before we can be ready to come again, girl/girl sex can often be longer and multi-orgasmic since we can keep coming all night long!

For some of us, the very idea of emotional bonding is restricted to interactions with guys, and getting down with girls offers a carefree pleasurable experience, minus the expectations and challenges of a relationship. With another woman, sex can be simply about sex. What's more, there is no possibility of reproduction! This is distinctly nonprocreative sex, but it can still be creative.

INDIA, 33 As I enter the salon, our eyes meet immediately and sparks of recognition soar between us. She is alone and has been waiting for me. Taking my hand, she walks a few steps backward before turning to lead me to the sink in the back. Her classic features are like those of Japanese courtesans in woodblock prints. Her enviable hair, gathered in a long, dense ponytail, caresses her ivory neck and brushes the top of her narrow waist. I recline with my neck over the sink as she instructs, and she gently rakes her fingers through my scalp, arranging every strand away from my face. My skin heats up from her touch, and my pussy wakes.

The water runs near my ear and lightly on my scalp, mingled with her touch. "Temperature okay?" she asks. I purr my approval (I'm speechless). She smiles as she massages my temples and the base of my neck, the weight of my head resting entirely in one of her hands. I think of her palm cupping my pussy, and I clench it, as I notice it's throbbing. As she leans over to grab the shampoo, I reach over and push the bottom of her tiny black peasant top over her breasts, and secure it above her nipples with the drawstring. Her exposed belly, soft but flat, and her pierced navel make my tongue restless. Her breasts are round and full, her nipples are coaxed out by the friction of the gauzy material.

As she shampoos, I watch her breasts' motion, circular, vertical, then motionless as she rinses me. One of my hands traverses the scalloped ridges of her backbone; the other palms the weight of her breasts hovering over my face. She nods approval down at me through thick strands of black. Lowering herself onto my face, she quivers while I devour her. Sliding her hands down my body, I lift my hips for her as she pushes my skirt up and spreads my knees wide. The triangle of my G-string is soaked with my juice and she works her expert thumb over it, stopping just north of my pulsing clit. I gasp when the air hits my wet labia as she pulls the strip of my panties to the side and lodges it next to my swelling pussy. She takes her last deep breath before going down. Lapping with such hunger, she makes her tongue broad and flat, licking me from my ass all the way up, lingering around the circumference of my vagina, savoring my engorged clit, even darting in and out of my navel. I unknot her ponytail while she drags her lower lip over my clit again and again. When she pulls her heavy hair over her head, it pools all over my belly like hot oil. I move her hair to one side and return her gaze. Her flushed cheeks are sparkling with perspiration and her breath comes in hot gusts from her nose onto my mound with passionate nasal sighs.

When I am just about to let go into her mouth, she leads me into a tiny side room and motions for me to sit up in the pedicure chair. As I climb, she pulls off my G-string and makes me sit forward, straddling the footbath, my open pussy at her eye level. With one hand she pulls up on my mound, spreading my flaming pink lips with her thumb and forefinger, and exposes my explosive clit. She runs warm water from the hand shower down my thigh. "Temperature okay?" she asks. She gazes up at me through damp hair, and I pant, "Perfect" (I've regained speech). From a distance, she floods my pussy, changing the stream, the pressure, moving it closer and aiming a stream up into my vagina, pushing low on my abdomen with the heel of her hand to send the warm flow back out.

She asks me to guide her and I put my hand over hers on the handle, pointing the pulsing stream where I love it—"Oh, there. It's just right . . ." I sink my hand deep into her hair and I can't hold back any longer. I recline and my legs kick up. My body rolling, words spilling out of my mouth in an uncontrollable mix of praise and profanity. She holds me down and open with one hand, wielding the shower with the other hand like a whip, taming me, a lioness. She keeps me coming, wave after wave, and immediately expects reciprocation. She pulls up her tiny denim skirt (no panties) and climbs up into the chair, reclining and immediately spreading her long legs unabashedly. I gaze in awe. Her pussy is practically bare, a few shimmering black hairs pointing toward a tantalizing slit. My eyes follow the trail down to a soft vertical line—so innocent and girly—just asking to be gently parted with my thumbs. Inside the pale, plump, velvety-white skin there is a tiny wet oyster—a perfect bite. I blow on her, and her pussy contracts then relaxes, reaching toward my mouth.

Locking my lips loosely around her, I delve with my tongue slowly around and inside her, tasting caramel, her liquid sugar pouring into my mouth, coating my teeth, my tongue, trickling down the back of my throat. I rub her with the tip of my chin; in her slickness, I draw circles around her clit. Her cheeks are burning red, strands of her hair stuck across her face with my juice—exquisite. I lick lightly upward over her clit and slowly tuck a pinky into her tight little pussy—that's all it seems she can take! Against her rising belly, the red stones of her navel ring twinkle, and I move my mouth up, satiating her clit with my thumb. With the sound of metal on my teeth, her eyes shoot open with a wild mixture of hope and fear, and I begin tugging lightly on the pendant. Once; twice; the third tug opens the door. She springs bolt upright, pulling my damp head in to her belly, and places one hand over mine on her clenched pussy. Fumbling for my fingers, she aids them all the way up into her tiny hole; our fingers intertwine, and the muscles high inside her pussy loosen around us. She shakes and moans from deep inside her core.

NATALIE, 34 I have three girlfriends whom I get together with about once a month for dinner. We eat, drink, and talk a lot. It's a fun bunch, all of us very playful, very attractive, and fun-loving. We joke about sex and sometimes chat about vibrators and orgasms, but we hadn't explored the topic much until recently. Last night we got together at my friend Donna's house, and after a lot of wine, we decided to hang out in the hot tub. Donna said she had bathing suits for us all, but I suggested that we just go naked. "It's just us girls, who cares?"

The others agreed, so we stripped inside and paraded out her back door and got into the tub.

I was last to walk out the door. Trailing behind them, I admired their bodies. I've seen plenty of naked women in my life, but I have to say that the four of us looked particularly fit and sexy. We're all runners, and my three friends are swimmers too. I always knew they had nice long legs and shapely arms and hard stomachs, but I only now noticed how nice their bottoms were. I love men, through and through, but I was so turned on looking at their bodies, I could barely keep my mouth shut about what I wanted to do. We all stepped into the tub. It was one of those crystal-clear nights, with a full moon, and the stars shining so brightly. It was almost magical.

Christy started moaning with pleasure about how good the hot water felt, since her back was so sore. I'm a good friend, so I offered to rub it. She seemed to enjoy my hands on her back, but I wondered if she might be thinking what I was thinking. I was sitting behind her on the hot tub bench in the water, my legs outside of hers, and she kept moving back toward me. Her bum started rubbing against my pussy, and at this point I wasn't wondering anymore. She leaned her head back against my neck, and then slid down my chest until her hair was flowing over my breasts in the water.

Then she furtively reached back with her hand and put two fingers on my pussy. Our two friends were chatting away, oblivious to the action on the other side of the tub. At first I was worried about how they'd react if they noticed, but at some point the pleasure completely overtook the concern, and right then, as if Christy could feel my response, she turned around to face me and kissed me softly and deeply, grabbing the back of my neck gently, as if to say, "We're doing this, whether you like it or not. You'll like it, trust me." I did. I was so turned on, I can't even describe it. We were hot and wet and excited, and her fingers were fucking me. I fondled her breasts and then lifted her up so I could suck on them, one and then the other. She wrapped her legs around my waist and rubbed her cunt up against mine. I

"Straight" as a Ruler?

could feel the moistness of her lips on my clit. I put a finger inside her pussy. I had never felt anyone else's pussy before. I liked it. She was wet and I liked turning her on.

Christy and I both noticed at about the same time that Donna and Angie had stopped talking. I don't know how long it took them to notice. At first I got worried again, but when I looked at their faces, I could tell they were jealous, perhaps shocked but totally titillated. Without a word, Donna moved over to us and put a finger in Christy's ass. Christy started moving slowly back and forth to get the most out of my finger and Donna's. Angie came over and started kissing me and sucking on my breasts. This was incredible and so comfortable. It all seemed so natural and easy, it occured to me to wonder why the hell we had never done this before. Before long, we were all playing with each other, moving from one to the other, in a chain of ecstasy. Each one of us was being fingered by someone else, we were all kissing each other, and we were all stroking or sucking on someone's beautiful breasts.

ROSE, 34 I've had this fantasy of you ever since that drunken night after our friend's bachelorette party. You couldn't make it home, so I offered you the guest room, but you said you didn't want to sleep alone, so I said you could sleep with me. We were so giggly, we just stripped off our sequined tops and ruffled skirts and climbed into bed, with smeared makeup, still wearing panty hose. I had on my sheer black bra, and you were wearing a white one with matching lacy thigh-highs.

I looked at you for a lingering clear moment of sobriety, my eyes taking in your pale skin. I wanted to push you down softly against my feathery bed and bite at the lace edges of your panties, grip them in my teeth, and rip them down. I desperately needed to unravel your secrets, breathe in your scent, push aside the layers, spread you open, and lick the slick mist of your ocean. In my fantasy, I do. You yield, like the night to the stars, and I find your clit glistening.

I begin to explore. I am rubbing myself up against the corner of the bed, stinging with my own desire, dripping into the fabric of my panty

hose. You coming is the same as me coming. No longer are you surprised; now you are desperate. Small, low animal sounds escape from
your throat, fragments of sentences and one-syllable sounds. "Mm, yes,
ohhhh, please . . . yes yes yes yes now yes please oooo mmmm
aaaaggggg ooooooo eeeeeee aaaaaaahhhhhhhh mmmmmmm
ooooooooooohhhhhhhhhh hhhhhh." "I want you to come. Come for
me, baby!" I am pleading inside my own head. You encourage me with
your sounds and your hands and I grab at your breasts, kneading them,
rubbing them, I want so badly to kiss you, but I cannot bring myself to
leave your pussy. You have spread the seas wide, and your clit is crashing
against the shore of my tongue. I gently nibble on the salty edges and
lavishly lick my way around the pink pulsating walls.

You are so swollen, so hungry. I slide my hands under your ass
and lift you up slightly; the angle is deeper now, and my movements
quicken to meet your need. Licking faster, faster, faster, I feel your
shudder build, and you release a flood of wetness, which rains down
into my lapping mouth. You are set free, and I slide to the floor. You
come to me, and kiss me, gathering me in your arms. You unhook my
bra, and my breasts spill out as I sigh in relief. Bending your head
down to kiss them, you take a hard nipple into your hot mouth,
swirling around it and sucking expertly. Your fingers travel down to
my wet pussy, but I am still wearing lacy tights.

You lay me down, like a wilted flower. You are totally in charge
now. You roll on top of me and kiss me. Your hands tear at the lace.
Penetrating my pink pussy with your flickering tongue, you make a
small hole, and with each push of your tongue into my pussy, you
make the hole wider, until you have ripped my stockings completely
open. You find my clit and circle it with your fingers, pressing into me;
you move your two fingers in semicircles around my aching clit, until
I am about to explode. Then you rub me with your fist. The sensation
is fierce and powerful, and I come quickly. You stretch out and lie on
top of me, in utter silence. I can feel your pussy still wet and dripping
onto mine. We fall asleep like that, bathing in moonlight.

CHAPTER 13

Power Play

I love to be tied up during sex—the loss of power and control is the aspect of submission that gets me off the most. Not being able to shove my lover's hand, lips, tongue, or teeth away from my sensitive spots is so delicious to me. I love that when I'm tied up, I really can't refuse the receipt of pleasure. The exciting feeling of not knowing what he'll tease, touch, tickle, lick, suck, or penetrate on my body gets me so wet. Give this girl a rope, a blindfold, and an eager, open-minded, explorative lover, and I'm one very happy chick.

—FRANCINE, 26

Throughout this book we have talked about how knowing our own anatomy is empowering, how vibrators are powerful tools for orgasm, how the morning-after pill allows us to control our lives, and how breaking taboos can make us feel good and strong. Sexual power requires that we know what we want so we can go out and get it.

Sometimes we want to explore power in very explicit ways, like getting tied up in bed, giving a partner a spanking, or fantasizing about a boss. Luckily, insisting on gender equality doesn't mean we have to erase the power dynamics of sex altogether. In fact, the position of equality is the best place from which to start to play.

The combination of sex and power has been a challenging issue for feminism, as a theory and a movement. We have been so focused on getting women out from under repressive power, we've had to ignore some of the ways playing with power can be positive for sexuality. But power dynamics do not always have to be about one party taking advantage of the other. Letting someone else take control does not mean you are weak, and wanting to be in control doesn't mean you are a bully. Even when we are taking the traditionally submissive role, we remain in control of our pleasure. In fact, being submissive can be at least as powerful as being "dominant." In the end, the submissive role calls the shots and dictates the action.

This philosophy is articulated by sadomasochist (S&M) communities and was introduced to the American public in the early stages of the sexual revolution when *The Story of O* was published in 1965. "O" searches for a new self through sadomasochism, and her submission is born completely of her own desire. More recently, *Secretary*, an S&M-themed independent film, reminds us that if feminism has done its job, an empowered female character can freely play the sexual submissive.

The "take me" turn-on is ever present for this generation of women. When we have opportunities to be in control in public, we can cognizantly choose to give up control during sex. We react to the intensity of someone else's sexual desire and the pleasure of exploring extreme physical sensations. Sometimes all you want at the end of a long day is for someone to dominate you in exactly the way that pleases you. Whether you want to direct or be directed, pleasurable power play is about an interaction in which each party must communicate what they want in order to get it.

Our motivations and desires to experiment and fantasize about domination and submission are just a part of how we define sexuality on our own terms, based on communication between consensual partners. Check out what other women like, to learn some new skills and have a grand ol' spankin' time.

226

THE POWER OF SEX
S&M for everyone!

In her everyday life, Michelle (31) is very much a dominant woman; her career requires her to assess and distribute work among many men, a task she has always enjoyed. Because she doesn't act submissive in her everyday life, she finds she likes to be submissive in the bedroom every now and then; it's a dirty little secret slice of her personality that she'll show only when she's really turned on and very comfortable. She's also not afraid to be aggressive by letting her partner know exactly what she wants, though she wouldn't call herself a dominatrix.

Bondage/discipline, domination/submission, or sadism/masochism —BDSM—is often stereotyped as an extreme sport played by a tight-knit community of like-minded people, donning leather, latex, whips, and crosses. While this community does exist, elements of BDSM are present in the most vanilla sex and the most typical fantasies.

While whips and chains have never turned Julie (27) on, she's always been aroused by power structures and the idea of violating roles in a social setting. Some of her favorite fantasies take place in an office where someone who outranks her abuses that power. In one, she is at a job interview, meeting with two really hot executive guys in a media company. After the interview concludes, one of the men gets up to leave. The remaining one says, "If you really want this job, you have to suck my dick." Nervously, she gets on her knees in her interview suit and does it.

She's then led down a hall into a large conference room where the other one is waiting, and they order her to take off her clothes. The first man starts kissing her, pushing her onto a table. He sits on a chair in front of her and eats her pussy, and then the second one takes a seat. Then they all get up on top of the table and she sucks one guy's dick while the other takes her from behind. After it's over, they parade her through the office and she feels everyone staring at her.

In the safety of our minds, we explore things we may never ask for from a partner, or never even want to actualize. But as powerful as the mind may be, sometimes fantasies just aren't enough, and it's time to get down and get it in action! Giving a spanking, having sex while blindfolded, or being cuffed to the bed requires only a playmate who respects your requests and gives you the freedom and ability to communicate exactly what you want.

Pleasure Tip: You don't need to go for the extreme and stylized roles of a Master/servant couple or a Mistress/slave scene to play with power. Imagine the most extreme version of BDSM and take one small element of that picture into the bedroom with you—whether it is a studded belt, an office chair, or a little dirty Daddy talk.

DOMINATE LIKE A SUBMISSIVE

You're tied up and blindfolded, strapped in a sling that hangs from the ceiling. The room you're in is part of a Love Hotel, where every door is open and people can wander in and out, watching and participating as they please. You don't know who your current lover is. He is doing delicious things to your body—kissing your lips softly, moving down to your neck and your breast, biting gently on your nipples, sucking and licking them. There is a very dominant man in the room who is directing the action. The director instructs your partner to tease you and not let you come right away. Moving down slowly, he licks your stomach and slides in between your legs, flicking your clit with his tongue, massaging it and sucking it while spreading apart your pussy with his fingers. You moan and breathe heavily as he slides a finger inside you.

He puts his cock in your mouth and holds your head in his hand while you suck him. The director says things like "Yeah, that's right, you little slut, suck him. Take that cock all the way in your mouth." You are so hot that you could come any second, but you're not allowed. You feel a huge rubber cock slide inside you, and you go crazy, screaming, coming, and squirting all over. After you calm down, the director unties you and orders you to get on your hands and knees so he can fuck you like an animal with his big hard cock and use your long hair as his reins.

Submission is a major fantasy of mine, but not in the sense of pain play. What is exciting is the exchange of power and being able to give up control to someone else. Abandon. In one of my fantasies, there is a man (sometimes a woman) who can make me give in to commands. I will accompany them somewhere unknown—a party, a friend's house, a club, or some other gathering. I will be instructed to wear no bra or panties under my clothing. I am asked to sit in suggestive ways. I may be asked to pull up my skirt and expose myself and touch myself. And because I will be wet with desire, aroused by my humiliating exposure, I will be asked to dip my fingers in my pussy and lick the wetness from my fingers. I will be asked to spread my legs wide so that others can see and touch my wetness. I am naked in front of the others. I am blindfolded so I can't see who is touching me. At some point someone begins to fuck me, but I am not allowed to move or do anything that might make me come faster. I am restrained so I can't move against the fucking, and I am wild with the need to come but do not want others to see me so uncontrolled. When I'm finally allowed to come, it is a convulsive, explosive rush that leaves me spent, dripping, weak.

—MIRTA, 48

Have you ever wanted to just find someone who will throw you up against a wall, down on the bed, or over the counter and take you like there's no tomorrow? No woman is alone in this "just do me" fantasy; it's one of the oldest in the book. Playing the submissive can be all about getting it like you need it, without having to lift a finger. You just have to define those desires before your hands are tied.

Alice (22) loves it when her boyfriend holds her wrists while fucking her. He doesn't let her move, and she feels as if he is in control. Her job is to please him and take him in her pussy, as hard as he is. She also likes it when he makes her blow him, pulling her hair to let her know what he wants her to do. While it's kind of hot when she's in control and tells him what she wants him to do, she thinks it's hotter when he takes the lead.

Her power thoughts extend to her masturbation fantasies, wherein she imagines a gorgeous woman watching her and her boyfriend fuck. Alice is on top of him and the woman comes to her, bossing her around, telling them both exactly what she wants them to do. The woman demands a kiss and Alice is dying to do it, hoping her boyfriend doesn't notice how much she likes it. On the woman's command, she and Alice fuck in front of her boyfriend, and both of them dominate Alice, making her give them what they want. All in all, she finds the whole politically incorrect scenario totally hot.

Pleasure Tip: Write a letter to your lover, explaining exactly the terms of *your* submission fantasy where loss of control (with a little spanking mixed in) is the basis for your pleasure. For inspiration, check out the juicy letter Fran wrote:

We've returned to your house after the party. You grab me by the waist and ask why I didn't wear what you had requested. Before I can answer, you kiss me; your hands make their way to my tits and you begin to slowly pinch my nipples, a little harder than usual, yet it still feels amazing. Your tongue plays with mine as your hands make their way down and remove my shirt. Next come my pants, till I am standing in front of you in just my black bra, thong, and heels. You stop kissing me and ask me again why I didn't wear what you had requested. Again I begin to answer and you just grab me by the back of the hair and tell me you don't want to hear my answer. Instead, you lead me over to the dining room and tell me to bend forward with my forearms on the tabletop and stand still, not saying a thing. Just then, I feel a sharp stinging sensation as you smack the right side of my ass. It hurts for a quick second and then the sensation is more invigorating than anything else. I then feel a smack to the other side, and you tell me that is just the beginning. In between smacks to either side of my ass, you list the things I did wrong at the party: I was too flirty, wore the wrong outfit, didn't get you a new drink in time, and therefore I need a little retraining on how to be your whore. There must have been about six smacks in all, and I can feel the warmth on both sides of my ass where your handprints are starting to appear. I've closed my eyes and I feel your hand move the crotch of my panties to the side and then your tongue darting across my clit. I am so wet, and I feel as though I could come at any moment. Your face is between my legs, and my wetness drips onto your chin as your finger slips inside my pussy. The feeling of your fingers and your tongue at the same time makes me moan, and just then you stop and stand up behind me and I feel your hand come down on the side of my ass again. You remind me that I am not to say anything unless you ask me to, and I nod. You take me by the hair again and tell me to stand up. You kiss me and I can taste my pussy on your tongue. Your hands unzip your pants and you lower me as you pull out your hard cock and thrust it into my mouth. I feel myself on the verge of coming, just sucking your hard cock. You thrust into my mouth and I struggle to take all of you in while your hand still grips the back of my hair. You thrust into my mouth hard a couple more times and you call me your whore and tell me to suck your dick. I feel your hand guiding me to stand up again and you bend me back over the table; you remind me not to say a word, and then I feel your hard cock push its way into my swollen pussy. I gasp at the sensation and just as I try to stop myself, I feel your hand come down on the other side of my ass. You tell me that you're not going to tell me again to be quiet and that good little whores need to learn respect. You are now fucking me harder than I've ever felt. The feeling of you slamming into my wet pussy is almost making me black out and I feel myself coming again and again.

—FRAN, 31

BECOME MISTRESS CAKE

What could be more powerful than grasping a man by his collar and leading him down your body till his mouth is between your legs? What could be more pleasurable than a man willing to submit to your every desire? Such is the luck of a woman who explores her ability and wish to dominate. The desire of the Dom is to be in charge, and to revel in sexual confidence.

In her power fantasy, Lola (22) envisions storming into her man's house. He and all his friends are sitting around, hanging out together, and she pretends to be furious about something, demanding he see her in the bedroom. He looks confused and annoyed because of the scene she's making, and because he has no clue what she could be upset about, which instantly turns her on. He grabs her arm, flinging her into the room, and slams the door, asking her what the hell her problem is. In turn, she swings the door back open and tells him that whatever she has to say, his friends can hear too.

She kicks off her shoes and takes off her shirt, and before he can protest, she starts kissing him really hard, taking off his shirt. He resists a little when she unbuttons his pants, remembering that his friends are watching, but she pushes his hands away and continues undressing him. His dick is rock-hard and she pushes him down, climbs on top of him, pins his arms to the bed, and rides him fast, getting more turned on by the pleasured yet embarrassed look on his face and the astonished looks on the faces of his friends. He picks her up and slams her up against the wall, fucking her like it's the last time he's ever going to get pussy like this.

He can't control himself anymore. He lets out a moan that she's never heard before and starts to come. She comes with him and they slide down the wall as if they are floating back to earth, kissing and staring at each other in amazement. She gets dressed, grabs her purse, and turns to him to say she never wants to discuss this issue again. As she leaves, his friends give her a standing ovation.

Women making the rules, and men following them: It's usually thought of as a male fantasy, that is, one lived out in a dungeon where men come to pay for the services of a dominatrix. But even while the woman is being paid to fulfill a male fantasy, she surely has control, and in turn expresses part of her own sexuality. No winners, no losers. There's something for everyone.

Men and women seek Layla (28) out and pay what she considers a goofy amount of money to spend time with her and share their fantasies. This makes her incredibly hot. She is a professional dominatrix, and in her explicit client dynamics, she is in control. No matter what the client wants her to be—the maid, the secretary, or the schoolteacher—she is always the character of her dreams; the object of desire.

Pleasure Tip: Play the Top. Figure out how much bossing around your partner can take, and then take charge. Take over in the director's chair and let him know *exactly* how fast and how hard you want it. And never, ever let him come before you.

MIXING IT UP

To be in complete control of your partner's pleasure can be heady. To feel completely at the mercy of your partner can be sexy as hell. We may want to be tied up one day, then want to use those same ropes to tie someone else up the very next day. While we can have fantasies about either domination or submission, the real fun comes when we explore both roles. In fact, the ability to move back and forth between these roles in one sitting can be the hottest aspect of BDSM.

Having a willing partner at her mercy, or begging for her Master to punish her—these are equal turn-ons for Missi (24). Threesomes usually make her feel like a tug-of-war rope, because the other two partners play "good cop, bad cop," one showing mercy with gentle and soft attention and the other teasing and torturing her with spanking and biting. In her favorite sex experience, a shy, quiet girlfriend of Missi's and Missi's bossy macho boyfriend traded personalities. When all three of them were in the bedroom together, Missi's girlfriend took her over her knee, spanking her until she had tears in her eyes, and her boyfriend brushed her hair back, petting her and kissing away the tears. Though their explorations have settled down a bit now that they are married, Missi still loves it when her husband wraps her hands around the headboard, telling her not to let go or he'll stop going down on her.

Pleasure Tip: Experiment with a role that's new to you. If you're used to taking charge, request a night off. If you're used to following the rules, make some new ones of your own. When exploring a fantasy, it's traditional in the BDSM world to establish a safe word for both partners. If you thought you wanted to try something, but you change your mind in the middle, all you have to do is say the word and both partners stop the action. Quick communication at its best.

MIND YOUR SENSES

You're lying nude, on the softest satin sheets, and he worships every inch of your body with gentle soft kisses and caresses. Blindfolded and tied to the bedpost, you are made to endure the most intense sensations of kisses and touches that go just far enough, yet stop just short of a full orgasm. Then they begin again, until you are begging for it never to stop, being pushed even further as he continues to tease every inch of you. The moving air feels like silk over your body.

Red alert! With no idea of what's coming next, you're ready to experience each physical sensation as it happens. When it does, you accept it completely, pushing yourself to the edge. You are totally submissive at this point, and loving it. He power-fucks you for 15 minutes, then stops and removes your bondage, carefully taking out the beautiful knots around your wrists. He then picks you up, places your four-inch black stilettos on your feet, and turns you around so that your ass is presented to him. He takes your hips and grips them hard, entering your ass gently at first. He begins to tease you to the point where you can't take it anymore. You start begging him to plunge his big fat cock into your ass, but he orders you to be quiet. As his sex slave, you do as you are told. He finally enters you, taking it slow at first, knowing that you want more. He begins to pick up the rhythm and starts to spank you, telling you what a naughty girl you've been. Your cheeks turn pink and you start to tingle with exquisite pleasure and pain. He then takes his cock out and starts masturbating over you, coming all over your ass. He cleans you up, places you on the chair, and removes the blindfold. He leaves without saying a word.

One night Rose and her husband stumbled into an S&M bar. There was a stage set up with all of the accoutrements, and a Mistress at a table giving professional "flogging" for 20 minutes, a temptation Rose succumbed to. Tied up by her wrists and ankles, standing with her legs spread and her skirt above her hips, she was blindfolded and flogged, tickled, whipped, burned (lightly), and spanked by a gorgeous, tall, muscular, powerful woman, all in front of her husband (and a number of really lucky men left at the bar!). For the next three days, she got wet every time she sat down. Her burning cheeks were a great souvenir!

Pleasure Tip: Explore the range of your physical sensations with props like feathers, crops, lotions, and paddles. Better yet, follow Rose's lead and check out your local dungeon for a proper spanking from an expert dominatrix.

THIS LITTLE KINKY PIGGY . . .

Strictly speaking, a fetish is an object or a body part, usually considered nonsexual in everyday life, that is required for sexual satisfaction, and a fetishist is someone who cannot get off without the fetish object present. In the context of female sexual pleasure, it makes sense to think of fetishes more loosely—as general turn-ons, on a continuum of extremes from total turn-off to "can't do without." Once upon a time, fetishes were thought of as a strictly male thing. No longer.

You are lying on your stomach with your feet and hands tied to a bed. Three girls enter the room and sit down beside you. One girl starts to tickle your feet with the tips of her fingers in a slow motion. Another girl starts to tickle your rib cage, working her way up to your armpits. The last one starts to tickle the back of your neck. All three are paying close attention to your body, especially the sexy redhead who is tickling your feet. She knows exactly what you like. The girls stop the erotic torture and start to fill their mischievous hands with lotion and begin to apply it to your body. The lotion, warmed by their hands, soothes your excited body, but when they finish, they take out their favorite tickling toys and resume their torture. This goes on for hours until you are so exhausted from the pleasure that you pass out. They untie you from the bed and leave you asleep, dreaming of the sexy encounter you just had.

Though the concept of a fetish may be something everyone can understand, the specifics of a fetish are very personal. It may be a specific body part that turns you on. Jennifer (34) has a fetish for the groin muscle on a man—you know, that definition that starts at the top of the groin. "Oh, God! When I see a man wearing baggy jeans and no top, or a guy at the beach who is toned, all I see is that muscle—you know the one—enticingly leading into his pants. It just makes me nuts."

Long before Victoria (25) discovered the joys of masturbation, she worked long, tedious hours in a fabric store. She thinks the time she spent there has affected her fantasy life, as her fantasies tend to include beautiful fabrics: medieval styles with burgundies, golds, and velvets;

silks; Asian wraps . . . any fabric with a bit of style and texture makes her wet. Sometimes her fantasies include hundreds of hands, caressing her blindfolded and tied-up body while she lies across a silky-smooth, incredibly detailed sheet. Other times she is behind a curtain on a movie stage, pushing her tongue into the cunt of a stranger with complex tattoos. As they rock back and forth, their bodies roll against the curtain. She knows it may be a bit odd for other people to read how fabric truly gets her off, but to her the appeal makes perfect sense. Sex is all about touch, and she likes each experience to be saturated with texture.

Pleasure Tip: Pick a sexy activity that you find very personal and unusual, and call it your fetish. Think you're alone? Look online and find worlds of boot-licking, nylon-ripping, or latex-wearing girls just like you!

OLIVIA, 31 Since I was a very young girl, I've always had spanking fantasies. Anything where I am not in control gets me off. In real life, I am always 100 percent in control and make all the decisions, and in my fantasies I want the exact opposite.

We are at a party and I've been shamelessly flirting with another guy. I've had a few drinks and am feeling very happy. It is late when we leave. In the car, you tell me that I've been a very bad girl and need to be punished. I get excited. You tell me to take off my clothes and remain naked until we get home. I comply, and sit in excruciating anticipation of my punishment.

While driving, you reach a hand over, pinch my nipples very hard, and order me to spread my legs wide. You tell me you want to see my pussy. You see how wet I've become and tell me that I will be given my proper punishment when we arrive home. When we get there, you have me stand up and you tie my wrists behind my back. You play with my nipples over and over, pinching, biting, and sucking them, driving me absolutely crazy. You bring out a chair and bend me over your lap and begin spanking me with your hand. Over and over you spank me; my ass is starting to get really red and feels as if it's on fire. My inner thighs are slippery wet.

You stand me back up, untie my wrists, and order me to spread my legs and bend over and touch my toes. You tell me how bad I am, what a whore I am, and that I deserve this punishment. You bring out a wooden paddle and order me to count out loud the number of times you spank me. "One, sir. Two, sir." It gets harder to count as you continue to paddle. After about 10, I am writhing in pain and excitement. You stand me up and tell me I am not allowed to come. I must ask your permission. You kneel down and start to eat my pussy. You do so very gently, making circles around my aching clit, fingering me, pushing on my G-spot. I am going crazy. You take my clit in your mouth and gently tug on it, sucking so softly. "Permission to come, sir?" I ask. "No, you may not," you answer. I cannot concentrate. I must come, and I will die if I don't get to come. You continue to suck on my clit and bring your hand up to play with my nipples. I cannot endure this. "Permission to come, sir?" "No, you may not." But I have no choice: As you continue to suck my pussy, I have the most glorious orgasm. My whole body shakes, my legs are weak. It is fantastic.

You know I have come. You stand up to berate me for my weakness, and tell me I need further punishment. You pull out your beautiful hard cock and order me to suck it. I kneel and begin to suck your cock, and every couple of minutes you hit my ass with the paddle. You order me to stand up and bend over the couch, then enter me slowly and fuck me just at the opening of my pussy. I want you all the way inside me. Instead, you put your hands on either side of my lips and pull apart, making me tighter for your dick. Eventually, you can't take any more and fuck me hard and deep, losing control. When you come, you pull my hair and my back arches. You kiss my neck and tell me to thank you for my punishment. And I do.

DAPHNE, 25 I have had so many different fantasies and have acted many of them out, beginning a few years ago, in my early twenties. I guess I am into S&M, since I am totally enamored by submission, bondage, and where just plain control lies. Usually I like it rough, to say the least. In my fantasy I am this sexy-as-hell dominatrix-type vixen, in a tight vinyl corset, a lace garter, and a thong. My long dark hair flows over my shoulders and breasts, and I am wearing spike-heeled lace-up vinyl boots. I have a frayed whip in my hand and I am gently smacking it against my thigh so that it's making the slightest sound of leather against skin. My man is really built, muscular, and just sexy as hell. He's on my bed, tied to the bedposts, with sweat dripping down his chest onto his tight, defined stomach, wearing these cute white Calvin Klein boxer briefs, and he is breathing heavily because he is blindfolded and doesn't know what the hell is happening, or coming to him.

So I walk over to the bed and drag my whip down his damp body and he breathes heavier and I can see the anticipation in his face. I whisper to him, "Do you want to taste my pussy?" and he answers back, "Yes," and I smack his chest with my whip and say to him, "Yes what?" and he says to me, "Yes, Goddess." So then I climb onto his face and give him my wet pussy; he is in total bliss as he tongues me and sucks me, my juices dripping down his face onto his neck. I say to him, "You like that wet pussy in your mouth, don't you?" He moans like an animal in a cage and I see his arms flexing to break free of his restraints, but he's not getting out of this.

I slide down his hard body, lick his lips so I can taste myself on his mouth, and rub my wet pussy up and down his big hard cock over his shorts. He groans, and squirms, so tense and excited. It's turning me on to see him in all this distress over me. So I say to him, "Whose cock is this, motherfucker?" and he pants his reply to me: "Yours." I smack him again with my whip across his chest, and yell in his face, "Now, answer me the right way!" He groans, "It's yours, Goddess." Then I take hold of his hard cock and slowly slide just the head inside me, and then pull it out and rub it against my clit, and he lets out this moan like he is going to go mad if I don't let him inside me.

I do it again, just to tease the shit out of him and to see the expression run across his face. Grinning devilishly, I watch him go crazy. I'm turned on by how badly he wants me. I jam his cock inside me and start fucking his brains out. My pussy becomes a river. I can tell he is almost at his limit, so I slide off him and pull his blindfold off so he can watch while I suck his big cock and then let him come all over my face.

ALLISON, 32 It's my first year as a teacher, and the undergrads are unfathomably beautiful. I can't seem to remember knowing I was ever that young, that ripe, and that perfect. Even as the girls eat too much and the boys drink too much, they remain crystalline in their beauty. I lecture, worried that because I have tattoos, they will think that I think that I am one of them. Aware of my breasts, I plead with the weather gods that the day will stay warm, because if it is cold, I know my nipples will show, and then what will they think? In the middle of a lecture about Hamlet the naughty Dane, I see that the jocks in the back are not asleep. They have their hands down their pants, each one fondling himself as slowly as possible. I think I hear the rustle of their running pants. The sharp sound of their breathing seems to be coming from right behind me. I'm wet and I'm standing there lecturing about the folly of youth and the pleasures of iambic pentameter.

I'm thinking, "They can't possibly get off in class, can they?" Eventually, they'll back off; it will be like those fraternity pranks you hear about, where they tie a brick to their testicles and drop it off the roof. It isn't for real, is it? I'm throbbing so hard that I can't seem to walk, so I lean on the podium. The heaters in the building make a hum that has turned the wooden podium into a five-foot-tall vibrator. Watching them do their thing, I want to put my own hand down my pants. Once I allow that thought into my mind, I realize that what I want is to mount each of these 18-year-olds, to let them fuck me—no, to fuck them, to ride them with all of my 14 years of experience in fucking. I want to get off on one and then climb onto the next. I suddenly find their white hats, their inability to stay awake during screenings, and their lame excuses about lamer papers all part of some erotic backstory.

I want each and every one of them. I know they have beautiful dicks, they have gorgeous trails of hair leading down stomachs not yet ruined, they smell like sour beer and cigarettes and sorority-girl blow jobs. They need me. They need to know what a real woman smells like, they need to know what happens when I get off, how I'll shiver and shudder, how the walls of my pussy will grab at their dicks, how I can make it do that at will. They need to know how to feel the oncoming orgasm, need to know they can tease it out of me. They need to know all this far more than they need to know about classic five-act structure and the use of set pieces at the Globe Theatre.

It all ends with nothing, with me going home and getting myself off four or five times before I can stop. Of course I think it is over, that somehow I've escaped this fantasy. I don't really want to mount the lacrosse team in the back row of the lecture hall. Or at least, I want it, but I want to keep my job more. Then I'm on the subway, headphones on, reading papers, willfully ignoring everyone around me, pretending to be a misanthrope. The energy changes slightly, like when a homeless person gets on, or all the rich people decide they are outnumbered by poor people: the silence of New York gone sour.

It's my boys. All six of them. White hats, baggy pants. Sprawled opposite me. I look up and one of them mouths the word "Professor" and then smiles. At this point I have some choices. I could make a joke, like "You caught me, I grade papers on the train!" Or I could just say, "Hey, guys," and go back to grading. I could pretend I need to see someone on 28th Street, and just hop off the train. I could . . . My lips are dry. I want to lick my lips. Somehow the idea of my lip licking becomes the first step toward being involved in the gang bang they'll jerk off to in 15 years when their wives are still too tired from getting up with the baby. I do what any self-respecting New Yorker would do. I place my right hand gently between my legs. I find the seam on my jeans and press so lightly, then harder.

I lick my lips. My breasts ache, I'm dripping, and my clit pokes out, eager to feel the friction from my thumb. The guys don't breathe. I'm not sure if I do. I look up for a second, expecting . . . I don't know, expecting jeers or knowing smiles. Instead I see, I swear, the look my sister has in church. That look that says they are seeing true beauty while simply allowing it to wash over them. They don't touch themselves, but they will tonight. And it will be my pussy they'll dream of fucking.

CHAPTER 14

Birth of the Cake Sam'ich

Since my late teens and early 20s, I have been giving the "flip the switch" threesome a thought. I've been with the same man for 15 years (married for almost 13). For the past decade, I've been seriously thinking about this. I want it. Just the thought of two men stimulating several erogenous zones on my body at the same time sends me over the edge. Being between two strong muscular men and feeling their bodies on both sides of me. It just has to be good. One could go down on me while the other paid attention to my other body parts. There is just so much you could do.

—TARA, 34

We all know at least a little, or maybe a lot, about threesomes. Either you've had one and it was amazing, you've had one and it was a disaster worthy of Jerry Springer, or you've wanted to have one but just haven't found quite the right fit, time, or excuse. Maybe you know someone who just had one, and that piques your curiosity! For many of us, our first on-screen threesome was the one between *Saved by the Bell*'s Elizabeth Berkley, the sizzling Gina Gershon, and Kyle MacLachlan in *Showgirls*. For the more "cultured" among us, two foreign films—*Y Tu Mamá También* and *The Dreamers*—recently captured the cinematic thrill of the threesome.

243

No matter whether it's two women and one man ("WMW") or two men and one woman ("MWM," or what we like to call the CAKE Sam'ich!), it's time to define the glorious threesome from the female perspective. Imagine being the center of attention, with four hands focused on your body. Picture yourself as the ultimate voyeur, with a live lovemaking session unfolding right before your very eyes. Moments later, you are the world's most ravishing exhibitionist, showing off all your special tricks for an observer, or maybe two. Consider all the possibilities of being with another woman while enjoying the pleasure of a man as well, or of seeing two men's bodies together. Envision bodies intertwined, simultaneous sex acts, and overwhelming pleasure. All of these possibilities, and more, fuel the fantasy and experience of the female-directed threesome.

Like girl-on-girl action, the threesome has long been the supposed cherry on the top of the male sexual fantasy cake. The experience of being with two women at one time is considered the ultimate proof of male virility. But women can also desire to have more than one person focused on our pleasure, and many of us are actively seeking out this experience. We may be with our partner, hunting for another girl or boy to complete the trio; with a girlfriend, on the prowl for a willing male third (how hard is that!); or just on our own, facing the challenge of seducing a couple or two male friends. Any which way you cut it, it's hot, hot, hot.

Many challenges make it hard to transform the threesome fantasy into a reality. Within a relationship, some women simply don't like to share, no matter who the third may be. If this describes you, it may be best to stick to what you've got. Then there's always the jealousy problem, the technical aspects, and the rules and regulations, not to mention the search for the right participants. While there are all these intangible and intimidating factors to deal with, threesomes are kind of like swimming. Just put your foot in the pool to test the water, and then take the plunge. We'll be your lifeguard.

FOR HER EYES ONLY

In its most common iteration, the threesome goes down as a WMW where a couple is in search of another woman to get in the mix. The ménage à trois is a girl's ultimate score—a 3-point, touchdown, K.O., home-run-with-the-bases-loaded, clean-up-hitter kind of score. It's a win-win-win situation, a never-ending night (or day!) of discovery. To take you all back to high school mathematics, it's that classic 3! equation: $3 \times 2 \times 1 = 6$. So, mathematically speaking, there are at *least* 6 combinations that will work in any given ménage. Here's an insider's view of this tripartite combination's voyeuristic/exhibitionist appeal.

1. You get to do another girl in front of your boyfriend.

2. You get to watch your boyfriend do another girl.

3. You get to be watched while you do your boyfriend.

4. Then, of course, you and your boyfriend can do the other girl together.

5. You and another girl can do your boyfriend.

6. Above all, you get to be done by two people at the same time!

> I often fantasize about trying out a threesome with another woman, sometimes out of a desire for more sensual sex and sometimes out of a desire to tease my partner. So many men love the thought of watching or joining two women at play, and I would like to fulfill his voyeuristic fantasy. I'm sorry if that sounds demeaning [to me] in any way, but I would definitely be the one getting the biggest kick out of it.
>
> —CHRISSIE, 30

Emma (25) slyly arranged her first threesome with a girl who she knew was desperate to be with her boyfriend. He would always joke around with Emma that the three of them should get down together, so Emma egged the other girl on by surreptitiously telling her about her boyfriend's exquisite bedroom talents. With all this dirty talk, Emma aroused the other girl to the point of no return. She and Emma grabbed the boyfriend, dragged him home, undressed him, and got straight to it. The nitty-gritty of having more than two people get it on was a complete and utter turn-on for Emma. Now she is dying to have another threesome with her boy, but this time with a girl who *she* thinks is hot and who really wants *her*!

Since threesomes are such a popular fantasy for women, it is no surprise that a supportive partner interested in the fulfillment of our fantasies gets high marks for participating in them. For Susan (29), it all started after she had gotten out of a long, boring relationship and on the rebound met an incredibly open and honest guy who enabled her to be herself sexually for the first time. They would talk about everything, even some sexual things she'd thought she could never share with anyone out of fear of being embarrassed or revealing too much. She had told him that she secretly wanted to have a threesome. On his birthday, he jokingly mentioned that this might be the occasion to finally experiment with her fantasy. At that moment, Susan finally accepted her desire to have a threesome. Now she was on a quest to find the right woman:

"There was a bisexual woman at work who would always tell me how I turned her on with what I wore to the office (dresses and suits). We'd always laugh about it. After thinking about it for a while, rehearsing what I'd say, etc., I asked her if she'd want to do something with a couple. We know what her answer was. I waited a bit to actually tell my man. I needed to be sure I wanted to do it. When I made my decision and told him, he did exactly what I knew he'd do: He asked me if it was what I had wanted and not something I was doing for him. He assured me that it didn't have to go past fantasy and that he was very okay with that. But I wanted to experience it. When that day came, I was anxious and I told him so. He gave me every opportunity to change my mind. I didn't. It was amazing. The three of us had a blast. It was nothing like I expected. No one was left out at any time unless they chose to be. It lasted all day. I have to admit, I wondered if my boyfriend would still be turned on by only me, or would be bored with just me. I was wrong to worry. We continued to have great sex, and he never suggested another encounter unless I did. So, what do you think I did with this man? I married him."

We are constantly competing in so many ways—for each other's attention, for the attention of men; there is an implied contest that is always raging (unfortunately) between members of the same sex. From the female perspective, a threesome is an amazing way to translate the traditionally heterosexual competition into good old-fashioned desire. Melissa (31) fantasizes about bringing another woman home to her boyfriend—a girl who is gorgeous and intimidating—and watching him enter their guest with his hard cock while she screams with pleasure. She imagines her boyfriend looking at her while he thrusts his hips into the other girl, imagines knowing that he really wants her, but is settling for the other girl because Melissa wants it that way. Instead of feeling intimidated by the beautiful girl's presence, she feels in control of the action, dictating when and if her boyfriend can come. The threesome is the ultimate way to join forces and put aside all female competition for the sake of mutual pleasure and exploration.

There are infinite numbers of personals placed by people looking to bring that special girl home as a birthday surprise for a boyfriend or girlfriend. Holidays are good times to have threesomes as well. A little eggnog, and suddenly one of your friends is hitting on you and your boyfriend at once, and it's kind of fun.

The best aspect of any threesome is that is has the potential to turn men and women on together! Mutual pleasure is where it's at—and the integration of male and female pleasure is a fantastic step forward. Whether you want to be the performer, the director, or the viewer, a threesome has a little something for everybody.

Pleasure Tip: One way to sample how a threesome might feel without actually committing to the whole experience is to go to a strip club with your partner so you can see what including another women in your sexual interaction might be like. Get a lap dance. (Female dancers have been known to be very receptive to female clientele and to relish the prospects of an open-minded young woman's first lap dance). Then switch it up and get him a lap dance. Spend a few minutes talking about what turned you on, and then head home, just the two of you, take all of that good energy, and have some full-on all-night-long booty-shakin' sex.

THE RULES

"Attractive, intelligent couple seeks new adventure!" Obviously the rules differ, depending on whether you're a swinging single girl out looking for a good time with another couple, or a member of a couple looking for that single girl. (Why isn't there a service for finding each other?)

> My advice is all about the selection of the third party. My experience was with one of my female friends from out of town, who was perfect because I already had a deep comfort level and affection for her, even though we had never been intimate before. She was just in for the weekend, which gave her a vacation mentality, and she left right when things might have gotten awkward. Now she's about to get married and we still laugh about it.
>
> —CAROLYN, 25

So, you are ready to rock the threesome. You've gone through it in your head, time and time again, and you're ready to hit the town. So, um, what now? The challenging thing about a threesome is how to find that special third.

Listen—it's hard enough to get one date, let alone two at a time. That said, once you get your mind around it, the possibilities are all around you. If you already have a partner and you're both game for the new addition to the family—well, then, it's time to go fishing. Something about merely having a threesome on the mind seems to yield results.

One of the safest and possibly most successful places to start looking is within your circle of friends. While that may seem strange to some, you would be surprised at how receptive many of your associates would be to a collective romp in the hay. Let's face it, attitude is everything, and if you start thinking threesome, you may be surprised at how quickly an opportunity presents itself.

The single girl

If you are a single girl looking for a threesome, you're in luck—basically every couple out there will probably want to get down with you! You also have considerable latitude when it comes to your options. You can choose two unsuspecting men; you and your girlfriend can pick up a hot single guy; late-night romping with new friends might reveal everyone's secret desires; or you can be a couple's fantasy come true.

There are a lot of advantages to being the odd girl out. Think of it this way: Single means independent, and you can be the first one to leave in the morning. True, you're alone and they're together, but you get to walk away with all potential complications behind you.

Pleasure Tip: When you are the third for a couple, you are in charge of maintaining the delicate between rocking sex and a relationship on the rocks. Be sure to pay lots of attention to the other girl and make her feel the extra love. Cheer her on as you sit back and live out your own voyeuristic tendencies. Watch the couple do it the way they do in private—this is the ultimate spying-through-the-window opportunity—and let them have the last moments of the night to themselves.

The couple

It gets a bit more complicated if you are part of a couple. One of the biggest considerations is who's going to find or approve the third person. It may be more than a bit off-putting for your boyfriend to come home and announce: "Hey, baby, I just met this fine young thing tonight. She digs me, and I'm thinking threesome—how 'bout you?" Opinions on this may vary, but we think female approval is essential. If you're not comfortable with the girl who's joining you in your bed, it's just not gonna happen. So, sometimes the best way to get the party started is for you to think of some third parties who might be receptive to the idea and then drop them on your partner.

If you're the one to break the ice, try being straightforward and just ask your boyfriend if he would want you and another woman. Chances are, the answer will be a resounding yes. But if you aren't comfortable asking, try complimenting another woman when you're with him. If you see a sexy girl, tell him what you think is sexy about her—her legs, her clothes, her pouty lips; whatever. If he's comfortable with your sexual attraction to her, it's a good indication that he could be persuaded to help you realize the attraction. If he's weirded out when you say things like "I'd like to bring her over wearing only a nightie," it probably isn't a good idea.

There are a couple of things to keep in mind with any potential threesome. Most important is to maintain complete respect for your partner's emotions as well as your own. You can go into a threesome completely open to the possibilities, or you can set some boundaries in advance. It can be intense to see your partner with another person, focusing his entire attention on giving her pleasure. It can be equally intense for your partner to watch you explore the newfound excitement of another woman.

Once you've located your prospective partner, there is no standard threesome etiquette; you can choose to participate in as many different variations as you feel comfortable with. You may simply want to be with another woman with your partner there. You may want to give up all control to two men and be ravished from head to toe without a care in the world, or you may wish to take control and dominate two men for your own pleasure. It can all be good!

Although it may sound trite, the solution is communication. It is good to talk with your partner, and maybe everyone involved, about what you expect the threesome will be like. The dynamic of bringing in a third person creates new issues that need to be discussed, both in advance and afterward, but it's probably best to try to get most of your talking done beforehand. Once it's on . . . it is on. Once it's done . . . it is done. You don't want to have to break mid-game to start discussing the whole "but you did" and "she did" and "you said you wouldn't." Establish clear boundaries well in advance and be mature enough to handle the consequences.

In the actual act of the threesome, no matter what side you are on (and even if you are in the middle!), you want to be sure that everyone involved is happy, comfortable, and experiencing their fair share of the fun. That's just good politics. Check in with your partner from time to time and just be sure that everything's a-okay.

Some couples embrace the other opportunities that the WMW offers: It can be a major turn-on to watch your boyfriend, your husband, or another couple having sex. Watching your man get it on with another woman offers a very different perspective.

The group

It started when I moved abroad and met four great people: two girls, two guys. My third week, we all went away to the mountains for the weekend. Late the first night, we bought some gin and fake eyelashes. After a few drinks, we convinced the guys that it would be a bonding experience to put on the eyelashes. They did, and strangely enough, it was a total turn-on. The power they surrendered to us women was sexy. We had another drink and decided to play Truth or Dare. It all started off innocently enough—strip for the group, etc. Then a Truth question to the girls: Have you made out with another girl? I was the only one who hadn't. My next turn, I opted for a Dare in hopes of them making me kiss one of the girls. I was right. With her long, wavy hair, she crawled in close to me and leaned her head to the side. For the first time, I touched the lips of another woman with my own. Our tongues mingled like old friends and before long, I could feel another set of lips joining ours. I opened my eyes to see that one of the guys had joined in. I backed off slightly and the third girl in our group took my place while the final guy grabbed me tightly, guided me gently to the ground, and quickly started to undress me. Someone turned off the lights, and from then on it was tough to tell who was doing what to whom.

—CARYN, 25

The three-way connection can be difficult to properly configure, and you always risk leaving one person out of the action. Everyone has had that experience with two friends, where one is always jealous of the other, or you are jealous of them. It's just hard to keep everybody included all the time! The solution? Go with foursomes or fivesomes. Already tried that? Well done. We're glad that someone has it figured out.

THE BIRTH OF THE CAKE SAM'ICH

Dear CAKE,

I am a sexy, pretty, intelligent, and liberated Latin woman. I've always done what I wanted sexually. I know how to make the first step with a man. I can do it easily. I am really elegant and discreet. Unfortunately, I have never been able to find two men to go to bed with at the same time. Yes, I have always fantasized about a threesome with two men, but it has never happened. Since I was a little girl, all those delicious moments of sex and desire were related to men. I have never desired women in my life. Anyway, it's very difficult, mission impossible, to find two straight men to go to bed with one woman. My thesis is this: Most men think that if they are with the same woman at the same time, then maybe they have to desire each other too. So, I keep trying, without any luck. I got very close twice. Two guys and I were kissing and touching in the same room, at a party, but both of them made clear that they would not take it to the "threesome" level. Maybe one day.

—VANESSA, 31

It is high time to announce the birth of the "CAKE Sam'ich." While the standard threesome offers a world of potential, we'd like to turn our focus to another thrill-filled configuration for the ladies. The CAKE Sam'ich is somewhere between a Fluffernutter and a 'smore, with one widely smiling woman smack dab in the middle of two men. As women, are we interested in being at the center of our own self-directed movie with two men in the supporting roles? Hell, yeah! Right?

The main challenge in fulfilling this fantasy is to find two men whom we find attractive and who are willing to risk the stigma involved with being anywhere near another naked man outside the locker room. Culturally speaking, if two men are in bed together, in any other context, they *must* be "gay," right? That's ridiculous! We don't assume that two women together in a threesome with a man are gay, do we?

But if you are going to get down with a second man in the mix, the men are most definitely going to have to be comfortable with their feet touching . . . at the very least. It'd be hard to properly implement the MWM configuration without the slightest bit of MM contact. That's going to be a real challenge for some men, and if your man can't get with that, then your sam'ich probably ain't happening.

I've yet to experience the MWM, but I would love to, under the right circumstances. I am much more turned on by the male bonding that occurs in a more direct sense: two men getting it on. This has totally frustrated me because it's hard enough to get guys to partake in the stereotypical gang bang, never mind finding two men (whom I'm attracted to and who are attracted to me) who are also down with enjoying another man's body. It works both ways: In my experience, members of the gay male community aren't too excited about including me in their frolicking. I can see why it would be so difficult for curious guys to have a dabble—I mean, the whole phenomenon is kind of ignored in most media, there's not really even much porn catering to bi-curious men and the women who love them. Generally, you're either gay or straight. Happily attracted to both men and women myself, I really appreciate the men who find my sexuality erotic, and I am still looking for ways to do the same for men.

—ANNE, 25

Alas, every woman knows the leaps and bounds most men would have to take to give it up to us with another man involved. It would seem nearly impossible to find two men who could share control of pleasuring their female companion, without constantly competing in the sack. On the other hand . . . competition might not be such a bad thing!

For the uptight straight guy, the MWM combo raises all sorts of semi-homophobic issues: What if I touch his penis, what if our bodies, our hands, our mouths (heaven forbid) come into contact. What if it happens and *I like it*? Yikes!

To dig even deeper, many men are inherently threatened by the notion that their partners may desire sexual interaction with another man, in any context. This is tied to an embedded and widespread sexual insecurity that we all share. Are we not enough? Not big enough? Tight enough? Pretty enough? Manly enough? Good enough? It's just going to be challenging to grasp the notion of "sharing" one's partner, and facing the threat of competition head-on.

While this gets to the heart of the matter for some men, we have found that there is no shortage of straight (yes, straight) men who are intrigued by the possibilities of the CAKE Sam'ich. Guys are growing accustomed to our desire to watch, touch, and feel two men by our side in bed, and there is a contingent out there of straight-up guys who are ready to rise to the challenge. Just as we have seen when we open the sexual dialogue between women, there can be a lot hiding behind the veil of what's acceptable for men, and lots of guys individually break the male mold.

The CAKE Sam'ich is twice the pleasure and twice the fun. It's like a pornographic Doublemint commercial for girls. Nancy (24) describes her Sam'ich experience in a way that's truly inspirational: She says there's nothing better than being fucked from behind while sucking off another guy with your mouth. It is exciting and totally surreal at the same time. Having more than one man want you and lust after you is a great compliment. Having control over two men who want to ravage her body sends chills down her spine. The best part is when the two men get creative and put their hands together with both their pointer fingers out and finger her while licking her breasts.

For Rose, the interaction between the two men, and the way both her partner and the third reacted to the companionship and competition of the threesome, are what made her Sam'ich worth reliving in her mind as a constant fantasy.

LET'S HEAR IT
FROM THE BOYS

I imagine it would drive any girl wild to have two mouths on her, one at each pair of lips, hands in her hair, hands caressing her all over; two cocks in turn or in tandem; two men overwhelming her, overloading her with stimuli. I'll address the discomfort I'd feel being naked and performing alongside another guy: Hell, yes, that would be uncomfortable! At first. But my focus would be on the girl. And if there were some preliminary nekkidness (i.e., let's take off our clothes, have a bottle of wine, and fondle this gorgeous young woman), I suspect that self-conscious period would pass. And I wouldn't be surprised if two guys in this situation didn't find occasion to congratulate each other—like, "Hey, nice job hitting her G-spot." Then again, if a girl wants two guys who would be more interactive, there are some switch hitters out there. I think if a girl is honest about what she wants and communicates it directly, she can put together any fantasy she wants.

—AARON, 29

I have had the pleasure of sharing a girl with another guy, and it was a great night. Yes, it does involve you being comfortable with yourself . . . but isn't that what we are all striving for? I spent a night out partying with friends, and had the fortune of ending the night with a good guy friend and a good girl friend. Since I had a history with the girl, we sank into our old tricks, and the girl was more than happy to have another player in the mix. Watching her get more and more steamed up about having not one but two boys to play with just made the situation hotter. She loved having one of us up by her mouth and another of us down below. She got more hot with each minute and said and did things even she thought she would never do . . . to the point where it ended with the two of us bathing her in our explosion and her smiling the entire time. The three of us still talk about it, and she still says it was one of her best nights ever. So trust me, it's a very sexual and fantastic way to spend an evening. Let your mind go and your body will follow.

—ANDREW, 32

Now, those are the boys we always want to hear from! We respect any guy's choice to be straight as straight can be—but if we are into the fantasy of two guys, we are going to give some props to the adventurous men. They may certainly be few and far between, but some lucky women have successfully smoked these would-be buns out of hiding.

I didn't even notice my boyfriend and John exchanging signals, my boyfriend silently letting John know that almost anything was okay, that he could fuck me all he wanted. He guided me onto John's enormous cock and let me ride him while he watched, jerking off. I couldn't hide the pleasure on my face when my boyfriend came around behind me and put a finger slowly inside my ass while my pussy was full of another man. There are few times in my life when I felt so empowered, so in control. I felt as if I had these two beautiful men working solely for my pleasure.... Things only got better. Very surprisingly, my boyfriend decided to initiate oral sex between the two men. They sucked each other off while I watched, leaning back on the headboard and masturbating. That was a new discovery for me.... I never knew how much watching men go down on each other turned me on! The total shock of watching my conservative boyfriend with a cock in his mouth put me over the edge! I could go on and on, but one of the more interesting parts of the experience was the next morning. When we all woke up together, my boyfriend had to leave early for work. Before he left, he pulled me into the bathroom, bent me over, and fucked me selfishly, not caring a bit about my pleasure, which is totally unlike him. John and I woke up a few hours later, and he did the exact same thing. Interesting commentary on men, power, their need to assert their sexuality, etc. I have to be honest with you: Their animalistic "marking" me the next morning was one of the biggest turn-ons of the whole experience.

—ROSE, 24

You may assume that exploring the Sam'ich in the context of your current, loving, and maybe monogamous relationship would present complications, but jealousy isn't always an issue. Julia (26) experienced such an occasion one night: She was having sex with her boyfriend in his room. When she got up to get a glass of water from the kitchen, she bumped into her boyfriend's roommate, who happened to be eavesdropping on them through the bedroom door in his boxers. When he saw Julia in her sheer, tiny negligee, he grabbed her and pinned her to the wall, breathing heavily in her ear and whispering her name with unadulterated, uncontrollable passion that instantly made her wet.

Her desperate hands rubbed his bare chest and she could feel him get hard against her thigh. By this point, she was so intensely aroused that she let him pull her panties off. He didn't push himself inside her. They just stayed like that, kissing, while he whispered into her ear, "I want to come inside you so bad." In the heat of the moment, neither of them noticed Julia's boyfriend standing in the doorway, watching them. Julia's heart almost exploded with the intensity of arousal and fear she was feeling. To her (delighted) surprise, her boyfriend just stood there and started massaging himself. As if on cue, and with her boyfriend's permission, the roommate entered Julia. One thing led to another, and by the end of the night, Julia found herself smack dab in the middle of two adoring men. She came intensely as she rode backward on the roommate's lap while giving her boyfriend the most incredible blow job.

Birth of the CAKE Sam'ich

I'm a professional woman in my early 30s, and it's always a challenge to balance my male-dominated professional life with my very adventurous desire to explore my sexuality—taking things to new heights while continually redefining and experiencing true satisfaction. Back in February, I met two men at a conference in Miami. They are business associates and very good friends. We have kept in touch over the past several months. As the phone calls & IM conversations became more and more sexual, it was very easy to figure out that I had found two completely uninhibited heterosexual males who would be into it. As luck would have it, I ended up traveling on a business trip to their hometown. The three of us met at my hotel; we had a few cocktails and a great dinner. The sexual tension among the three of us was off the charts the entire night! When they drove me back to my hotel, I invited them both up to my room. They practically ran over each other getting to the elevator! I had never experienced two men at the same time and was very curious. Let me tell you, it was the most amazing 6 hours of my life. Having two uninhibited, ravenous men focusing on my pleasure was astounding—not to mention addictive! Rendezvous Number 2 is already scheduled in NYC.

—TAMMY, 31

Pleasure Tip: The possibility of the CAKE Sam'ich will always be there, so there's no rush to realization. When you find yourself single, confident, and ready to find a willing twosome for your threesome, go ahead—check out all the resources at your disposal and make it happen. Take some advice from Tammy and go for it. Think happy thoughts. Think threesomes!

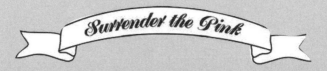
JACQUELINE, 34 After dinner at a beautiful hotel, my boyfriend leads me upstairs to a room that he has booked for the evening. He kisses me deeply and sensuously, telling me he has a big surprise for me. On the bed are silk ropes and a blindfold. He slowly undresses me and caresses my body with his hands and lips. I am so incredibly turned on. He won't let me touch him or undress him at all. He lays me down on the bed, on my back, and ties my wrists to the bedposts. He puts the blindfold on me, making sure that I can't see anything. It both thrills and scares me to be so vulnerable, lying naked, blindfolded, and tied up. He runs his hands all over my body, massaging my breasts and teasing my very wet pussy.

I hear a knock at the door. My boyfriend gets up and answers it. There's a muffled conversation and I am very nervous. I hear his voice reassure me that it will be the experience of a lifetime and to trust him. He tells the mystery person (persons?) to feel free to do whatever he (*they?*) wants to me. My body tingles with anticipation. I feel a strange pair of hands begin to massage my breasts. The hands are rough and callused and I like the way they feel against my smooth skin. He takes my breasts and pushes them together. I feel his tongue flick my nipples, making them very hard. He takes one nipple into his mouth and gently nibbles and sucks. Suddenly I feel another mouth on my other breast. I hear my boyfriend from across the room moan softly as he watches two strange men pleasure me. The men continue to fondle and massage me, and then I feel a hard cock being pushed into my mouth.

I know my lover is still across the room, so this means that there are three strangers here to fuck me. I open my mouth and taste the cock. One man moves down and strokes my thighs, pushing them apart. My impulse reaction is to resist. I hear my man laugh softly at my "prudishness." He tells the man between my legs, "Eat her cunt." The man forces my legs wide open and plunges his tongue deep in my pussy. The man at my mouth has straddled my face and is slowly pushing his cock in and out of my mouth. The third man is still concentrating on my breasts. I'm writhing with pleasure and feel myself getting ready to come. I hear my lover approach the bed. He is telling the men that I am here for their pleasure (but I know that they are really here for mine) and that they can do anything they want except fuck me in the ass.

The cock is taken out of my mouth and my blindfold is untied. All three men are touching and sucking and licking me. My boyfriend is naked, with a huge hard-on. He goes back to a chair across the room and watches, stroking his cock. The men untie my hands and I get on all fours. Immediately a cock is put in my pussy and one in my mouth. The other man gets under me and licks my clit while I'm being fucked. The man fucking me is pounding his extremely large cock deep into my pussy. I know I'm about to come any second. He lets out a loud moan and pulls his cock out and comes all over my ass. I am still sucking the third man when my boyfriend gets up out of the chair and comes over. "Come on her face," he tells the stranger. The other men move off to the side and my lover runs his hand over my swollen pussy. I'm still on all fours, and he gets behind me. He opens my cheeks and licks my asshole. The third man grabs my hair with both hands and squirts his hot come on my face. At the same time my lover slowly puts his dick in my ass. The pain and pleasure are almost unbearable. The other men are watching intently, stroking themselves as he begins to pump my ass. I am moaning and screaming so loudly I'm afraid someone will call security. I can't help being so loud—the pleasure is indescribable. He slams his cock into me and asks me if I liked his surprise. My only response is an orgasm so strong I almost pass out. I can't wait to pay him back for the surprise someday soon.

CHARLIE, 35 Weekend in New Orleans. We're looking for a girl. A girl for me. And you're going to watch. I need a couple of drinks to bolster my confidence; we've already decided what we're looking for. She should look very different from me, and be tall with dark hair. We roam from club to club, watching all the dancers, getting turned on, but it takes a few hours to find her. But we do. She's dancing, wearing a pink bikini, looking a little bored. We decide that's perfect. Maybe she's bored because she wants a little more, and we want more too. She's tall, has beautiful breasts, long dark brown hair, and big eyes.

We watch her for while, you and I sitting close together. You run your hand up and down my back and make me feel safe. Eventually you get up, and I get a little stab of fear because I know you're going to make "the deal." I look at her; she looks right at me and smiles. Does she want me? What does it feel like to be desired by a woman? Tonight I'll find out. You return to me, taking my hand to pull me up and whisper, "Come on, baby," leading me into the dark recesses of the club. The room is nothing special: a small stage with a pole, a leather couch, and no windows. You don't really want to ask if I'm afraid. I don't want to admit it.

Sexy stripping music starts to play and our girl comes in and steps onto the stage. She dances for us a bit, and I relax, thinking maybe you paid for just a private dance. You are staring at her and stroking my leg. She comes toward us, steps off the stage, and holds both hands out to me. "This is why we're here," I keep telling myself. I take her hands and let her pull me onto those high heels I now regret wearing—it's going to be hard enough to stand. She leads me up onto the stage, turns me so I'm facing her with my back to the pole. She dances for me, and on me, turning to rub her ass against my pussy, turning again to push her breasts into my face, like I imagine she's done at a hundred bachelor parties before. I'm still a little bit in shock that it's all happening. I take some degree of comfort in knowing somebody up here knows what she's doing.

Birth of the CAKE Sam'ich

She pushes my arms over my head and holds them there; I never really see it coming, but she leans down and kisses me, her tongue is in my mouth, and it feels . . . it feels good. They say nobody knows how to kiss a woman like another woman, and I think of that as I let go and kiss her back. I desperately want to look at you, but she won't let me. She turns me around to face the pole, bends me over a bit, and runs her hands up and down my legs, touching my ass. She turns me around to face her again, and continues dancing.

Then he comes in. You and I are both a little surprised; he wasn't part of the deal. We'd seen him outside, working in the main part of the club. Big, young, so strong, very clean-cut, like a law student moonlighting in this seedy club. I'm scared again. He smiles, and I steal a glance and see in your face everything I need to, the look that says, "It's okay to stop, it's okay to go on, I'm getting off because it's you up there." Your pants are unzipped. The man steps behind me, locking my arms behind my back; he is so much bigger than me, and so is she, it's the land of the fucking giants up here.

He nuzzles my neck playfully, and I'm less scared. Our girl is in front of me; she slows her dancing and reaches out, running her hands over my breasts. My dress offers little protection. The boy moves, arms still locked behind me, and now I'm facing you. You are so hard, slowly stroking your cock as you watch, a little smile on your face. I look into your eyes and I'm not 100 percent sure you really see me, you look a little far away. . . . But your smile gets bigger and I know for sure you're there with me. The girl is on her knees now, in front of me. She touches my legs again, and I gasp a little as she reaches under my dress, slides my thong off, and throws it to you on the couch. The boy's grip on my arms tightens while her hands move up my thighs, under my dress, and I fall back onto him.

I feel what it's like to have another woman's delicate fingers touch me, go inside me. Her fingers are magic, she knows just what to do. I get so wet, staring at you while her fingers move in and out. . . . She lifts my dress up just enough to begin licking me, still on her knees, her tongue swirling around and making me so hot and so dizzy. . . . She brings me so close to orgasm, but then suddenly moves away, I stagger a little, the boy helps me down off the stage and more or less hands me to you, you pull me down to you, I climb onto your lap, your cock is rock-hard, I slide you in and we come together, arms around each other tightly, suddenly alone now, in that dirty little room.

Birth of the CAKE Sam'ich

On the Road

FINAL EXAM

Invite your girlfriends over for a night of CAKE. Here's how to get talking. Below are some sexy questions. Pair up with someone in the room, and start asking away, beginning with the first question. If she says yes to a question you ask her, she must sign her name under the statement on your sheet. When she signs off on a question, ask her to tell you the related story. Once your friend has signed 4 or 5 statements, move on to talk with another friend. Ask your next friend the questions that your last one couldn't sign off on. Provide a prize for the first person to get all the questions signed.

Have you had an orgasm in the last 24 hours?   _____

Have you bought a vibrator for yourself?   _____

Have you masturbated in the last 24 hours?   _____

Have you acted out your favorite fantasy?   _____

Have you had a female ejaculation?   _____

Have you had an orgasm during intercourse?   _____

Do you know where your G-spot is? _____

Have you had an orgasm with vaginal stimulation only? _____

Have you made out with another girl? _____

Do you get turned on watching porn? _____

Have you had a "no-hands" orgasm? _____

Have you experimented with S&M? _____

Have you given oral-sex instructions? _____

Have you had an orgasm while dreaming? _____

Have you stripped for a partner? _____

Do you like anal sex? _____

Have you fantasized about anonymous sex? _____

Have you had sex in a public space? _____

Do you own a porno? _____

Have you tied a partner up? _____

Have you been to a strip club and enjoyed it? _____

Have you had a spanking? _____

Have you had a lap dance? _____

Have you given a spanking? _____

Have you masturbated using water? _____

Do you enjoy being dominant? _____

Have you made your own sexy video? _____

Do you enjoy being submissive? _____

Have you checked out Internet porn? _____

Have you masturbated in your car? _____

Have you been tied up? _____

Have you given a lap dance? _____

Do you have a fetish? _____

Have you performed a striptease? _____

Have you stripped in front of the mirror? _____

Have you gotten a happy-ending massage? _____

Do you fantasize during sex? _____

Have you had a threesome? _____

Have you had multiple orgasms? _____

Have you fantasized about a friend? _____

SEX ACCESSORIES

Bullet

Crystal Wand

Hitachi Magic Wand

Pearl Thong underwear

Pocket Rocket

Rabbit Pearl

Strawberry Kiss

EYE CANDY

Behind the Green Door

Bend Over Boyfriend

Emmanuelle

Eyes of Desire

Female Ejaculation for Couples

G Marks the Spot

House of Dreams

How to Female Ejaculate

I Dream of Jenna

Insatiable

Justine

Nina Hartley's Guide to Private Dancing

Squirters 2

The Opening of Misty Beethoven

The Ultimate Guide to Anal Sex for Women

*Select CAKE Seal of Approval and Pleasure Tip items are available through www.cakenyc.com.

The Cake Card

Member Name
CAKE GIRL

Become a member of CAKE—where the girls make the rules. Apply now! Go to www.cakeny.com.

Acknowledgments

Over the past five years many people have supported our work with CAKE. First and foremost we could not have published this book without the help of our business partner, Matthew Kramer. His ambition, drive, vision, patience, friendship, and love helped us put the fun back in our feminist politics.

Thanks to those who came before us: Alfred Kinsey, Shere Hite, and Masters and Johnson for their groundbreaking research and for making sexuality a field of study, and Betty Dodson, Carol Queen, Nancy Friday, Candida Royalle, Tristan Taromino, Deborah Sundahl, Milan Zaviacic, and Rebecca Chalker for their work, inspiration, support for this project, and for their correspondence and feedback.

We owe a debt of gratitude to Bob Levine and Kim Schefler, our agents, for believing in the future of this project and for matching us up with our editors, Greer Hendricks and Suzanne O'Neill, who transformed our initial manuscript into a true resource.

People often ask us how our parents feel about our work, so we officially thank Lynn Kramer, Roger Kramer, and Melinda and Ernie Dahlman for loving each and every small success along the way. We are grateful to our mentors Betsy Blackmar and Dr. Ronald Moglia for supporting our search for pleasure in the world of academia.

Special thanks also to all our friends who provided expertise both profession and personal, especially Amy Levine, Robin Steinfeld, Elizabeth Kramsky, the Moxie Girls, Loretta Mulcare, Allie Alvarado, Melissa Rosenstein, Jennifer Smith, Deborah Apsel, Andrew Wan, Aron Wahl, and Jagger the dog.

Resources

CAKE APPROVED: Recommendations for your pleasure and resources that informed the content of this book.

Publications

Angier, Natalie. *Woman: An Intimate Geography.* New York: Anchor Books, 1999.

Archer, Bert. *The End of Gay (And the Death of Heterosexuality).* Toronto: Doubleday, 1999.

Bataille, Georges. *The Story of the Eye.* City Lights Books, 1987.

Blackledge, Catherine. *The Story of V: A Natural History of Female Sexuality.* New Brunswick, NJ: Rutgers University Press, 2003.

Bentley, Toni. *The Surrender: An Erotic Memoir.* New York: Regan Books, 2004.

Birkhead, Timothy. *Promiscuity: An Evolutionary History of Sperm Competition*. Cambridge, MA: Harvard University Press, 2000.

Blank, Joani. *Good Vibrations: The New Complete Guide to Vibrators*. Down There Press, 2000.

Boston Women's Health Book Collective. *Our Bodies, Ourselves: A New Edition for a New Era*. New York: Touchstone, 2005.

Bright, Susie, ed. *The Best American Erotica* series. New York: Touchstone.

Bright, Susie. *Sexual State of the Union*. Cleis Press, 1995.

Chalker, Rebecca. *The Clitoral Truth*. New York: Seven Stories Press, 2000.

Comfort, Alex. *The Joy of Sex*. New York: Pocket Books, 1974.

Dodson, Betty. *Orgasms for Two: The Joy of Partnersex*. New York: Harmony Books, 2002.

———. *Sex for One: The Joy of Selfloving*. New York: Harmony, 1987.

Federation of Feminist Women's Health Centers. *A New View of A Woman's Body*, 2nd ed. Los Angeles, CA: Feminist Health Press, 1991.

Ferrato, Donna. *Love & Lust*. New York: Aperture, 2004.

Friday, Nancy. *My Secret Garden: Women's Sexual Fantasies*. New York: Simon & Schuster, 1973.

Greenfield, Lauren. *Girl Culture*. Chronicle Books, 2002.

Haffner, Debra W. *From Diapers to Dating: A Parent's Guide to Raising Sexually Healthy Children*. New York: Newmarket Press, 1999.

Hatcher, Robert A. *Contraceptive Technology.* Ardent Media, 2004.

Hite, Shere. *The Hite Report.* New York: Macmillian, 1976.

Johnson, Merri Lisa, ed. *Jane Sexes It Up: True Confessions of Feminist Desire.* New York: Four Walls Eight Windows, 2002.

Jong, Erica. *Fear of Flying.* New York: Holt, 1973.

Kerner, Ian. *She Comes First: The Thinking Man's Guide to Pleasuring a Woman.* New York: Regan Books, 2004.

Kinsey, Alfred C., et al. *Sexual Behavior of the Human Female.* Indiana University Press, 1953.

Klein, Fritz. *The Bisexual Option.* Birmingham, AL: Harrington Park, 1993.

Koedt, Anne. *The Myth of Vaginal Orgasm.* New York: Signet, 1970.

Laqueur, Thomas. *Solitary Sex: A Cultural History of Masturbation.* Zone Books, 2003.

Madonna. *Sex.* Ediciones B, 1992.

Maines, Rachel. *The Technology of Orgasm: "Hysteria," the Vibrator, and Women's Sexual Satisfaction.* Baltimore, MD: Johns Hopkins University Press, 1999.

Masters, William, et al. *Human Sexuality.* New York: Pearson Education, 1997.

Melissa P. *100 Strokes of the Brush Before Bed.* New York: Grove Press, 2004.

Merritt, Natacha. *Digital Diaries.* Taschen, 2000.

Miller, Henry. *Tropic of Capricorn.* New York: Random House, 1987.

Millet, Catherine. *The Sexual Life of Catherine M.* New York: Grove Press, 2003.

Mohanraj, Mary Anne, ed. *Aqua Erotica: 18 Stories for a Steamy Bath.* New York: Three Rivers Press, 2000.

Nin, Anaïs. *Delta of Venus.* Harcourt, 1977.

Palac, Lisa. *The Edge of the Bed: How Dirty Pictures Changed My Life.* Boston: Little, Brown, 1998.

Réage, Pauline. *The Story of O.* New York: Ballantine Books, 1981.

Rich, Frank. "Naked Capitalists." *The New York Times Magazine,* May 20, 2001.

Sevely, Josephine Lowndes. *Eve's Secrets.* New York: Random House, 1987.

Sprecher, Susan, Anita Barbee, and Pepper Schwartz. "Was It Good for You, Too?: Gender Differences in First Sexual Intercourse Experiences." *The Journal of Sex Research* vol. 32, no. 1, 1995, 3–15.

Sundahl, Deborah. *Female Ejaculation and the G-Spot.* Berkeley, CA: Hunter House, 2003.

Talese, Gay. *Thy Neighbor's Wife.* New York: Ballantine, 1980.

Taormino, Tristan. *The Ultimate Guide to Anal Sex for Women.* Cleis Press, 1997.

Vance, Carole. *Pleasure and Danger.* London: Pandora Press, 1992.

Vatsyayana, Indra Sinha, trans. *The Love Teachings of Kama Sutra: With Extracts from Koka Shastra, Ananga Ranga and Other Famous Indian Works on Love.* Marlowe & Company, 1997.

Venning, Rachel, and Claire Cavanah. *Sex Toys 101: A Playful Uninhibited Guide.* New York: Simon & Schuster, 2003.

Winks, Cathy. *The Good Vibrations Guide: The G-Spot.* San Francisco: Down There Press, 1998.

Wolf, Naomi. *The Beauty Myth.* New York: Morrow, 1991.

Zaviacic, Milan. *The Human Female Prostate: From Vestigial Skene's Paraurethral Glands and Ducts to Woman's Functional Prostate.* Bratislava, Slovakia: Slovak Academic Press, 1999.

Index

Friedan, Betty, 25
Friends (television program), 204
From Diapers to Dating (Haffner), 11

G

General Motors (GM), 186
Gershon, Gina, 183, 243
girl-on-girl sex, 203–23
  in childhood, 17–18
  emotional needs and, 214–15
  exploring, 210–12
  getting over labels, 205–6
  physical attraction in, 213–14
  in pornography, 192–93
  skills in, 214
  taboo, power, and, 215–17
Glaser, Adam. *See* Seymore Butts
G Marks the Spot (film), 190
Good Vibrations (store), 62, 64
Good Vibrations: The Complete Guide to Vibrators (Blank), 64
Granville, Joseph Mortimer, 63
Grease (film), 7
grind (position), 104–5
G-spot (female prostate), 47, 53–54, 185, 190
  anatomy of, 50
  ejaculation and, 78, 80, 81–82
  intercourse and, 105

Guide to Private Dancing (video), 150
gynecological exams, 33

H

Haffner, Debra W., 11
hand job (self-arousal technique), 53
Hartley, Nina, 150
Harvard University, 185
Hatcher, Robert A., 112
Hitachi Magic Wand (vibrator), 54, 61, 68, 69, 71, 83, 125
Holmes, John, 191
Hopefuls (CAKE Scale category), 207
Hot Mamas, 115
hot stone massage, 162–63
House of Dreams (film), 193
human papillomavirus (HPV), 33, 34
Hunger, The (film), 204
hymen, 20

I

I Dream of Jenna (film), 189
Insatiable (film), 191
intercourse. *See* sexual intercourse
Internet pornography, 184, 186
In the Cut (film), 183

J

Jacuzzi, 57
Jameson, Jenna, 179
Jeremy, Ron, 193
Jerry Maguire (film), 183
Jong, Erica, 156, 159
Justine (film), 193

K

Kama Sutra, 101–2
Kerner, Ian, 98
Kidman, Nicole, 183
Kinsey, Alfred, 39, 47, 208–9
Kinsey scale, 208–9
Klass, Alisha, 84–85
Klein, Fritz, 209
Koedt, Anne, 47
Kristel, Sylvia, 191

L

Ladas, Alice, 47
lap dancing, 76, 147, 248
Laqueur, Thomas, 38
Laurel Canyon (film), 183, 204
Law, Jude, 183
lesbian sex. *See* girl-on-girl sex
Lesbos, 208
Liberating Masturbation (Dodson), 64
libido. *See* arousal

location, location, location (position), 105
"Lovemaking of the Crow, The" *(Kama Sutra),* 101–2
Lover, The (film), 183
lubrication, 99, 107, 108, 109
luteal phase, 32
luteinizing hormone, 32

M

MacLachlan, Kyle, 243
Madonna, 40, 150, 204
Maines, Rachel, 63
male gaze, 144
massage, hot stone, 162–63
Masters and Johnson, 39, 47
masturbation, 35–59
  censure of, 9–10, 38–39
  in childhood, 8–10, 14
  exhibitionist, 148–50
  mutual, 93–94, 149
  outlandish places for, 45
  percentage of women performing, 39
  self-exploration and, 46
  tips, tricks, and techniques for, 52–57
McDormand, Frances, 183
Merritt, Natacha, 145
Miller, Henry, 40
Minders (CAKE Scale category), 207